# Berlitz®

# Thai

phrase book & dictionary

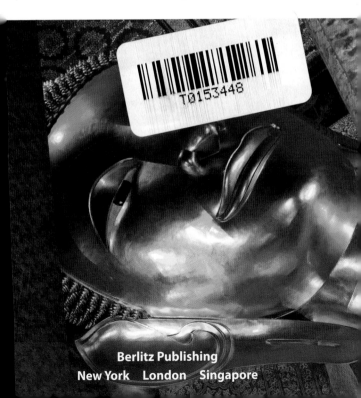

**Berlitz Publishing**
**New York   London   Singapore**

**Contacting the Editors**
Every effort has been made to provide accurate information in this publication, but changes are inevitable. The publisher cannot be responsible for any resulting loss, inconvenience or injury. We would appreciate it if readers would call our attention to any errors or outdated information. We also welcome your suggestions; if you come across a relevant expression not in our phrase book, please contact us at: **comments@berlitzpublishing.com**

All Rights Reserved
© 2019 Apa Digital (CH) AG and Apa Publications (UK) Ltd.
Berlitz Trademark Reg. U.S. Patent Office and other countries. Marca Registrada. Used under license from Berlitz Investment Corporation.

Printed in China

**Editor:** Helen Fanthorpe
**Translation:** updated by Wordbank
**Cover Design:** Rebeka Davies
**Interior Design:** Beverley Speight
**Picture Researcher:** Beverley Speight
**Cover Photos:** All photos Shutterstock

**Interior Photos:** Peter Stuckings/APA 1, 14, 33, 36, 52, 55, 58, 65, 66, 69, 71, 72, 79, 85, 91, 101, 104, 106, 111, 112, 117, 119, 121, 128, 130, 135 ; Nikt Wong/APA 16, 39, 81; istockphoto 22, 142, 143; Britta Jachinski/APA 42; Mina Patria/APA 25; James Macdonald/APA 165

## Distribution

**UK, Ireland and Europe**
Apa Publications (UK) Ltd
sales@insightguides.com
**United States and Canada**
Ingram Publisher Services
ips@ingramcontent.com
**Australia and New Zealand**
Woodslane
info@woodslane.com.au
**Southeast Asia**
Apa Publications (SN) Pte
singaporeoffice@insightguides.com

**Worldwide**
Apa Publications (UK) Ltd
sales@insightguides.com

**Special Sales, Content Licensing, and CoPublishing**
Discounts available for bulk quantities. We can create special editions, personalized jackets, and corporate imprints. sales@insightguides.com; www.insightguides.biz

# Contents

## Survival

## Food & Drink

## People

## Leisure Time

## Special Requirements

## In an Emergency

## Dictionary

# Pronunciation

This section is designed to make you familiar with the sounds of Thai using our simplified phonetic transcription. You'll find the pronunciation of the Thai letters and sounds explained below, together with their 'imitated' equivalents. This system is used throughout the phrase book; simply read the pronunciation as if it were English, noting any special rules below.

## Consonants

Consonants are considerably easier to pronounce in Thai than vowels since all but a few have English equivalents. The consonants producing the same sound are grouped together. The initial consonants at the beginning of syllables are:

| Letter(s) | Approximate Pronunciation | Symbol | Example | Pronunciation |
|---|---|---|---|---|
| ก | g as in gas | **g** | กิน | *gihn* |
| ข, ค, ฆ | k as in king | **k** | ค้า, ขาย, ฆ่า | *kár, kıě, kâr* |
| จ | j as in jet | **j** | จาน | *jarn* |
| ง | ng as in singer | **ng** | งาน | *ngarn* |
| ฉ, ช | ch as in cheese | **ch** | ฉัน, ช้าง | *cháhn, chárng* |
| ซ, ศ, ษ, ส | s as in sun | **s** | ซ้าย, ศาล, ภาษา, สิบ | *síe, sărn, par•săr, sìhp* |
| ญ, ย | y as in year | **y** | ใหญ่, เย็น | *yì, yehn* |
| ด, ฎ | d as in dog | **d** | ดอกไม้, ชฎา | *dòrk•mí, chah•dar* |
| ต, ฏ | t as in star (sharp t) | **\*dt** | เต่า ปฏัก | *dtòu, bpà•dtàhk* |
| ฐ, ท, ฒ, ฑ, ธ | t as in tan | **t** | ฐาน, ทหาร, ผู้เฒ่า, ถนน, ธรรมชาติ | *tărn, tah•hǎrn, pôo•tôu, tah•nDn, tahm•mah•chârt* |
| ณ, น | n as in new | **n** | เณร, น้ำ | *nen, nárm* |

\* A combination of two letters, *d* and *t*, are used here to indicate the sharp sound *t* in order to differentiate this sound from the normal sound of *t*.

| Letter(s) | Approximate Pronunciation | Symbol | Example | Pronunciation |
|---|---|---|---|---|
| บ | b as in band | **b** | บอก | *bòrk* |
| ป | p as in speak (sharp p) | **\*bp** | ไป | *bpi* |
| ผ, พ, ภ | p as in pen | **p** | ผึ้ง, เพื่อน, รูปภาพ | *pûeng, pûean, rôop·pârp* |
| ฝ, ฟ | f as in fun**f** | | ฝน, สีฟ้า | *fŏn, seĕ·fár* |
| ม | m as in man | **m** | แม่ | *mâe* |
| ร | r as in run**r** | | รถยนต์ | *rót·yon* |
| ล, ฬ | l as in love | **l** | ลิง, นาฬิกา | *lihng, nar·lih·gar* |
| ว | w as in work | **w** | วัน | *wahn* |
| ห, ฮ | h as in happy | **h** | แห้ง, นกฮูก | *hâeng, nók·hôok* |
| อ | o as in on**o** | | อ่อน | *òrn* |

\* Similarly, *b* and *p* are used to indicate the sharp sound *p*.

As **final consonants of syllables**, the letters *p, t* and *k* are pronounced as the sharp sounds *p, t* and *k*.

## Vowels

| Letter | Sound Duration | Approximate Pronunciation | Symbol | Example | Pronunciation |
|---|---|---|---|---|---|
| -ะ, -ั- | short | a as in about | **ah** | จะ, รัก | *jah, ráhk* |
| -า- | long | ar as in cart, without pronouncing the r | **ar** | ขา | *kăr* |
| -ิ | short | i as in pit | **h** | บิน | *bihn* |
| -ี | long | ee as in bee | **ee** | ปีก | *bpèek* |
| -ึ | short | u as in put + e as in exam | **ue** | ลึก | *lúek* |

| Letter* | Sound Duration | Approximate Pronunciation | Symbol | Example | Pronunciation |
|---|---|---|---|---|---|
| ◌ือ | long | u as in put + e as in exam, with the e sound lengthened | **uee** | กลางคืน | *glarng•kueen* |
| ◌ุ | short | u as in put | **uh** | ขุด | *kùht* |
| ◌ู | long | oo as in root | **oo** | พูด | *pôot* |
| เ-ะ, เ-็ | short | e as in get | **eh** | เตะ, เล็ก | *dtèh, léhk* |
| เ- | long | e as in bed with the e sound lengthened | **e** | เพลง | *pleng* |
| แ-ะ, แ-็ แข็งแรง | short | a as in match | **a** | แกะ, | *gà, kǎng•raeng* |
| แ- | long | a as in band | **ae** | สีแดง | *seě•daeng* |
| โ-ะ | short | o as in no with a short duration | **o** | โต๊ะ | *dtó* |
| โ- | long | oe as in toe | **oe** | โรงเรียน | *roeng•rean* |
| เ-าะ | short | o as in spot | **oh** | เกาะ | *gòh* |
| -อ- | long | or as in worn, without pronouncing the r | **or** | รอ, ทอง | *ror, torng* |
| ◌ีย | long | ea as in spear | **ea** | เปลี่ยน | *bplèan* |
| เ-ือ | long | like ue + a sound | **uea** | มะเขือเทศ | *máh•kuěa•têt* |

The dash (-) indicates the position of the consonant in relation to the vowel or vowel cluster.

| Letter | Sound Duration | Approximate Pronunciation | Symbol | Example | Pronunciation |
|--------|----------------|---------------------------|--------|---------|---------------|
| -ัว, -ว- | long | oar as in boar without pronouncing the r | **oar** | กลัว, สวม | *gloar, sŏarm* |
| เ-ิ, เ-อ | long | er as in per without pronouncing the rer | **er** | เดิน, เจอ | *dern, jer* |
| ำ | short | a as in about + m | **ahm** | ทำ | *tahm* |
| ำ | long | a as in cart + m | **arm** | น้ำ | *nárm* |
| ไ-, ใ- | short | i as in bicycle | **i** | ไป, ใหม่ | *bpi, mì* |
| -าย | long | ie as in pie | **ie** | สาย | *sĭe* |
| เ-า | short | ou as in count | **ou** | เขา | *kŏu* |
| -าว | long | ow as in how | **ow** | ขาว | *kŏw* |

In Thai, each vowel is pronounced with either a short or a long duration; try to mimic these durations when speaking Thai, as they indicate different meanings. Following are the approximate pronunciation of short and long vowels.

Standard Thai is the official language of Thailand, though it has several different forms, which are used in special social situations, especially in informal, formal, religious and royal contexts.

# Tones

Thai is a tonal language. The phonetic transcriptions in this phrase book include the following tone marks:

| Tone | Pitch | Symbol |
|------|-------|--------|
| mid tone | normal speaking with the voice at a steady pitch | no mark |
| high tone | pitched slightly higher than normal | ´ |
| low tone | pitched slightly lower than normal | ` |
| falling tone | pitched high and falling sharply | ^ |
| rising tone | pitched low and rising sharply | ˇ |

Here are examples of how tone changes the meaning of a word:

| Thai Script | Pronunciation | Tone | Meaning |
|-------------|---------------|------|---------|
| คา | kar | mid tone | to dangle |
| ข่า | kàr | low tone | galanga (a cooking spice) |
| ฆ่า | kâr | falling tone | to kill |
| ค้า | kár | high tone | to trade |
| ขา | kǎr | rising tone | a leg |

Two Thai letters, อ and ว, function as both consonants and vowels. When used as consonants, they will always be initial consonants in a syllable and take an initial sound as listed in the consonant table. But when they are used as vowels their sounds will be as follows:

อ has an or sound as in torn and can be in the middle or at the end of a syllable.

ว has an oar sound as in boar and will always be in the middle of a syllable.

# How to use this Book

> Sometimes you see two alternatives separated by a slash. Choose the one that's right for your situation.

## ESSENTIAL

I'm on vacation [holiday]/business.    ผม *m* /ฉัน *f* มา เที่ยว/ธุระ *pŏm/cháhn mar têaw/túh•ráh*

I'm going to...    ผม *m* /ฉัน *f* จะไปที่... *pŏm/cháhn jah bpi têe...*

I'm staying at the...Hotel.    ผม *m* /ฉัน *f* พักอยู่ที่โรงแรม... *pŏm/cháhn páhk yòo têe roeng•raem...*

> Words you may see are shown in YOU MAY SEE boxes.

## YOU MAY SEE...

ขาเข้า *kăr kôu*    arrivals
ขาออก *kăr òrk*    departures
ที่รับกระเป๋า *têe ráhp grah•bpŏu*    baggage claim

> Any of the words or phrases listed can be plugged into the sentence below.

## Somewhere to Stay

Can you recommend...?    ช่วยแนะนำ...หน่อยได้ไหม? *chôary ná•nahm...nòhy dîe mí*

   a hotel    โรงแรม *roeng•raem*
   a hostel    ที่พักเยาวชน *têe páhk you•wah•chon*
   a campsite    ที่ตั้งแค้มป์ *têe dtâhng káem*

Thai phrases appear in purple.

Read the simplified pronunciation as if it were English. For more on pronunciation, see page 7.

## Personal

How old are you? คุณอายุเท่าไหร่? *kuhn ar·yúh tôu·rì*

I'm... ผม *m* /ฉัน *f* อายุ... *pŏm /cháhn ar·yúh...*

Are you married? คุณแต่งงานแล้วหรือยัง? *kuhn dtàng·ngarn láew rúe yahng*

I'm... ผม *m* /ฉัน *f* ... *pŏm/cháhn...*

single/in a relationship ยังโสด/มีแฟนแล้ว *yahng sòet/mee faen láew*

engaged/married มีคู่หมั้นแล้ว/แต่งงานแล้ว *mee kôo·mâhn láew/ dtàng·ngarn láew*

For Numbers, see page 158.

Related phrases can be found by going to the page number indicated.

When different gender forms apply, the masculine form is followed by *m*; feminine by *f*

Rather than shaking hands, in Thailand it is polite to greet people with a ไหว้ *wîe* ('wai', Thai gesture of greeting).

Information boxes contain relevant country, culture and language tips.

### YOU MAY HEAR...

ผม *m* /ฉัน *f* พูดภาษาอังกฤษได้ นิดหน่อย *pŏm/cháhn pôot par·săr ahng·griht dîe níht·nòhy*  I only speak a little English.

ผม *m* /ฉัน *f* พูดภาษาอังกฤษไม่ได้ *pŏm/cháhn pôot par·săr ahng·griht mi dîe*  I don't speak English.

Expressions you may hear are shown in You May Hear boxes.

Color-coded side bars identify each section of the book.

# Survival

# Arrival & Departure

## ESSENTIAL

| | |
|---|---|
| I'm on vacation [holiday]/business. | ผม *m* /ฉัน *f* มา เที่ยว/ธุระ *pŏm/cháhn mar têaw/ túh•ráh* |
| I'm going to… | ผม *m* /ฉัน *f* จะไปที่… *pŏm/cháhn jah bpi têe…* |
| I'm staying at the …Hotel. | ผม *m* /ฉัน *f* พักอยู่ที่ โรงแรมมี… *pŏm/cháhn páhk yòo têe roeng•raem…* |

## YOU MAY HEAR…

| | |
|---|---|
| ขอดูพาสปอร์ตหน่อย *kŏr doo párs•sah•bpòrt nòhy* | Your passport, please. |
| จุดประสงค์ในการมาครั้งนี้คืออะไร? *jùht•bprah•sŏng ni garn mar kráhng née kuee ah•ri* | What's the purpose of your visit? |
| คุณพักที่ไหน? *kuhn páhk têe•nĭ* | Where are you staying? |
| คุณจะอยู่ที่นี่นานเท่าไหร่? *kuhn jah yòo têe•nêe narn tôu•rì* | How long are you staying? |
| คุณมาที่นี่กับใคร? *kuhn mar têe•nêe gàhp kri* | Who are you here with? |

## Border Control

| | |
|---|---|
| I'm just passing through. | ผม *m* /ฉัน *f* แค่แวะผ่านเท่านั้น *pŏm/cháhn kâe wá pàrn tôu•náhn* |
| I'd like to declare… | ผม *m* /ฉัน *f* มี…ที่ต้องการแสดง *pŏm/cháhn mee…têe dtôhng•garn sah•daeng* |
| I have nothing to declare. | ผม *m* /ฉัน *f* ไม่มีสิ่งของต้องแสดง *pŏm/cháhn mî mee sihng•kŏrng dtôrng sah•daeng* |

### YOU MAY HEAR...

มีอะไรจะแสดงไหม? *mee ah•ri jah sah•daeng mí*  Anything to declare?

คุณจะต้องจ่ายภาษีสำหรับสิ่งนี้ *kuhn jah dtôrng jie par•sĕe săhm•ràhp sìhng née*  You must pay duty on this.

ช่วยเปิดกระเป๋าใบนี้หน่อย *chôary bpèrt grah•bpŏu bi née nòhy*  Open this bag.

### YOU MAY SEE...

ศุลกากร *sĭhn•lah•gar•gorn*  customs

สินค้าปลอดภาษี *sĭhn•kár bplòrt par•sĕe*  duty-free goods

จุดตรวจหนังสือเดินทาง *jùht dtròart năhng•sĕue dern•tarng*  passport control

ตำรวจ *dtahm•ròart*  police

# Money

## ESSENTIAL

| | |
|---|---|
| Where's...? | ...อยู่ที่ไหน? ...yòo têe•nǐ |
| the ATM | ตู้เอทีเอ็ม dtôo e•tee•ehm |
| the bank | ธนาคาร tah•nar•karn |
| the currency exchange office | ที่รับแลกเงิน têe ráhp lâek ngern |
| When does the bank open/close? | ธนาคาร เปิด/ปิด เมื่อ ไหร่? tah•nar•karn bpèrt/bpìht mûea•rì |
| I'd like to change dollars/pounds into baht. | ผม m /ฉัน f อยากแลกเงินดอลลาร์/ปอนด์เป็น เงินบาท pǒm/cháhn yàrk lâek ngern dohn•lâr/bporn bpehn ngern bàrt |
| I'd like to cash traveler's checks [cheques]. | ผม m /ฉัน f อยากขึ้นเงินเช็คเดินทาง pǒm/cháhn yàrk kûen•ngern chéhk dern•tarng |

## At the Bank

| | |
|---|---|
| I'd like to... | ผม m /ฉัน f อยากจะ... pǒm/cháhn yàrk jah... |
| change money | แลกเงิน lâek ngern |
| change dollars/ pounds into baht | แลกเงินดอลลาร์/ปอนด์เป็นเงินบาท lâek ngern dohn•lâr/ bporn bpehn ngern bàrt |
| cash traveler's checks [cheques]/ Eurocheques | ขึ้นเงิน เช็คเดินทาง/ยูโรเช็ค kûen•ngern chéhk dern•tarng/yoo•roe chéhk |
| get a cash advance | เบิกเงินสดล่วงหน้า bèrk ngern•sòt lôarng nâr |
| What's the exchange rate/fee? | อัตรา/ค่าธรรมเนียม แลกเปลี่ยนเท่าไหร่? àht•dtrar/ kâr•tahm•neam lâek•bplèan tôu•rì |
| I think there's a mistake. | ผม m /ฉัน f คิดว่ามีอะไรผิดพลาด pǒm/cháhn kíht wâr mee ah•ri pìht•plârt |

Thai currency is the บาท *bàrt* (baht), divided into สตางค์ *sah•dtarng* (satang).

Coins: 25 and 50 **satang**; 1, 2, 5, and 10 **baht**.

Bills: 20 (green bill), 50 (blue bill), 100 (red bill), 500 (purple bill) and 1000 (gray bill) **baht**.

## YOU MAY SEE...

| | |
|---|---|
| สอดบัตรที่นี่ *sòrt bàht têe•nêe* | insert card here |
| ยกเลิก *yók•lêrk* | cancel |
| ลบคำ *lob kâr* | clear |
| ป้อนคำ *bporn kâr* | enter |
| รหัส *ra•hàht* | PIN |
| ถอน *tǒrn* | withdrawal |
| จากบัญชีกระแสรายวัน *jarg bahn•chee grah•sae•rie•wahn* | from checking [current] account |
| จากบัญชีออมทรัพย์ *jarg bahn•chee orm•sahb* | from savings account |
| ใบบันทึกรายการ *bi bahn•túek rie•garn* | receipt |

| | |
|---|---|
| I lost my traveler's checks [cheques]. | ผม *m* /ฉัน *f* ทำเช็คเดินทางหาย *pǒm/cháhn tahm chéhk dern•tarng hǐe* |
| The ATM ate my card. | ตู้เอทีเอ็มกินบัตรของผม *m* /ฉัน *f* ไป *dtôo e•tee•ehm gihn bàht kǒhng pǒm/cháhn bpi* |
| My card... | บัตรของผม *m* /ฉัน *f* ... *bàht kǒhng pǒm/cháhn...* |
| was lost | หาย *hǐe* |
| was stolen | ถูกขโมย *tòok kah•moey* |
| doesn't work | ใช้ไม่ได้ *chí mî dîe* |

Cash can be obtained from ATMs throughout Thailand, though some machines may be unreliable. Some debit cards and most major credit cards are accepted. Be sure to confirm this with your card-issuing bank. Also, know whether your PIN is compatible with Thai machines, which usually expect a four-digit, numeric code. ATMs usually offer good rates, though there may be some hidden fees. Currency exchange offices and banks are an option for exchanging currency. Banks across the country are generally open Monday to Friday 8:30 a.m. to 3:30 p.m.

## Getting Around

### ESSENTIAL

| | |
|---|---|
| How do I get to town? | ผม *m* /ฉัน *f* จะเข้าเมืองยังไง? *pŏm/cháhn jah kôu mueang yahng•ngi* |
| Where's…? | …อยู่ที่ไหน? …*yòo têe•nĭ* |
| the airport | สนามบิน *sah•nărm•bihn* |
| the train [railway] station | สถานีรถไฟ *sah•tăr•nee rót•fi* |
| the bus station | สถานีขนส่ง *sah•tăr•nee kŏn•sòng* |
| the subway [underground] station | สถานีรถไฟใต้ดิน *sah•tăr•nee rót•fi tîe dihn* |
| the skytrain station | สถานีรถไฟฟ้า *sah•tăr•nee rót•fi•fár* |
| How far is it? | มันอยู่ไกลแค่ไหน? *mahn yòo gli kâe nĭ* |
| Where do I buy a ticket? | ผม *m* /ฉัน *f* จะซื้อตั๋วได้ที่ไหน? *pŏm/cháhn jah súee dtŏar dîe têe•nĭ* |

| A one-way/round-trip [return] ticket to… | ตั๋ว เที่ยวเดียว/ไปกลับ ไป… *dtŏar têaw deaw/bpi glàhp bpi…* |
|---|---|
| How much? | เท่าไหร่? *tôu•rì* |
| Is there a discount? | มีส่วนลดไหม? *mee sòarn•lót mí* |
| Which…? | …ไหน? *…nĭ* |
| gate | ประตู *bprah•dtoo* |
| line | แถว *tăew* |
| platform | ชานชาลา *charn•char•lar* |
| Where can I get a taxi? | ผม *m*/ฉัน *f* จะเรียกแท็กซี่ได้ที่ไหน? *pŏm/cháhn jah rêark ták•sêe dîe têe•nĭ* |
| Take me to this address. | พาผม *m*/ฉัน *f* ไปส่งที่ที่อยู่นี้ด้วย *par pŏm/cháhn bpi sòng têe têe•yòo née dôary* |
| Where's the car rental [hire]? | ผม *m*/ฉัน *f* จะเช่ารถได้ที่ไหน? *pŏm/cháhn jah chôu rót dîe têe•nĭ* |
| Can I have a map? | ผม *m*/ฉัน *f* ขอแผนที่หน่อยได้ไหม? *pŏm/cháhn kŏr păen•têe nòhy dî mí* |

## Tickets

| When's… to Bangkok? | …ไปกรุงเทพออกเมื่อไหร่? *…bpi gruhng•têp òrk mûea•rì* |
|---|---|
| the (first) bus | รถบัส (เที่ยวแรก) *rót báhs (têaw râek)* |
| the (next) flight | เที่ยวบิน (เที่ยวต่อไป) *têaw bihn (têaw dtòr•bpi)* |
| the (last) train | รถไฟ (ขบวนสุดท้าย) *rót•fi (kah•boarn sùht•tíe)* |
| Is there… trip? | มีเที่ยว…ไหม? *mee têaw…mí* |
| an earlier | เร็วกว่านี้ *rehw gwàr née* |
| a later | หลังจากนี้ *lăhng jàrk née* |
| a cheaper | ถูกกว่านี้ *tòok gwàr née* |
| Is it a direct train? | นี่เป็นรถไฟเที่ยวตรงใช่ไหม? *nee bpehn rót•fi têaw trong chî mí* |
| Is the train on time? | รถไฟเที่ยวนี้ตรงเวลาหรือไม่? *rót•fi têaw nee trong we•la rúe mî* |

| Where do I buy a ticket? | ผม *m* /ฉัน *f* จะซื้อตั๋วได้ที่ไหน? *pŏm/cháhn jah súee dtŏar dîe têe•nǐ* |
|---|---|
| One ticket/Two tickets, please. | ขอซื้อตั๋ว หนึ่ง/สอง ใบ *kŏr súee dtŏar nùeng/sŏrng bi* |
| For today/tomorrow. | สำหรับ วันนี้/พรุ่งนี้ *săhm•ràhp wahn•née/prûhng•née* |
| ...ticket. | ตั๋ว... *dtŏar...* |
| A one-way | เที่ยวเดียว *têaw deaw* |
| A round-trip [return] | ไปกลับ *bpi glàhp* |
| A first class | ชั้นหนึ่ง *cháhn nùeng* |
| A business class | ชั้นธุรกิจ *cháhn túh•rá•gìht* |
| An economy class | ชั้นประหยัด *cháhn bprah•yàht* |
| How much? | เท่าไหร่? *tôu•rì* |
| Is there... discount? | มีส่วนลดสำหรับ...ไหม? *mee sòarn•lót săhm•ràhp...mí* |
| a child | เด็ก *dèhk* |
| a student | นักศึกษา *náhk•sùek•săr* |
| a senior citizen | ผู้สูงอายุ *pôo•sŏong•ar•yúh* |
| a tourist | นักท่องเที่ยว *náhk•tôhng•têaw* |
| I have an e-ticket. | ผม *m* /ฉัน *f* มีตั๋วอิเล็กทรอนิกส์ *pŏm/cháhn mee dtŏar ee•léhk•tror•nìhk* |
| Can I buy a ticket on the bus/train? | ผม *m* /ฉัน *f* จะซื้อตั๋วบน รถบัส/รถไฟ ได้ไหม? *pŏm/cháhn jah súee dtŏar bon rót báhs/rót•fi dî mí* |
| Do I have to stamp the ticket before boarding? | ฉันต้องประทับตราตั๋วก่อนขึ้นรถไฟหรือไม่? *cháhn tong bpra•tahb dtrar dtoar gorn kuen rót•fi rúe mí?* |
| How long is this ticket valid? | ตั๋วใช้ได้จนถึงเมื่อไหร่? *dtoar chî dîe jon tueng muea•rì* |
| Can I return on the same ticket? | ผม/ฉันใช้ตั๋วนี้เพื่อนั่งรถไฟขากลับได้หรือไม่? *pŏm/cháhn chî dtoar nee púea nahng rót•fi kăr•glahb dîe rúe mí?* |

| | |
|---|---|
| I'd like to... | ผม *m*/ฉัน *f* อยากจะ...การจองตั๋ว *pǒm/cháhn yàrk jah...* |
| my reservation. | *garn jorng•dtǒar* |
| cancel | ยกเลิก *yók•lêrk* |
| change | เปลี่ยนแปลง *bplèan•bplaeng* |
| confirm | ยืนยัน *yueen•yahn* |

## Plane

### Airport Transfer

| | |
|---|---|
| How much is a taxi to the airport? | ค่าแท็กซี่ไปสนามบินเท่าไหร่? *kâr ták•sêe bpi sah•nǎrm•bihn tôu•rì* |
| To...Airport, please. | ไปสนามบิน... *bpi sah•nǎrm•bihn...* |
| My airline is... | ผม *m*/ฉัน *f* ไปสายการบิน... *pǒm/cháhn bpi sǐe•garn•bihn...* |
| My flight leaves at... | เครื่องของผม *m*/ฉัน *f* จะออกเวลา... *krûeang kǒhng pǒm/ cháhn jah òrk we•lar...* |
| I'm in a rush. | ผม *m*/ฉัน *f* ต้องรีบไป *pǒm/cháhn dtôhng rêep bpi* |
| Can you take an alternate route? | คุณไปทางอื่นได้ไหม? *kuhn bpi tarng ùen dî mí* |
| Can you drive faster/slower? | คุณช่วยขับ เร็วขึ้น/ช้าลง หน่อยได้ไหม? *kuhn chôary kàhp rehw kûen/chár long nòhy dî mí* |

## YOU MAY SEE...

| | |
|---|---|
| ขาเข้า *kǎr kôu* | arrivals |
| ขาออก *kǎr òrk* | departures |
| ที่รับกระเป๋า *têe ráhp grah•bpǒu* | baggage claim |
| รักษาความปลอดภัย *ráhk•sǎr kwarm bplòrt•pi* | security |
| เช็คอิน *chéhk ihn* | check-in |
| เช็คอินด้วยตั๋วอิเล็กทรอนิกส์ *chéhk ihn dôary dtǒar ee•léhk•tror•nìhk* | e-ticket check-in |
| ประตูทางออกขึ้นเครื่อง *bprah•dtoo tarng•òrk kûen krûeang* | departure gates |

## YOU MAY HEAR...

| | |
|---|---|
| คุณเดินทางด้วยสายการบินอะไร? *kuhn dern•tarng dôary sie•garn•bihn ah•ri* | What airline are you flying? |
| ในประเทศหรือระหว่างประเทศ? *ni bprah•têt rǔee rah•wàrng bprah•têt* | Domestic or international? |
| เทอร์มินอลไหน? *ter•mih•nôrn nǐ* | What terminal? |

## Checking In

| | |
|---|---|
| Where's check-in? | เคาน์เตอร์เช็คอินอยู่ที่ไหน? *kóu•têr chéhk ihn yòo têe•nǐ* |
| My name is... | ผม *m* /ฉัน *f* ชื่อ... *pǒm/chán chûee...* |
| I'm going to... | ผม *m* /ฉัน *f* จะไป... *pǒm/chán jah bpi...* |
| Here's my reservation. | นี่คือรายการจองตั๋วของฉัน *nee kuee rary•garn jorng toar korng chán* |
| I have... | ผม *m* /ฉัน *f* มี... *pǒm/chán mee...* |
| one suitcase | กระเป๋าหนึ่งใบ *grah•bpǒu nùeng bi* |
| two suitcases | กระเป๋าสองใบ *grah•bpǒu sǒrng bi* |

| | |
|---|---|
| one carry-on [piece of hand luggage] | กระเป๋าถือขึ้นเครื่องหนึ่งใบ *grah•bpŏu tŭee kûen krûeang nùeng bi* |
| How much luggage is allowed? | อนุญาตให้นำสัมภาระไปได้เท่า ไหร่? *àh•núh•yârt hî nahm săhm•par•ráh bpi dîe tôu•rì* |
| Is that pounds or kilos? | นั่นเป็นหน่วยปอนด์หรือกิโล? *nahn bpehn noar bporn rúe gih•lo* |
| Which terminal/gate? | เทอร์มินอล/ประตู ไหน? *ter•mih•nôrn/bprah•dtoo nǐ* |
| I'd like a window/ an aisle seat. | ผม *m*/ฉัน *f* อยากได้ที่นั่ง ริมหน้าต่าง/ริมทางเดิน *pŏm/cháhn yàrk dîe têe•nâhng rihm nâr•dtàrng/rihm tarng dern* |
| When do we leave/ arrive? | เราจะ ออก/ถึง เมื่อไหร่? *rou jah òrk/tŭeng mûea•rì* |
| Is the flight delayed? How late? | เที่ยวบินล่าช้าหรือเปล่า? *têaw bihn lâr•chár rúe•bplòw* ช้าแค่ไหน? *chár kâe nǐ* |

---

## YOU MAY HEAR...

คนต่อไป! *kon dtòr•bpi*

ขอดู หนังสือเดินทาง/ตั๋ว หน่อย *kŏr doo năhng•sŭee dern•tarng/dtŏar nòhy*

คุณมีสัมภาระที่จะเช็คขึ้นเครื่อง ไหม? *kuhn mee săhm•par•ráh têe jah chéhk kûen krûeang mí*

สัมภาระของคุณน้ำหนักเกิน *săhm•par•ráh kŏhng kuhn nárm•nàhk gern*

กระเป๋าใบนั้นใหญ่เกินกว่าที่ จะอนุญาตให้ถือขึ้นเครื่อง *grah•bpŏu bi náhn yì gern gwàr têe jah ah•núh•yârt hî tŭee kûen krûeang*

ขึ้นเครื่องได้ย *kûen krûeang dîe...*

Next!

Your passport/ticket, please.

Are you checking any luggage?

You have excess luggage.

That's too large for a carry-on [to carry on board].

Now boarding...

## Luggage

| | | |
|---|---|---|
| Where is/are…? | …อยู่ที่ไหน? | …yòo têe•nĭ |
| the luggage carts [trolleys] | รถเข็นสัมภาระ | rót kĕhn săhm•par•ráh |
| the luggage lockers | ตู้เก็บสัมภาระ | dtôo gèhp săhm•par•ráh |
| the baggage claim | ที่รับกระเป๋า | têe ráhp grah•bpŏu |
| My luggage has been lost/stolen. | กระเป๋าของผม *m* /ฉัน *f* หาย/ถูกขโมย | grah•bpŏu kŏhng pŏm/cháhn hĭe/tòok kah•moey |
| My suitcase is damaged. | กระเป๋าของผม *m* /ฉัน *f* เสียหาย | grah•bpŏu kŏhng pŏm/ cháhn sĕa•hĭe |

## Finding your Way

| | | |
|---|---|---|
| Where is/are…? | …อยู่ที่ไหน? | …yòo têe•nĭ |
| the currency exchange office | ที่แลกเปลี่ยนสกุลเงิน | têe laeg bplèan sah•guhn ngern |
| the car rental [hire] | รถเช่า | rót chôu |
| the exit | ทางออก | tarng òrk |
| the phones | โทรศัพท์ | toe•rah•sàhp |
| the taxis | รถแท็กซี่ | rót ták•sêe |
| Is there… into town? | มี…เข้าเมืองไหม? | mee…kôu mueang mí |
| a bus | รถเมล์ | rót•me |

| a train | รถไฟ *rót•fi* |
| a subway [underground] | รถไฟใต้ดิน *rót•fi tîe•dihn* |
| a skytrain | รถไฟฟ้า *rót fi•fár* |

## Train

| Where's the train [railway] station? | สถานีรถไฟอยู่ที่ไหน? *sah•tăr•nee rót•fi yòo têe•nĭ* |
| How far is it? | อยู่ไกลแค่ไหน? *yòo gli kâe nĭ* |
| Where is/are…? | …อยู่ที่ไหน? …*yòo têe•nĭ* |
| the ticket office | ที่ขายตั๋ว *têe kĭe dtŏar* |
| the information desk | ประชาสัมพันธ์ *bprah•char•săhm•pahn* |
| the luggage lockers | ตู้เก็บสัมภาระ *dtôo gèhp săhm•par•ráh* |
| the platforms | ชานชาลา *charn•char•lar* |
| Can I have a schedule [timetable]? | มีตารางเดินรถไหม? *mee dtar•rarng dern rót mí* |
| How long is the trip? | ใช้เวลาเดินทางเท่าไหร่? *chí we•lar dern•tarng tôu•rì* |
| Is it a direct train? | เป็นรถไฟสายตรงหรือเปล่า? *bpehn rót•fi sĭe dtrong rúe•bplòw* |

## YOU MAY SEE…

| ชานชาลา *charn•char•lar* | platforms |
| ประชาสัมพันธ์ *bprah•char•săhm•pahn săhm•pahn* | information |
| แผนกสำรองที่นั่ง *pah•nàek săhm•rorng rorng têe•nâhng* | reservations |
| ห้องรอ *horng ror* | waiting room |
| ขาเข้า *kăr kôu* | arrivals |
| ขาออก *kăr òrk* | departures |

The Thai train network connects towns across the mainland and the peninsula. Though travel by train may be somewhat slow, it is inexpensive and a great way to enjoy the scenery. You should be aware, though, that in some towns, the station is some distance from the city center, so double check before you start making plans. There are a variety of train options, differentiated by speed. Express trains are the fastest. Trains also have first, second and third class cars, as well as sleepers, which are all priced accordingly.

## YOU MAY HEAR...

| | |
|---|---|
| ไปไหน? *bpi nǐ* | Where to? |
| ตั๋วกี่ใบ? *dtǎar gèe bi* | How many tickets? |
| ขอตั๋วด้วยค่ะ *ko˘r toar dôary kâh* | Tickets, please. |
| ป้ายต่อไปคือ... *bpie dtor bpi kuee...* | Next stop... |

| | |
|---|---|
| Do I have to change trains? | ผม *m*/ฉัน *f* จะต้องเปลี่ยนรถหรือเปล่า? *pǒm/cháhn jah dtôhng plèan rót rúe•bplòw* |
| Is the train on time? | รถไฟมาตรงเวลาไหม? *rót•fi mar dtrong we•lar mí* |

### Departures

| | |
|---|---|
| Which track [platform] to...? | ชานชาลาไหนที่จะไป...? *charn•char•lar nǐ têe jah bpi...* |
| Is this the track [platform] train to...? | ชานชาลานี้เป็นรถไฟที่จะไป...ใช่ไหม? *charn•char•lar née bpehn rót•fi têe jah bpi...chî•mí* |

| Where is track [platform]…? | ชานชาลา…อยู่ที่ไหน? charn•char•lar…yòo têe•nî |
| Where do I change for…? | ผม *m*/ฉัน *f* จะเปลี่ยนรถไฟไป…ได้ที่ไหน? pŏm/cháhn jah bplèan rót•fi bpi…dîe têe•nî |

---

## YOU MAY HEAR…

คุณจะต้องเปลี่ยนรถที่… kuhn jah dtôhng plèan rót tée…

You have to change at…

สถานีต่อไป… sah•tǎr•nee dtòr•bpi…

Next stop…

---

## On Board

| Can I sit here/open the window? | ผม *m*/ฉัน *f* นั่งตรงนี้/เปิดหน้าต่างได้ไหม? pŏm/cháhn nâhng dtrong née/bpèrt nâr•dtàrng dî mí |
| That's my seat. | ตรงนั้นเป็นที่นั่งของผม *m*/ฉัน *f* dtrong náhn bpehn tée•nâhng kŏhng pŏm/cháhn |
| Here's my reservation. | นี่คือที่ที่ผม *m*/ฉัน *f* จองไว้ née kuee tée tée pŏm/cháhn jorng wí |

## Bus

| Where's the bus station? | สถานีขนส่งอยู่ที่ไหน? sah•tǎr•nee kŏn•sòng yòo têe•nî |
| How far is it? | อยู่ไกลแค่ไหน? yòo gli kâe nî |
| How do I get to…? | ผม *m*/ฉัน *f* จะไป…ได้ยังไง? pŏm/cháhn jah bpi…dîe yahng•ngi |
| Is this the bus to…? | นี่เป็นรถที่จะไป…ใช่ไหม? nêe bpehn rót tée jah bpi…chî•mí |
| Please tell me when to get off. | ช่วยบอกให้ผม *m*/ฉัน *f* รู้ด้วยเมื่อ ไปถึง chôary bòrk hî pŏm/cháhn róo dôary mûea bpi tǔeng |
| Do I have to change buses? | ผม *m*/ฉัน *f* จะต้องเปลี่ยนรถหรือเปล่า? pŏm/cháhn jah dtôhng plèan rót rúe•bplòw |
| How many stops to…? | ไป…ประมาณกี่ป้าย? bpi…bprah•marn gèe bpîe |
| Stop here, please! | จอดด้วย! jòrt dôary |

Both the Thai government and private companies offer bus service. Prices between the two are competitive and rates are usually based on distance. Bus travel is common and usually packed at rush hour in the bigger cities. Buying round-trip tickets will often get you a discount.

## YOU MAY SEE...

| | |
|---|---|
| ป้ายรถเมล์ *bpîe rót•me* | bus stop |
| ทางขึ้น/ทางลง *tarng kûen/tarng long* | enter/exit |
| หยุด *yùhd* | stop |

## Subway

| | |
|---|---|
| Where's the subway/ skytrain station? | สถานี รถไฟใต้ดิน/รถไฟฟ้า อยู่ที่ไหน? *sah•tăr•nee rót•fi tîe•dihn/rót•fi•fár yòo têe•nĭ* |
| A map, please. | ขอแผนที่หน่อย *kŏr păen•têe nòhy* |
| Which line for...? | สายไหนไปที่...? *sĭe nĭ bpi têe...* |
| Which direction? | ไปทางไหน? *bpi tarng nĭ* |
| Do I have to transfer [change]? | ผม *m* /ฉัน *f* ต้องเปลี่ยนขบวนไหม? *pŏm/chán dtôrng plèan kah•boarn mí* |
| Is this the subway [train]/skytrain to...? | รถไฟใต้ดิน/รถไฟฟ้า ขบวนนี้ไป...ใช่ไหม? *rót•fi tîe dihn/rót•fi•fár kah•boarn née bpi...chî•mí* |
| How many stops to...? | ไป...ประมาณกี่ป้าย? *bpi...bprah•marn gèe bpîe* |
| Where are we? | เราอยู่ที่ไหน? *rou yòo têe•nĭ* |

For Tickets, see page 20.

Bangkok has its own skytrain and subway services that offer the fastest and most convenient way to travel within the city center. The skytrain, known as บีทีเอส (BTS), currently has two lines: the Sukhumvit Line and the Silom Line. Both routes cover the city center and its commercial and tourist areas. The subway (MRT) currently has only one line that runs mostly north-south along the eastern part of Bangkok. Both the skytrain and the subway operate from 6:00 a.m. until midnight daily. Though subway and skytrain lines intersect at some stations, the ticketing system is separate at present. However, the plan for common ticketing between BTS skytrain and MRT is now in progress. Both services offer a discounted-fare smart card, which can be refilled with credit at the ticket office. For shorter stays, you can buy either a 1-day BTS pass, or a 1-day or 3-day MRT pass valid for unlimited travel within those periods. MRT also offers a 30-day unlimited ride pass.

## Boat & Ferry

| | |
|---|---|
| When is the ferry to...? | เรือข้ามฟากไป...ออกเมื่อไหร่? *rua kârm fârk bpi. . . òrk mûea•rì* |
| Where are the life jackets? | เสื้อชูชีพอยู่ที่ไหน? *sûea choo•chêep yòo têe•nǐ* |
| Can I take my car? | เอารถไปด้วยได้ไหม? *ou rót bpi dôary dîe mí* |
| What time is the next sailing? | เรือเที่ยวต่อไปออกเมื่อไร? *ru ̆ea têaw dtor bpi òrk muea•rì* |
| Can I book a seat/cabin? | ขอจองที่นั่ง/เคบินได้ไหม? *kor jorng têe•nahng/ke•bihn dîe mí* |
| How long is the crossing? | ใช้เวลาข้ามฟากนานเท่าไร? *chí we•la karm•fark narn tôu•rì* |

For Tickets, see page 20.

Boat travel in Thailand may offer some of your trip's most unforgettable experiences, since it is a unique method of transportation, which allows you to see the city from another perspective. Service is convenient and usually functions regularly between sunrise to sunset. One of the most popular routes in Bangkok is along the Chao Phraya river.

## YOU MAY SEE...

| | |
|---|---|
| เรือชูชีพ *reua choo•chêep* | life boat |
| เสื้อชูชีพ *sûea choo•chêep* | life jacket |

## Taxi

| | |
|---|---|
| Where can I get a taxi? | ผม *m* /ฉัน *f* จะ เรียกแท็กซี่ได้ที่ที่ไหน? *pŏm/cháhn jah rêak ták•sêe dîe têe•nĭ* |
| Do you have the number for a taxi? | คุณมีเบอร์โทรเรียกแท็กซี่ไหม? *kuhn mee ber toe rêak ták•sêe mí* |
| I'd like a taxi now/ in an hour. | ผม *m* /ฉัน *f* ต้องการแท็กซี่ เดี๋ยวนี้/ภายใน หนึ่ง ชั่วโมง *pŏm/cháhn dtôhng•garn ták•sêe dĕaw née/pie•ni nùeng chôar•moeng* |
| I'd like a taxi for tomorrow at... | ผม *m* /ฉัน ต้องการรถแท็กซี่พรุ่งนี้ที่...*pŏm /cháhn tong•garn rót tak•see pruhng•nee têe...* |
| Pick me up at... | รับผม *m* /ฉัน *f* ที่... *ráhp pŏm/cháhn têe...* |
| I'm going to... | ผม *m* /ฉัน *f* จะ ไปที่... *pŏm/cháhn jah bpi têe...* |
| this address | ที่อยู่นี้ *têe•yòo née* |
| the airport | สนามบิน *sah•nărm•bihn* |
| the train [railway] station | สถานีรถไฟ *sah•tăr•nee rót•fi* |
| I'm late. | ผม *m* /ฉัน *f* สายแล้ว *pŏm/cháhn sĭe láew* |

Taxis can be hailed in the street. Just look for the Taxi Meter sign for car taxis, since metered taxis are cheaper than non-metered taxis. Motorcycle taxis are also an option, if you're game. Fares are all-inclusive, so tipping is not necessary, but you may round up, if you like. When you take a taxi outside of Bangkok, the fare may have to be negotiated before the start of the trip.

ตุ๊ก ตุ๊ก *dtúhk•dtúhk* (three-wheeled taxi), both motorized and man-powered, is an alternative to taking taxis. These are not metered, so you should negotiate the fare. Tipping is generally not necessary, though you may choose to round up the fare.

You'll also find that, especially in rural areas, you also have the option of สองแถว *sŏrng tăew* that is actually a truck with two benches in the back. Like for the three-wheeled taxi, you should negotiate the fare with the driver before starting off.

| | | |
|---|---|---|
| Can you drive faster/ slower ? | คุณช่วยขับ เร็วขึ้น/ช้าลง หน่อยได้ไหม? | *kuhn chôary kàhp rehw kûen/chár long nòhy dî mí* |
| Stop/Wait here. | จอด/รอ ตรงนี้ | *jòrt/ror dtôhng•née* |
| How much? | เท่าไหร่? | *tôu•rì* |
| Can I have a receipt? | ขอใบเสร็จด้วยได้ไหม? | *kŏr bi•sèht dôary dî mí* |
| You said it would cost... | คุณบอกว่ามันแค่... | *kuhn bòrk wâr mahn kâe...* |
| Keep the change. | ไม่ต้องทอน | *mî dtôhng torn* |

## Bicycle & Motorbike

| | | |
|---|---|---|
| I'd like to rent [hire]... | ผม *m* /ฉัน *f* อยากจะเช่า... | *pŏm/cháhn yàrk jah chôu...* |
| a bicycle | จักรยาน | *jàhk•grah•yarn* |
| a moped | จักรยานมอเตอร์ไซค์ | *jàhk•grah•yarn mor•dter•si* |
| a motorcycle | มอเตอร์ไซค์ | *mor•dter•si* |

## YOU MAY HEAR...

ไปไหน? bpi nǐ

ที่อยู่อะไร? têe•yòo ah•ri

มีค่าบริการ ช่วงกลางคืน/สนามบิน เพิ่มด้วย mee kâr bor•rih•garn chôarng glarng•kueen/ sah•nǎrm•bihn pêrm dôary

Where to?

What's the address?

There's a nighttime/ airport surcharge.

| | |
|---|---|
| How much per day/week? | ค่าเช่าวัน/อาทิตย์ ละเท่าไหร่? kâr•chôu wahn/ar•tíht lah tôu•rì |
| Can I have a helmet/lock? | ผม m /ฉัน f ขอ หมวกกันน็อค/กุญแจล็อค ด้วยได้ไหม? pǒm/cháhn kǒr màork•gahn•nóhk/guhn•jae lóhk dôary dì mí |

Thai driving is much less tame than at home and Americans must adapt to the fact that traffic drives on the left side of the road. Though car rental is cheap by Western standards, renting a car without a chauffeur is generally discouraged. Privately-hired excursion drivers are customarily tipped.

## YOU MAY SEE...

| | |
|---|---|
| เบนซิน *ben•sihn* | gas [petrol] |
| ดีเซล *dee•sen* | diesel |
| แก๊สโซฮอล์ *gáes•soe•horn* | gasohol* |

*Gasohol is a mixture of gasoline and ethanol.

## Car Hire

| | |
|---|---|
| Where's the car rental [hire]? | บริการรถเช่าอยู่ที่ไหน? *bor•rih•garn rót chôu yòo têe•nǐ* |
| I'd like... | ผม *m*/ฉัน *f* อยากได้... *pǒm/chán yàrk dîe...* |
|   an automatic/ | รถ เกียร์อัตโนมัติ/เกียร์ธรรมดา *rót gea* |
|   a manual | *àht•dtah•noe•máht/gea tahm•mah•dar* |
|   a cheap/small car | รถราคาไม่แพง/คันเล็ก *rót rar•kǎr mî paeng/kahn lek* |
|   a car with air conditioning | รถที่มีแอร์ *rót têe mee ae* |
|   a car seat | รถที่มีเบาะสำหรับเด็ก *rót têe mee bòh sǎhm•ràhp dèhk* |
| How much...? | ...เท่าไหร่? *...tôu•rì* |
|   per day/week | วัน/สัปดาห์ ละ *wahn/sàhp•dar lah* |
|   for...days | สำหรับ...วัน *sǎhm•ràhp...wahn* |
|   per kilometer | กิโลเมตร ละ *gih•loe•mét lah* |
|   for unlimited mileage | แบบ ไม่จำกัดระยะทาง *bàep mî jahm•gàht rah•yáh•tarng* |

|  |  |
|---|---|
| with insurance | รวมประกัน *roarm bprah•gahn* |
| Are there any discounts? | มีส่วนลดไหม? *mee sòarn•lót mí* |

## Fuel Station

|  |  |
|---|---|
| Where's the gas [petrol] station? | ปั๊มน้ำมันอยู่ที่ไหน? *bpáhm•náhm•mahn yòo têe•nǐ* |
| Fill it up. | เติมเต็มถัง *dterm dtehm tǎhng* |
| ...baht, please. | ...บาท ...*bàrt* |
| I'll pay in cash/by credit card. | ผม *m*/ฉัน *f* จะจ่ายด้วย เงินสด/บัตรเครดิต *pǒm/cháhn jah jìe dôary ngern•sòt/bàht•kre•dìht* |

For Numbers, see page 158.

## Asking Directions

|  |  |
|---|---|
| Is this the way to...? | ทางนี้ไป...ใช่ไหม? *tarng née bpi...chî•mí* |
| How far is it to...? | ไป...อีกไกลไหม? *bpi...èek gli mí* |
| Where's...? | ...อยู่ที่ไหน? ...*yòo têe•nǐ* |
| ...Street | ถนน... *tah•nǒn...* |
| this address | ที่อยู่นี้ *têe•yòo née* |
| the highway [motorway] | ทางหลวง *tarng•lǒarng* |

### YOU MAY SEE...

| | |
|---|---|
| หยุด *yùht* | stop |
| ให้ทาง *hî tarng* | yield |
| ห้ามเข้า *hârm kôu* | no entry |
| ห้ามจอด *hârm jòrt* | no parking |
| หยุดตรวจ *yùht dtròart* | police check point |
| ห้ามแซง *hârm saeng* | no passing |
| ห้ามกลับรถ *hârm glàhp rót* | no u-turn |

35

| | |
|---|---|
| Can you show me on the map? | คุณช่วยชี้ในแผนที่ให้หน่อยได้ไหม? *kuhn chôary chée ni pàen•têe hî nòhy dî mí* |
| I'm lost. | ผม *m*/ฉัน *f* หลงทาง *pŏm/cháhn lŏng tarng* |

## YOU MAY HEAR...

| | |
|---|---|
| ตรงไป *dtrong bpi* | straight ahead |
| ซ้าย *síe* | left |
| ขวา *kwăr* | right |
| ตรง/เลย หัวมุม *dtrong/lery hŏar•muhm* | on/around the corner |
| ด้านตรงข้าม *dârn dtrong•kârm* | opposite |
| ด้านหลัง *dârn lăhng* | behind |
| ติดกับ *dtìht gàhp* | next to |
| หลังจาก *lăhng•jàrk* | after |
| ทิศเหนือ/ทิศใต้ *tíht nŭea/tíht dtie* | north/south |
| ทิศตะวันออก/ทิศตะวันตก *tíht dtah•wahn•òrk/ tíht dtah•wahn•dtòk* | east/west |
| ตรงไฟแดง *dtrong fi•daeng* | at the traffic light |
| ตรงสี่แยก *dtrong sèe•yâek* | at the intersection |

## Parking

| Can I park here? | ผม *m* /ฉัน *f* จอดรถตรงนี้ได้ไหม? *pŏm/cháhn jòrt rót dtrong•née dî mí* |
| Where's...? | ...อยู่ที่ไหน? ...*yòo têe•nǐ* |
| the parking garage | อาคารจอดรถ *ar•karn jòrt rót* |
| the parking lot [car park] | ลานจอดรถ *larn jòrt rót* |
| the parking meter | มิเตอร์จอดรถ *míh•dtêr jòrt rót* |
| How much...? | ...เท่าไหร่? ...*tôu•rì* |
| per hour | ชั่วโมงละ *chôar•moeng lah* |
| per day | วันละ *wahn lah* |
| overnight | คืนละ *kueen lah* |

## Breakdown & Repair

| My car broke down/ won't start. | รถของผม *m* /ฉัน *f* เสีย/สตาร์ทไม่ติด *rót kŏhng pŏm/ cháhn sĕa/sah•dtárt mî dtìt* |
| Can you fix it (today)? | คุณซ่อม (วันนี้) ได้ไหม? *kuhn sôhm (wahn•née) dîe mí* |
| When will it be ready? | จะเสร็จเมื่อไหร่? *jah sèht mûea•rì* |
| How much? | เท่าไหร่? *tôu•rì* |
| I have a puncture/ flat tyre. | ล้อรถของฉันแตก/แบน *lor rót korng cháhn dtaek/baen* |

## Accidents

| There was an accident. | มีอุบัติเหตุ *mee uh•bàht•tìh•hèt* |
| Call an ambulance/ the police. | เรียก รถพยาบาล/ตำรวจ ให้หน่อย *rêak rót pah•yar•barn/ dtahm•ròart hî nòhy* |

## Places to Stay

### ESSENTIAL

| | |
|---|---|
| Can you recommend a hotel? | ช่วยแนะนำโรงแรมให้หน่อยได้ไหม? *chôary ná•nahm roeng•raem hî nòhy dî mí* |
| I have a reservation. | ผม *m* /ฉัน *f* จองห้องไว้ *pǒm/cháhn jorng hôhng wí* |
| My name is… | ผม *m* /ฉัน *f* ชื่อ… *pǒm/cháhn chûee…* |
| Do you have a room…? | คุณมีห้อง…ไหม? *kuhn mee hôhng…mí* |
| for one/two | สำหรับ คนเดียว/สองคน *sǎhm•ràhp kon deaw/sǒrng kon* |
| with a bathroom | ที่มีห้องน้ำ *têe mee hôhng nárm* |
| with air conditioning | ที่มีแอร์ *têe mee ae* |
| For… | สำหรับ… *sǎhm•ràhp…* |
| tonight | คืนนี้ *kueen née* |
| two nights | สองคืน *sǒrng kueen* |
| one week | หนึ่งสัปดาห์ *nùeng sàhp•dar* |
| How much? | เท่าไหร่? *tôu•rì* |
| Is there anything cheaper? | มีอะไรที่ถูกกว่านี้ไหม? *mee ah•ri têe tòok gwàr née mí* |
| When's check-out? | ต้องเช็คเอาท์กี่โมง? *dtôrng chéhk•ou gèe moeng* |
| Can I leave this in the safe? | ผม *m* /ฉัน *f* จะฝากของไว้ในเซฟได้ไหม? *pǒm/cháhn jah fàrk kǒrng wí ni sép dî mí* |
| Can I leave my bags? | ผม *m* /ฉัน *f* จะฝากกระเป๋าไว้ได้ไหม? *pǒm/cháhn jah fàrk grah•bpǒu wí dî mí* |
| Can I have my bill/ a receipt? | ขอ บิล/ใบเสร็จ ด้วยได้ไหม? *kǒr bihn/bi•sèht dôary dî mí* |
| I'll pay in cash/ by credit card. | ผม *m* /ฉัน *f* จะจ่ายด้วย เงินสด/บัตรเครดิต *pǒm/cháhn jah jìe dôary ngern•sòt/bàht•kre•dìht* |

## Somewhere to Stay

| | |
|---|---|
| Can you recommend…? | ช่วยแนะนำ…ให้หน่อยได้ไหม? *chôary ná•nahm…hî nòhy dîe mí* |
| a hotel | โรงแรม *roeng•raem* |
| a hostel | ที่พักเยาวชน *têe páhk you•wah•chon* |
| a guesthouse | เกสต์เฮ้าส์ *gét•hóus* |
| a campsite | ที่ตั้งแค้มป์ *têe dtâhng káem* |
| What is it near? | มันอยู่ใกล้กับอะไร? *mahn yòo glî gàhp ah•ri* |
| How do I get there? | ผม *m* /ฉัน *f* จะไปที่นั่นได้ยังไง? *pǒm/chán jah bpi têe nâhn dîe yahng•ngi* |

## At the Hotel

| | |
|---|---|
| I have a reservation. | ผม *m* /ฉัน *f* จองห้องไว้ *pǒm/chán jorng hôhng wí* |
| My name is… | ผม *m* /ฉัน *f* ชื่อ *pǒm/chán chûee…* |
| Do you have a room…? | คุณมีห้อง…ไหม? *kuhn mee hôhng…mí* |
| for one/two | สำหรับ คนเดียว/สองคน *sǎhm•ràhp kon deaw/sǒrng kon* |
| with a bathroom [toilet]/shower | ที่มี ห้องน้ำ/ห้องอาบน้ำ *têe mee hôhng nárm/hôhng àrp•nárm* |
| with air conditioning | ที่มีแอร์ *têe mee ae* |

In Thailand, there are many accommodation options available, ranging from extreme luxury to the bare essentials. Various western hotel chains offer high-end accommodations throughout the country; Amari and Dusit are top-level Thai-owned chains. You can also find many moderately-priced hotels that offer very good value for the money. Budget travelers wil have their pick of inexpensive hotels, guestrooms and hostels.

If you didn't reserve any accommodations before your trip, visit the local Tourist Information Office (Tourism Authority of Thailand, TAT) for recommendations on places to stay.

| | | |
|---|---|---|
| that's handicapped [disabled-] accessible | ที่มีทางเข้าออกสำหรับคนพิการ | *têe mee tarng kôu òrk săhm•ràhp kon píh•garn* |
| on the ground floor | ที่อยู่ชั้นล่าง | *têe•yòo cháhn lârng* |
| that's smoking/ non-smoking | ที่สูบบุหรี่ได้/ห้ามสูบบุหรี่ | *têe sòop buh•rèe dîe/hârm sòop buh•rèe* |
| For... | สำหรับ... | *săhm•ràhp...* |
| tonight | คืนนี้ | *kueen née* |
| two nights | สองคืน | *sŏrng kueen* |
| a week | หนึ่งสัปดาห์ | *nùeng sàhp•dar* |
| Do you have...? | คุณมี...ไหม? | *kuhn mee...mí* |
| a computer | คอมพิวเตอร์ | *kohm•pihw•dtêr* |
| an elevator [a lift] | ลิฟต์ | *lihp* |
| (wireless) internet service | บริการอินเตอร์เน็ต (ไร้สาย) | *bor•rih•garn ihn•dter•nèht (rí sĭe)* |
| room service | รูมเซอรวิส | *room ser•wiht* |
| Do you have...? | คุณมี...ไหม? | *kuhn mee...mí* |
| a TV | โทรทัศน์ | *toe•rah•táht* |

### YOU MAY HEAR...

| | |
|---|---|
| ขอดู พาสปอร์ต/บัตรเครดิต หน่อย *kŏr doo párs•sah•bpòrt/bàht•kre•dìht nòhy* | Your passport/credit card, please. |
| กรุณากรอกเอกสารนี้ *gah•rúh•nar gròrk èk•gah•sărn née* | Fill out this form. |
| เซ็นชื่อตรงนี้ *sehn chûee dtrong née* | Sign here. |

| | | |
|---|---|---|
| a pool | สระว่ายน้ำ | *sàh wîe•nárm* |
| a gym | ห้องออกกำลังกาย | *hôhng òrk•gahm•lahng•gie* |
| I need... | ผม *m*/ฉัน *f* ต้องการ... | *pŏm/cháhn dtôhng•garn...* |
| an extra bed | เตียงเสริม | *dteang sěrm* |
| a cot | เตียงพับ | *dteang•páhp* |
| a crib | เปลเด็ก | *bple dèhk* |

For Numbers, see page 158.

## Price

| | |
|---|---|
| How much per night/week? | วัน/สัปดาห์ ละเท่าไหร่? *wahn/sàhp•dar lah tôu•rì* |
| Does that include breakfast/sales tax [VAT]? | รวม อาหารเช้า/ภาษี ด้วยไหม? *roarm ar•hărn chóu/par•sěe dôary mí* |
| Are there any discounts? | มีส่วนลดไหม? *mee sòarn•lót mí* |

## Preferences

| | |
|---|---|
| Can I see the room? | ผม *m*/ฉัน *f* ขอดูห้องก่อนได้ไหม? *pŏm/cháhn kŏr doo hôhng gòrn dî mí* |
| I'd like...room. | ผม *m*/ฉัน *f* อยากได้ห้องที่... *pŏm/cháhn yàrk dîe hôhng têe...* |
| a better | ดีกว่านี้ *dee gwàr née* |

| | |
|---|---|
| a bigger | ใหญ่กว่านี้ *yì gwàr née* |
| a cheaper | ถูกกว่านี้ *tòok gwàr née* |
| a quieter | เงียบกว่านี้ *ngêap gwàr née* |
| I'll take it. | ผม *m* /ฉัน *f* เอาห้องนี้ *pŏm/cháhn ou hôhng née* |
| No, I won't take it. | ผม *m* /ฉัน *f* ไม่เอาห้องนี้ *pŏm/cháhn mî ou hôhng née* |

## Questions

| | |
|---|---|
| Where's…? | …อยู่ที่ไหน? …*yòo têe•nĭ* |
| the bar | บาร์ *bar* |
| the restroom [toilet] | ห้องน้ำ *hôhng•nárm* |
| the elevator [lift] | ลิฟต์ *lihp* |
| the pool | สระว่ายน้ำ *sàh wîe•nárm* |
| Can I have…? | ผม *m* /ฉัน *f* ขอ…หน่อยได้ไหม? *pŏm/cháhn kŏr…nòhy dî mí* |
| a blanket | ผ้าห่ม *pâr•hòm* |
| an iron | เตารีด *dtou•rêet* |
| the room key/ key card | กุญแจห้อง/คีย์การ์ด *guhn•jae hôhng/kee•gárt* |
| a pillow | หมอน *mŏrn* |
| soap | สบู่ *sah•bòo* |

| toilet paper | กระดาษชำระ *grah•dàrt chahm•ráh* |
| a towel | ผ้าเช็ดตัว *pâr•chéht•dtoar* |
| Do you have an adapter for this? | คุณมีปลั๊กแปลงไฟฟ้าสำหรับนี่ไหม? *kuhn mee bpláhk bplaeng fi•fár săhm•ràhp nêe mí* |
| How do I turn on the lights? | ผม *m* /ฉัน *f* จะเปิดไฟยังไง? *pŏm/cháhn jah bpèrt fi yahng•ngi* |
| Can you wake me at…? | ช่วยปลุกผม *m* /ฉัน *f* เวลา… ได้ไหม? *chôary bplùhk pŏm/cháhn we•lar…dî mí* |
| When does breakfast start/end? | อาหารเช้าจะ เริ่ม/หยุด เสิร์ฟเมื่อไหร่? *ar•hărn chóu jah rêrm/yùht sèrp mûea•rì* |
| Can I leave this in the safe? | ผม *m* /ฉัน *f* จะฝากของไว้ในเซฟได้ไหม? *pŏm/cháhn jah fàrk kŏrng wí ni sép dî mí* |
| Can I have my things from the safe? | ผม *m* /ฉัน *f* จะขอของที่ฝากไว้ในเซฟได้ไหม? *pŏm/cháhn jah kŏr kŏrng têe fàrk wí ni sép dî mí* |
| Is there mail [post]/ a message for me? | มี จดหมาย/ข้อความ ถึงผม *m* /ฉัน *f* ไหม? *mee jòt•mĭe/kôr•kwarm tŭeng pŏm cháhn mí* |
| Do you have a laundry service? | มีบริการรับซักรีดไหม? *mêe bah•rih•karn ráhp sáhk•reed mí?* |

## YOU MAY SEE…

| ห้องน้ำ *hôhng•nárm* | restroom [toilet] |
| ห้องอาบน้ำ *hôhng àrp•nárm* | shower |
| ประตูหนีไฟ *bprah•dtoo nĕe fi* | fire door |
| ทางออก(ฉุกเฉิน) *tarng òrk (chùhk•chĕrn)* | (emergency) exit |
| ตู้ขายเครื่องดื่ม *dtoo kie krŭeang•dueem* | vending machines |
| น้ำแข็ง *nárm•kăng* | ice |

## Problems

| | |
|---|---|
| There's a problem. | ผม *m* /ฉัน *f* มีปัญหา *pŏm/cháhn mee pahn•hăr* |
| I lost my key/key card. | ผม *m* /ฉัน *f* ทำ กุญแจ/คีย์การ์ด หาย *pŏm/cháhn tahm guhn•jae/kee•gárt hǐe* |
| I'm locked out of the room. | ผม *m* /ฉัน *f* เข้าห้องไม่ได้ *pŏm/cháhn kôu hôhng mî dîe* |
| There's no hot water/ toilet paper. | ไม่มีน้ำร้อน/กระดาษชำระ *mî mee nárm rórn/grah•dàrt chahm•ráh* |
| The room is dirty. | ห้องสกปรก *hôhng sòk•grah•bpròk* |
| There are bugs in the room. | มีแมลงในห้อง *mee mah•laeng ni hôhng* |
| The...doesn't work. | ...ไม่ทำงาน *...mî tahm•ngarn* |
| Can you fix...? | คุณช่วยซ่อม...ให้หน่อยได้ไหม? *kuhn chôary sôhm...hî nòhy dî mí* |
| the air conditioning | แอร์ *ae* |
| Can you fix...? | คุณช่วยซ่อม...ให้หน่อยได้ไหม? *kuhn chôary sôhm...hî nòhy dî mí* |
| the fan | พัดลม *páht•lom* |
| the heat [heating] | เครื่องทำความร้อน *krûeang tahm kwarm•rórn* |
| the light | หลอดไฟ *lòrt•fi* |
| the TV | โทรทัศน์ *toe•rah•táht* |
| the toilet | โถส้วม *tŏe•sôarm* |
| I'd like another room. | ผม *m* /ฉัน *f* อยากจะเปลี่ยนห้อง *pŏm/cháhn yàrk•jah bplèan hôhng* |

## Checking Out

| | |
|---|---|
| When's check-out? | ต้องเช็คเอาท์กี่โมง *dtôrng chéhk•óu gèe moeng* |
| Can I leave my bags here until...? | ผม *m* /ฉัน *f* จะฝากกระเป๋าไว้ที่นี่ถึง...ได้ไหม? *pŏm/cháhn jah fàrk grah•bpŏu wí têe•nêe tŭeng...dî mí* |
| Can I have an itemized bill/a receipt? | ผม *m* /ฉัน *f* ขอบิลแยกตามรายการ/ใบเสร็จได้ ไหม? *pŏm/cháhn kŏr bihn yâek dtarm rie•garn/bi•sèht dî mí* |

44

| I think there's a mistake. | ผม **m** /ฉัน **f** คิดว่ามีอะไรผิดชักอย่าง *pŏm/cháhn kíht wâr mee ah•ri pìht sáhk yàrng* |
| I'll pay in cash/by credit card. | ผม **m** /ฉัน **f** จะจ่ายด้วย เงินสด/บัตรเครดิต *pŏm/cháhn jah jìe dôary ngern•sòt/bàht•kre•dìht* |

## Renting

| I reserved an apartment/a room. | ผม **m** /ฉัน **f** จอง อพาร์ตเมนต์/ห้องไว้ *pŏm/cháhn jorng ah•párt•méhn/hôhng wí* |
| My name is... | ผม **m** /ฉัน **f** ชื่อ... *pŏm/cháhn chûee...* |
| Can I have the key/key card? | ผม **m** /ฉัน **f** ขอกุญแจ/คีย์การ์ดหน่อย *pŏm/cháhn kŏr guhn•jae hôhng/kee•gárt nòhy* |
| Are there...? | มี...ไหม? *mee...mí* |
| dishes | ถ้วยชาม *tôary•charm* |
| pillows | หมอน *mŏrn* |
| sheets | ผ้าปูที่นอน *pâr bpoo têe•norn* |
| towels | ผ้าเช็ดตัว *pâr•chéht•dtoar* |
| utensils | เครื่องใช้ *krûeang•chí* |
| When do I put out the bins/recycling? | ผม **m** /ฉัน **f** จะทิ้ง ขยะ/ขยะรีไซเคิล ได้เมื่อไหร่? *pŏm/cháhn jah tíhng kah•yàh/kah•yàh ree•si•kêrn dîe mûea•rì* |
| ...is broken. | ...เสีย *...sĕa* |
| How does...work? | ...ใช้งานยังไง? *...chí ngarn yahng•ngi* |
| the air conditioner | แอร์ *ae* |
| the dishwasher | เครื่องล้างจาน *krûeang lárng•jarn* |
| the freezer | ตู้แช่แข็ง *dtôo•châe•kăeng* |
| the heater | เครื่องทำน้ำร้อน *krûeang tahm náhm•rórn* |
| the microwave | ไมโครเวฟ *mi•kroe•wef* |
| the refrigerator | ตู้เย็น *dtôo•yehn* |
| the stove | เตา *dtou* |
| the washing machine | เครื่องซักผ้า *krûeang•sáhk•pâr* |

## Domestic Items

| I need... | ผม *m*/ฉัน *f* ต้องการ... *pŏm/cháhn dtôhng•garn...* |
| an adapter | ปลั๊กแปลงไฟฟ้า *bpláhk bplaeng fi•fár* |
| aluminum [kitchen] foil | กระดาษฟอยล์ *grah•dàrt fory* |
| a bottle opener | ที่เปิดขวด *têe•bpèrt•kòart* |
| a broom | ไม้กวาด *míe•gwàrt* |
| I need... | ผม *m*/ฉัน *f* ต้องการ... *pŏm/cháhn dtôhng•garn...* |
| a can opener | ที่เปิดกระป๋อง *têe bpèrt grah•bpŏhng* |
| cleaning supplies | อุปกรณ์ทำความสะอาด *ùhp•bpah•gorn tahm kwarm sah•àrt* |
| a corkscrew | ที่เปิดจุกก๊อก *têe bpèrt jùhk•góhk* |
| detergent | ผงซักฟอก *pŏng•sáhk•fôrk* |
| dishwashing liquid | น้ำยาล้างจาน *náhm•yar lárng•jarn* |
| garbage [rubbish] bags | ถุงใส่ขยะ *tŭhng sì kah•yàh* |
| a lightbulb | หลอดไฟ *lòrt•fi* |
| matches | ไม้ขีด *míe•kèet* |
| a mop | ไม้ถูพื้น *mí•too•pueen* |
| napkins | กระดาษเช็ดปาก *grah•dàrt chéht bpàrk* |
| paper towels | กระดาษเช็ดมือ *grah•dàrt chéht muee* |
| plastic wrap [cling film] | ฟิล์มถนอมอาหาร *feem tah•nŏrm ar•hărn* |
| a plunger | ที่ดูดส้วม *têe dòot sôarm* |
| scissors | กรรไกร *gahn•gri* |

For Oven Temperatures, see page 164.

## At the Hostel

| | | |
|---|---|---|
| Is there a bed available? | มีเตียงว่างไหม? | *mee dteang wârng mí* |
| Can I have…? | ขอ…ได้ไหม? | *kŏr…dî mí* |
| a single/ double room | ห้องเดี่ยว/ห้องคู่ | *hôhng dèaw/hôhng kôo* |
| a blanket | ผ้าห่ม | *pâr•hòm* |
| a pillow | หมอน | *mŏrn* |
| sheets | ผ้าปูที่นอน | *pâr bpoo têe•norn* |
| a towel | ผ้าเช็ดตัว | *pâr chéht•dtoar* |
| Do you have lockers? | มีล็อคเกอร์ไหม? | *mee lóhk•gêr mí* |
| When do you lock up? | คุณปิดกี่โมง? | *kuhn bpìht gèe moeng* |
| Do I need a membership card? | ผม *m*/ฉัน *f* ต้องแสดงบัตรสมาชิกหรือเปล่า? | *pŏm/cháhn dtôrng sah•daeng bàht sah•mar•chíhk rúe•bplòw* |
| Here's my international student card. | นี่คือบัตรนักเรียนนานาชาติของฉัน | *nee kuee bahd•nahk•rean nar•nar•chârt korng cháhn* |

## Going Camping

| | | |
|---|---|---|
| Can I camp here? | ผม *m*/ฉัน *f* ตั้งแค้มป์ตรงนี้ได้ไหม? | *pŏm/cháhn dtâhng kaem dtrong•née dîe mí* |
| Where's the campsite? | ที่ตั้งแค้มป์อยู่ตรงไหน? | *têe dtâhng kaem yòo dtrong nĭ* |
| What is the charge per day/week? | วัน/สัปดาห์ ละเท่าไหร่? | *wahn/sàhp•dar lah tôu•rì* |
| Are there…? | มี…ไหม? | *mee…mí* |
| cooking facilities | ที่ทำอาหาร | *têe tahm ar•hărn* |
| electric outlets | ปลั๊กไฟ | *bpláhk•fi* |
| laundry facilities | ที่ซักผ้า | *têe sáhk•pâr* |
| Are there…? | มี…ไหม? | *mee…mí* |
| showers | ห้องอาบน้ำ | *hôhng àrp•nárm* |
| tents for rent [hire] | เต็นท์ให้เช่า | *dtéhn hî chôu* |

For Domestic Items, see page 46.

47

## Communications

### ESSENTIAL

| | |
|---|---|
| Where's an internet cafe? | อินเตอร์เน็ตคาเฟ่อยู่ที่ไหน? *ihn•dter•nèht kar•fê yòo têe•nî* |
| Can I access the internet/check e-mail here? | ผม *m* /ฉัน *f* ใช้อินเตอร์เน็ต/เช็คอีเมล์ ที่นี่ได้ไหม? *pǒm/ cháhn chí ihn•dter•nèht/chéhk ee•mew têe•nee dî mí* |
| How much per hour/half hour? | ชั่วโมงละ/ครึ่งชั่วโมง เท่าไหร่? *chôar•moeng lah/ krûeng chôar•moeng tôu•rì* |
| How do I connect/ log on? | ผม *m* /ฉัน *f* จะ เชื่อมต่อ/เข้าระบบ ได้ยังไง? *pǒm/cháhn jah chûeam•dtòr/kôu rah•bòp dî yahng•ngi* |
| A phone card, please. | ขอซื้อบัตร โทรศัพท์หน่อย *kǒr súee bàht toe•rah•sàhp nòhy* |
| Can I have your phone number? | ผม *m* /ฉัน *f* ขอเบอร์โทรศัพท์คุณหน่อยได้ไหม? *pǒm/ cháhn kǒr ber toe•rah•sàhp kuhn nòhy dî mí* |
| Here's my number/ e-mail. | นี่ เบอร์โทรศัพท์/อีเมล์ ของผม *m* /ฉัน *f* nêe ber toe•rah•sàhp/ee•mew kǒhng pǒm/cháhn* |
| Call me. | โทรหาผม *m* /ฉัน *f* นะ *toe hǎr pǒm/cháhn náh* |
| E-mail me. | อีเมล์หาผม *m* /ฉัน *f* นะ *ee•mew hǎr pǒm/cháhn náh* |
| Hello. This is… | ฮัลโหล นี่… *hahn•lǒe nêe…* |
| Can I speak to…? | ขอพูดกับคุณฯ *kǒr pôot gàhp kuhn…* |
| Can you repeat that? | พูดอีกทีได้ไหม? *pôot èek tee dî mí* |
| I'll call back later. | ผม *m* /ฉัน *f* จะ โทรกลับมาใหม่ *pǒm/cháhn jah toe glàhp mar mì* |
| Bye. | สวัสดี *sah•wàht•dee* |
| Where's the post office? | ที่ทำการ ไปรษณีย์อยู่ที่ไหน? *têe•tahm•garn bpri•sah•nee yòo têe•nî* |
| I'd like to send this to… | ผม *m* /ฉัน *f* อยากจะส่งของนี้ไปที่… *pǒm/cháhn yàrk jah sòng kǒrng née bpi têe…* |

## Online

| | |
|---|---|
| Where's an internet cafe? | อินเตอร์เน็ตคาเฟ่อยู่ที่ไหน? *ihn•dter•nèht kar•fê yòo têe•nî* |
| Does it have wireless internet? | มีอินเตอร์เน็ตไร้สายไหม? *mee ihn•dter•nèht rí sǐe mí* |
| What is the WiFi password? | รหัสผ่านของไวไฟคืออะไร? *rah•hahd•p ̂arn korng wi•fi kuee ar•ri* |
| Is the WiFi free? | ใช้ไวไฟได้ฟรีไหม? *chî wi•fi dîe free mí* |
| Do you have bluetooth? | คุณมีบลูทูธไหม? *kuhn mêe bloo•tooth mí* |
| Can I access Skype? | ฉันสามารถใช้สไกป์ได้ไหม? *cháhn sar•mard chî Sa•gibp dîe mí* |
| How do I turn the computer on/off? | ผม *m* /ฉัน *f* จะ เปิดเครื่อง/ปิดเครื่องคอมพิวเตอร์ ยังไง *pǒm/cháhn jah bpert krûeang/bpiht krûeang kohm•pihw•dtêr yahng•ngi* |
| How much per hour/ half hour? | ชั่วโมงละ/ครึ่งชั่วโมง เท่าไหร่? *chôar•moeng lah/krûeng chôar•moeng tôu•rì* |
| How do I...? | ผม *m* /ฉัน *f* จะ... ได้ยังไง *pǒm/cháhn jah. . .dîe yahng•ngi* |
| connect/disconnect | เชื่อมต่อ/ตัดการเชื่อมต่อ *chûeam•dtòr/dtàht garn chûeam•dtòr* |
| log on/off | เข้าระบบ/ออกจากระบบ *kôu rah•bòp/òrk jàrk rah•bòp* |
| type this symbol | พิมพ์สัญลักษณ์นี้ *pihm sǎhn•yah•láhk née* |
| What's your e-mail? | ขออีเมล์ของคุณหน่อยได้ไหม *kǒr ee•mew kuhn nòhy dî mí* |
| My e-mail is... | อีเมล์ของผม *m* /ฉัน *f* คือ *ee•mew kǒhng pǒm/cháhn kuee...* |
| Can I...? | ฉันสามารถ... ได้ไหม? *cháhn sar•mard...dîe mí* |
| access the internet | ใช้อินเตอร์เน็ต *chî ihn•ter•neht* |
| check my e-mail | เช็กอีเมล *chehk ee•mel* |
| print | พิมพ์ *pihm* |
| plug in/charge my laptop/iPhone/iPad? | เสียบปลั๊ก/ชาร์จไฟแล็ปท็อป/ไอโฟน/ไอแพ็ด? *seab bpahk/chart fi lap•torp/i•phoen/i•paed* |

| Do you have a scanner? | คุณมีสแกนเนอร์ไหม? *kuhn mêe sah•gaen•ner mí* |
|---|---|

## Social Media

| Are you on Facebook/ Twitter? | คุณเล่นเฟซบุ๊ค/ทวิตเตอร์ไหม? *kuhn l`ehn fes•buhk/ tah•wiht•ter mí* |
|---|---|
| What's your user name? | ชื่อผู้ใช้ของคุณคืออะไร? *chuee poo•chi korng kuhn kuee ar•ri* |
| I'll add you as a friend. | ฉันจะเพิ่มคุณเป็นเพื่อน *cháhn jah perm kuhn bpehn pûean* |
| I'll follow you on Twitter. | ฉันจะติดตามคุณในทวิตเตอร์ *cháhn jah dtihd•dtarm kuhn ni tah•wiht•ter* |
| Are you following...? | คุณติดตาม....ไหม? *kuhn dtihd•dtarm…mí* |
| I'll put the pictures on Facebook/Twitter. | ฉันจะใส่รูปลงในเฟซบุ๊ค/ทวิตเตอร์ *cháhn jah si roob long ni fes•buhk/tah•wiht•ter* |
| I'll tag you in the pictures. | ฉันจะแท็กคุณในรูปด้วย *cháhn jah tag kuhn ni roob dôary* |

### YOU MAY SEE...

| | |
|---|---|
| ปิด *bpìht* | close |
| ลบ *lóp* | delete |
| อีเมล์ *ee•mew* | e-mail |
| ออก *òrk* | exit |
| ตัวช่วย *dtoar•chôary* | help |
| อินเตอร์เน็ต *ihn•dter•nèht* | internet |
| เปิด *bpèrt* | open |
| ปริ๊นต์ *bpríhn* | print |
| บันทึก *bahn•túek* | save |
| ส่ง *sòng* | send |
| ชื่อผู้ใช้/รหัส *chûee pôo•chí/rah•hàht* | username/password |
| อินเตอร์เน็ตไร้สาย *ihn•dter•nèht rí sǐe* | wireless internet |

Internet service in Thailand is widespread. You can find internet cafes throughout Bangkok, at tourist attractions and even in small towns. Many areas, especially business districts, have hotspots; pre-registration may be required.

## Phone

| | |
|---|---|
| A phone card/prepaid phone, please. | ขอซื้อ บัตร โทรศัพท์/บัตรเติมเงินหน่อย *kŏr súee bàht toe•rah•sàhp/bàht dterm ngern nòhy* |
| How much? | เท่าไหร่? *tôu•rì* |
| Can I recharge/buy minutes for this phone? | ผม *m*/ฉัน *f* จะ เติมเงิน/เพิ่มเวลา ในโทรศัพท์นี้ได้ไหม? *pŏm/cháhn jah dterm ngern/pêrm we•lar ni toe•rah•sàhp née dîe mí* |
| Where's the pay phone? | ตู้โทรศัพท์อยู่ที่ไหน? *dtôo toe•rah•sàhp yòo têe•nî* |
| What's the area/country code for...? | รหัส พื้นที่/ประเทศ ของนรหัสอะ ไร? *rah•hàht púeen•têe/bprah•têt kŏrng...rah•hàht ah•ri* |
| What's the number for Information? | เบอร์โทรศัพท์ของประชาสัมพันธ์เบอร์อะไร? *ber toe•rah•sàhp kŏrng bprach•char•săhm•pahn ber ah•ri* |
| I'd like the number for... | ผม *m*/ฉัน *f* ต้องการเบอร์โทรศัพท์ของ... *pŏm/cháhn dtôhng•garn ber toe•rah•sàhp kŏhng...* |
| I'd like to call collect [reverse the charges]. | ผม *m*/ฉัน *f* ต้องการ โทรเก็บเงินปลายทาง *pŏm/cháhn dtôhng•garn toe gèhp ngern bplie tarng* |
| My phone doesn't work here. | โทรศัพท์ของผม *m*/ฉัน *f* ใช้ไม่ได้ที่นี่ *toe•rah•sàhp kŏhng pŏm/cháhn chí mî dîe têe•nêe* |
| What network are you on? | คุณใช้เครือข่ายอะไร? *kuhn chí kruea•k`ar ah•rì* |
| Is it 3G? | ใช่สามจีไหม? *chî sarm•jee chî mí* |
| I have run out of credit/minutes. | ฉัน ไม่มีเครดิต/นาทีเหลือแล้ว *cháhn mi•mee cre•dit/nar•tee luea laew* |

| Can I buy some credit? | ฉันจะซื้อเครดิตเพิ่ม ได้ไหม? *cháhn jah suee cre•dit perm die mí* |
| Do you have a phone charger? | คุณมีที่ชาร์จโทรศัพท์ไหม? *kuhn mee têe chart toe•rah•sahb mí* |
| Can I have your number? | ผม *m* /ฉัน *f* ขอเบอร์โทรศัพท์ของคุณหน่อย ได้ไหม? *pŏm/cháhn kŏr ber toe•rah•sàhp kŏhng kuhn nòhy dî mí* |
| Here's my number. | นี่เบอร์โทรศัพท์ของผม *m* /ฉัน *f* *nêe ber toe•rah•sàhp kŏhng pŏm/cháhn* |
| Please call me. | ช่วยโทรมาหาผม *m* /ฉัน *f* หน่อย *chôary toe mar hăr pŏm/ cháhn nòhy* |
| Please text me. | ช่วยส่งข้อความมาหาผม *m* /ฉัน *f* หน่อย *chôary sòng kôr•kwarm mar hăr pŏm/cháhn nòhy* |
| I'll call you. | ผม *m* /ฉัน *f* จะโทรหาคุณ *pŏm/cháhn jah toe hăr kuhn* |
| I'll text you. | ผม *m* /ฉัน *f* จะส่งข้อความถึงคุณ *pŏm/cháhn jah sòng kôr•kwarm tŭeng kuhn* |

## Telephone Etiquette

| Hello. This is... | ฮัลโหล นี่... *hahn•lŏe nêe...* |
| Can I speak to...? | ขอพูดกับคุณ... ได้ไหม? *kŏr pôot gàhp kuhn...dî mí* |
| Extension... | ต่อหมายเลข... *dtòr mĭe•lêk...* |

In Thailand, public phones are yellow and accept prepaid phone cards, which can be bought in convenience stores. Public phones are frequently found in major areas, but you may have a harder time finding one in the countryside.

To call the U.S. or Canada from Thailand, dial 00 + 1 + area code + phone number. To call the U.K., dial 00 + 44 + area code (minus the first 0) + phone number.

## YOU MAY HEAR...

ใครโทรมา? *kri toe mar*

รอสักครู่ *ror sáhk krôo*

เขา/เธอไม่อยู่/ติดสายอยู่ *kóu/ter mî yòo/ dtiht•sǐe yòo*

จะให้ เขา/เธอ โทรกลับไหม? *jah hî kóu/ter toe glàhp mí*

เบอร์โทรศัพท์ของคุณเบอร์อะไร? *ber toe•rah•sàhp kǒhng kuhn ber ah•ri*

Who's calling?

Hold on.

He/She is not here/on another line.

Can he/she call you back?

What's your number?

| | |
|---|---|
| Speak louder/more slowly, please. | ช่วยพูด ดังขึ้น/ช้าลง หน่อยได้ไหม *chôary pôot dahng kêuhn/chár long nòhy dî mí* |
| Can you repeat that? | พูดอีกทีได้ไหม? *pôot èek tee dî mí* |
| I'll call back later. | ผม *m*/ฉัน *f* จะโทรกลับมาใหม่ *pǒm/cháhn jah toe glàhp mar mì* |
| Bye. | สวัสดี *sah•wàht•dee* |

Most Thai post offices are open from approximately 8:00 a.m. to 4:00 p.m. and provide the typical range of services, including phone services. The central service in Bangkok, the General Post Office, located on Charoen Krung Road, is open 24 hours a day.

### YOU MAY HEAR...

กรอกข้อความในใบศุลกากรด้วย *gròrk kôr•kwarm ni bi sŭhn•lah•gar•gorn dôary*

Fill out the customs declaration form.

มูลค่าของเท่าไหร่? *moon•lah•kâr kŏrng tôu•rì*

What's the value?

มีอะไรอยู่ในนี้? *mee ah•ri yòo ni née*

What's inside?

## Fax

| | |
|---|---|
| Can I send/receive a fax here? | ผม *m* /ฉัน *f* ส่ง/รับแฟ็กซ์ที่นี่ได้ไหม? *pŏm/cháhn sòng/ráhp fàk têe•nêe dî mí* |
| What's the fax number? | แฟ็กซ์เบอร์อะไร? *fàk ber ah•ri* |
| Please fax this to... | กรุณาแฟ็กซ์อันนี้ไปที่... *gah•rúh•nar fàk àhn née bpi têe...* |

## Post

| | |
|---|---|
| Where's the post office/mailbox [postbox]? | ที่ทำการไปรษณีย์/ตู้ไปรษณีย์ อยู่ที่ไหน? *têe tahm garn bpri•sah•nee/dtôo bpri•sah•nee yòo têe•nî* |
| A stamp for this postcard/letter to... | ขอซื้อแสตมป์สำหรับส่งจดหมาย/โปสการ์ด นี้ไปที่... *kŏr súee sah•dtaem sãhm•ràp sòng jòt•mǐe/bpóet•sah•gárt née bpi têe...* |
| How much? | เท่าไหร่? *tôu•rì* |
| Send this package by airmail/express. | ช่วยส่งพัสดุนี้ทาง ไปรษณีย์อากาศ/อีเอ็มเอส *chôary sòng páht•sah•dùh née tarng bpri•sah•nee ar•gàrt/ee•ehm•ét* |
| A receipt, please. | ขอใบเสร็จด้วย *kŏr bi•sèht dôary* |

# Food & Drink

## ESSENTIAL

| | |
|---|---|
| Can you recommend a good restaurant/ bar? | คุณช่วยแนะนำ ร้านอาหาร/บาร์ ดีๆให้หน่อยได้ไหม? *kuhn chôary ná•nahm rárn ar•hărn/bar dee dee hî nòhy dî mí* |
| Is there a traditional Thai/an inexpensive restaurant nearby? | มี ร้านอาหารไทย/ร้านที่ราคา ไม่แพง ใกล้ๆแถวนี้ไหม? *mee rárn ar•hărn ti/rárn têe rar•kar mî paeng glî glî tă ew née mí* |
| A table for..., please. | ขอโต๊ะสำหรับ...คน *kŏr dtó săhm•ràhp...kon* |
| Can we sit...? | ขอนั่งตรง...ได้ไหม? *kŏr nâhng dtrong...dî mí* |
| here/there | นี้/นั้น *née/náhn* |
| outside | ด้านนอก *dârn nôrk* |
| in a non-smoking area | บริเวณห้ามสูบบุหรี่ *bor•rih•wen hârm sòop bu•rèe* |
| I'm waiting for someone. | ผม *m*/ฉัน *f* กำลังรอเพื่อนอยู่ *pŏm/cháhn gahm•lahng ror pûean yòo* |
| Where's the restroom [toilet]? | ห้องน้ำไปทางไหน? *hôhng•nárm bpi tarng nî* |
| A menu, please. | ขอเมนูหน่อย *kŏr me•noo nòhy* |
| What do you recommend? | มีอะไรแนะนำบ้าง? *mee ah•ri ná•nahm bârng* |
| I'd like... | ผม *m*/ฉัน *f* อยากได้... *pŏm/cháhn yàrk dîe...* |
| Some more..., please. | ขอ...เพิ่มอีกหน่อย *kŏr...pêrm èek nòhy* |
| Enjoy your meal! | ทานให้อร่อย! *tarn hî ah•ròhy* |
| The check [bill], please. | เช็คบิลด้วย *chéhk bihn dôary* |
| Is service included? | รวมค่าบริการแล้วหรือยัง? *roarm kâr bor•rih•garn láew rúe yahng* |
| Can I pay by credit card? | ผม *m*/ฉัน *f* จ่ายด้วยบัตรเครดิตได้ไหม? *pŏm/cháhn jìe dôary bàht kre•dìht dî mí* |

| | |
|---|---|
| Can I have a receipt? | ผม *m*/ฉัน *f* ขอใบเสร็จด้วยได้ไหม? *pŏm/cháhn kŏr bi•sèht dôary dî mí* |
| Thank you! | ขอบคุณ! *kòrp•kuhn* |

## Where to Eat

| | |
|---|---|
| Can you recommend...? | คุณช่วยแนะนำ...ให้หน่อยได้ไหม? *kuhn chôary ná•nahm... hî nòhy dî mí* |
| a restaurant | ร้านอาหาร *rárn ar•hărn* |
| a bar | บาร์ *bar* |
| a cafe | ร้านกาแฟ *rárn gar•fae* |
| a fast-food place | ร้านอาหารฟาสต์ฟู๊ด *rárn ar•hărn fárt•fóot* |
| a cheap restaurant | ร้านอาหารราคาไม่แพง *rarn•ar•harn rar•kar mí paeng* |
| an expensive restaurant | ร้านอาหารราคาแพง *rarn•ar•harn rar•kar paeng* |
| a restaurant with a good view | ร้านอาหารที่มีวิวสวย *rarn•ar•harn têe mee wihw sŏary* |
| an authentic/a non-touristy restaurant | ร้านอาหารดั้งเดิม/ที่ไม่ใช่สำหรับนักท่องเที่ยว *rarn•ar•harn dahng•derm/têe mí chî sahm•rahb nahk•torng•teaw* |

## Reservations & Preferences

| | |
|---|---|
| I'd like to reserve a table... | ผม *m*/ฉัน *f* อยากจะจองโต๊ะ... *pŏm/cháhn yàrk jah jorng dtó...* |
| for two | สำหรับสองคน *săhm•ràhp sŏrng kon* |
| for this evening | สำหรับเย็นนี้ *săhm•ràhp yehn née* |
| for tomorrow at... | สำหรับพรุ่งนี้ตอน... *săhm•ràhp prûhng née dtorn...* |
| A table for two, please. | ขอโต๊ะสำหรับสองที่ *kŏr dtó săhm•ràhp sŏrng têe* |
| We have a reservation. | เราจองไว้แล้ว *rou jorng wí láew* |
| My name is... | ผม *m*/ฉัน *f* ชื่อ... *pŏm/cháhn chûee...* |
| Can we sit...? | ขอนั่งตรง...ได้ไหม? *kŏr nâhng dtrong...dî mí* |

**YOU MAY HEAR…**

คุณจะสั่งอาหารเลยไหม? *kuhn jah sàhng ar•hǎrn lery mí* — Are you ready to order?

ผม *m* /ฉัน *f* อยากจะแนะนำ… *pǒm/cháhn yàrk jah ná•nahm…* — I recommend…

ทานให้อร่อย *tarn hî ah•ròhy* — Enjoy your meal.

| | |
|---|---|
| here/there | นี้/นั้น *née/náhn* |
| outside | ด้านนอก *dârn nôrk* |
| in the shade | ในร่ม *ni rom* |
| in the sun | ข้างนอก *karng nork* |
| in a non-smoking area | บริเวณห้ามสูบบุหรี่ *bor•rih•wen hârm sòop bu•rèe* |
| by the window | ริมหน้าต่าง *rihm nâr•dtàrng* |
| Where's the restroom [toilet]? | ห้องน้ำไปทางไหน? *hôhng•nárm bpi tarng nǐ* |

## How to Order

| | |
|---|---|
| Waiter/Waitress! | บ๋อย/คุณ! *bǒhy/kuhn* |
| We're ready to order. | เราต้องการสั่งอาหาร *rou dtôhng•garn sàhng ar•hǎrn* |

| | |
|---|---|
| The wine list, please. | ขอรายการไวน์หน่อย *kŏr rie•garn wie nòhy* |
| I'd like... | ผม *m* /ฉัน *f* อยากได้... *pŏm/cháhn yàrk dîe...* |
| a bottle of... | ...หนึ่งขวด ...*nùeng kòart* |
| a carafe of... | ...หนึ่งเหยือก ...*nùeng yùeek* |
| a glass of... | ...หนึ่งแก้ว ...*nùeng gâew* |
| The menu, please. | ขอเมนูหน่อย *kŏr me•noo nòhy* |
| Do you have...? | คุณมี...ไหม? *kuhn mee...mí* |
| a menu in English | เมนูเป็นภาษาอังกฤษ *me•noo bpehn par•sǎr ahng•grìht* |
| a fixed-price menu | เมนูอาหารชุด *me•noo ar•hǎrn chúht* |
| a children's menu | เมนูสำหรับเด็ก *me•noo sǎhm•ràhp dèhk* |
| What do you recommend? | มีอะไรแนะนำบ้าง? *mee ah•ri ná•nahm bârng* |
| What's this? | นี่อะไร? *nêe ah•ri* |
| Is it spicy? | เผ็ดไหม? *pèht mí* |
| I'd like... | ผม *m* /ฉัน *f* ขอ... *pŏm/cháhn kŏr...* |
| More..., please. | ขอ...เพิ่มหน่อย *kŏr...pêrm nòhy* |
| With/Without... | ใส่/ไม่ใส่... *sì/mî sì...* |
| Without..., please. | ไม่ใส่...นะ *mî sì...náh* |
| I can't have... | ผม *m* /ฉัน *f* กิน...ไม่ได้ *pŏm/cháhn gihn...mî dîe* |
| rare | ไม่ค่อยสุก *mî•kôhy sùhk* |
| medium | สุกปานกลาง *sùhk bparn•glarng* |
| well-done | สุกมาก *sùhk mârk* |
| It's to go [take away]. | ใส่ห่อไปกินที่บ้าน *sì hòr bpi gin têe bârn* |

59

## YOU MAY SEE...

| | |
|---|---|
| ราคาตายตัว *rar•kar dtie•dtoar* | fixed-price |
| เมนูพิเศษวันนี้ *me•noo píh•sèt wahn•née* | menu of the day |
| (ไม่)รวมค่าบริการ *(mî) roarm kǎr bor•rihgarn* | service (not) included |
| พิเศษ *píh•sèt* | specials |

## Cooking Methods

| | |
|---|---|
| baked | อบ *òp* |
| boiled | ต้ม *dtôm* |
| breaded | ชุบขนมปัง *chúhp kah•nŏm•bpahng* |
| diced | หั่น *hàhn* |
| fileted | แล่ *lâe* |
| deep-fried | ทอด *tôrt* |
| stir-fried | ผัด *pàht* |
| grilled | ปิ้ง/ย่าง *bpîhng/yârng* |
| poached | เคี่ยว *kêaw* |
| roasted | อบ *òp* |
| sautéed | ผัด *pàht* |
| smoked | รมควัน *rom kwahn* |
| steamed | นึ่ง *nûeng* |
| stewed | ตุ๋น *dtŭhn* |
| stuffed | ยัดไส้ *yáht sî* |

## Dietary Requirements

| | |
|---|---|
| I'm diabetic. | ผม *m*/ฉัน *f* เป็น โรคเบาหวาน *pŏm/cháhn bpehn rôek bou•wărn* |
| I'm... | ผม *m*/ฉัน *f* กิน... *pŏm/cháhn kihn...* |
| lactose intolerant | นมไม่ได้ *nom mî dîe* |
| vegetarian | มังสวิรัติ *mahng•sàh•wíh•ráht* |
| vegan | เจ *je* |
| I'm allergic to... | ผม *m*/ฉัน *f* แพ้... *pŏm/cháhn páe...* |
| I can't eat... | ผม *m*/ฉัน *f* กิน...ไม่ได้ *pŏm/cháhn gihn...mî dîe* |
| dairy | นม *nom* |
| gluten | สารกลูเตน *sărn gloo•dtêhn* |
| nuts | ถั่ว *tòar* |
| pork | เนื้อหมู *núea mŏo* |

| Is it halal/kosher? | อันนี้เป็นอาหาร ฮาลาล/โคเชอร์ หรือเปล่า? *ahn née bpehn ar•hǎrn har•larn/koe•chêr rúe•bplòw* |
|---|---|
| Do you have... | คุณมี... ไหม? *kuhn mee...mí* |
| skimmed milk | นมพร่องไขมัน *nom prorng ki•mahn* |
| whole milk | นมครบส่วน *nom krob so˘arn* |
| soya milk | นมถั่วเหลือง *nom toar•lueang* |

## Dining with Children

| Do you have children's portions? | คุณมีขนาดสำหรับเด็กหรือเปล่า? *kuhn mee kah•nàrt sǎhm•ràhp dèhk rúe•bplòw* |
|---|---|
| A highchair/child's seat, please. | ขอ เก้าอี้เด็ก/ที่นั่งเด็ก หน่อย *kǒr gôu•ee dèhk/têe•nâhng dèhk nòhy* |
| Where can I feed/ change the baby? | ผม *m* /ฉัน *f* จะ ให้นม/เปลี่ยนผ้าอ้อม เด็กได้ที่ไหน? *pǒm/ cháhn jah hî nom/bplèan pâr•ôrm dèhk díe têe•nǐ* |
| Can you warm this? | ช่วยอุ่นนี่ให้หน่อยได้ไหม? *chôary ùhn nêe hî nòhy díe mí* |

## How to Complain

| How much longer will our food be? | อีกนานไหมกว่าอาหารจะมา? *èek narn mí gwàr ar•hǎrn jah mar* |
|---|---|
| We can't wait any longer. | เรารอต่อไปไม่ไหวแล้ว *rou ror dtòr bpi mî wǐ láew* |
| We're leaving. | เราจะกลับแล้ว *rou jah glahp láew* |
| I didn't order this. | ผม *m* /ฉัน *f* ไม่ได้สั่งอันนี้ *pǒm/cháhn mî dî sàhng ahn née* |
| I ordered... | ผม *m* /ฉัน *f* สั่ง... *pǒm/cháhn sàhng...* |
| I can't eat this. | ผม *m* /ฉัน *f* กินอันนี้ไม่ได้ *pǒm/cháhn gihn ahn née mî dìe* |
| This is too... | นี่...เกินไป *nee...gern bpi* |
| cold/hot | เย็น/ร้อน *yehn/rorn* |
| salty/spicy | เค็ม/เผ็ด *kehm/pehd* |
| tough/bland | เหนียว/จืด *neaw/jueed* |
| This isn't clean/fresh. | อันนี้ไม่ สะอาด/สด *ahn née mî sah•àrt/sòt* |

A 10% service charge is usually included in the restaurant bill. When locals tip, they typically just leave behind some loose change. Tipping is not customary at food shops or roadside stands.

## Paying

| | | |
|---|---|---|
| The check [bill], please. | เช็คบิลด้วย | chéhk bihn dôary |
| Separate checks [bills], please. | แยกบิลด้วย | yâek bihn dôary |
| It's all together. | รวมบิลเลย | roarm bihn lery |
| Is service included? | รวมค่าบริการแล้วหรือยัง? | roarm kâr bor•rih•garn láew rúe yahng |
| What's this amount for? | อันนี้ค่าอะไร? | ahn née kâr ah•ri |
| I didn't have that. I had… | ผม m /ฉัน f ไม่ได้สั่งอันนี้ ผม m /ฉัน f สั่ง… | pŏm/cháhn mî dî sàhng ahn née pŏm/cháhn sàhng… |
| Can I have a receipt/ an itemized bill? | ผม m /ฉัน f ขอ ใบเสร็จ/บิลแยกตามรายการ ได้ไหม? | pŏm/cháhn kŏr bi•sèht/bihn yâek dtarm rie•garn dîe mí |
| That was delicious! | อาหารอร่อยมาก! | ar•hǎrn ah•ròhy mark |
| I've already paid | จ่ายเงินแล้ว | jàry ngern laew |

## Meals & Cooking

### Breakfast

| | | |
|---|---|---|
| apple juice | น้ำแอปเปิ้ล | nárm áep•bpêrn |
| bacon | เบคอน | be•kôhn |
| bread | ขนมปัง | kah•nŏm•bpahng |
| butter | เนย | nery |
| (cold/hot) cereal | ซีเรียล (เย็น/ร้อน) | see•rêal (yehn/rórn) |
| cheese | เนยแข็ง | nery•kǎng |

Food in Thailand is usually eaten with a fork and spoon, though Chinese-style noodle dishes are often eaten with chopsticks. Knives at the table are not necessary since food is cut into bite-sized chunks during cooking. It is common for the whole table to share several main dishes. While this is a great opportunity for you to try many new recipes at once, put only a spoonful at a time on your plate. In Thailand, it is impolite to fill your plate with food.

| | | |
|---|---|---|
| coffee/tea... | กาแฟ/ชา... | gar•fae/char... |
| black | ดำ | dahm |
| decaf | ชนิดไม่มีคาเฟอีน | chah•níht mî mee kar•fe•een |
| with milk | ใส่นม | sì nom |
| with sugar | ใส่น้ำตาล | sì náhm•dtarn |
| with artificial sweetener | ใส่น้ำตาลเทียม | sì náhm•dtarn team |
| ...eggs | ไข่... | kì... |
| hard-/soft-boiled | ต้มสุก/ลวก | dtôm sùhk/lôark |
| fried | ดาว | dow |
| scrambled | คน | kon |
| fruit juice | น้ำผลไม้ | nárm pǒn•lah•mí |
| jam/jelly | แยม/เยลลี่ | yaem/yen•lêe |
| milk | นม | nom |
| muffin | มัฟฟิน | máhp•fîhn |
| oatmeal | ข้าวโอ๊ต | kôw•óet |
| omelet | ไข่เจียว | kì•jeaw |
| orange juice | น้ำส้ม | nárm sôm |
| pineapple juice | น้ำสับปะรด | nárm sàhp•bpah•rót |
| rice porridge with pork/chicken | โจ๊ก หมู/ไก่ | jóek mǒo/gì |

| | |
|---|---|
| rice soup with… | ข้าวต้ม… *kôw dtôm…* |
| chicken | ไก่ *gì* |
| pork | หมู *mŏo* |
| shrimp [prawn] | กุ้ง *gûhng* |
| roll | ขนมปังก้อน *kah•nŏm•bpahng gôrn* |
| sausage | ไส้กรอก *sî•gròrk* |
| toast | ขนมปังปิ้ง *kah•nŏm•bpahng bpîhng* |
| yogurt | โยเกิร์ต *yoe•gèrt* |

## Appetizers

| | |
|---|---|
| deep-fried bread with ground [minced] pork/ shrimp [prawn] | ขนมปังหน้า หมู/กุ้ง *kah•nŏm•bpahng nâr mŏo/gûhng* |
| deep-fried, crispy wanton | เกี๊ยวทอด *géaw tôrt* |
| deep-fried pastry cup with ground [minced] pork | กระทงทอง *grah•tong•torng* |
| deep-fried, spicy fishcake | ทอดมันปลา *tôrt•mahn bplar* |
| deep-fried spring roll | เปาะเปี๊ยะทอด *bpoh•bpéa tôrt* |
| fresh spring roll | เปาะเปี๊ยะสด *bpoh•bpéa sòt* |
| grilled squid | ปลาหมึกย่าง *bplar•mùek yârng* |
| …satay | สะเต๊ะ… *sah•dtéh…* |
| beef | เนื้อ *núea* |
| chicken | ไก่ *gì* |
| pork | หมู *mŏo* |
| shrimp [prawn] rice cracker | ข้าวเกรียบกุ้ง *kôw•grèap gûhng* |
| spicy pork sausage salad | แหนมสด *năem•sòt* |

| | | |
|---|---|---|
| spicy northeastern sausage | ไส้กรอกอีสาน | *sî•gròrk ee•sărn* |
| stuffed chicken wing | ปีกไก่ยัดไส้ | *bpèek•gì yáht sî* |

## Soup

| | | |
|---|---|---|
| chicken and coconut milk soup flavored with galanga | ต้มข่าไก่ | *dtôm•kàr gì* |
| chicken soup | ซุปไก่ | *súhp gì* |
| clear soup with... | แกงจืด... | *gaeng•jùeet...* |
|     Chinese glass noodles, pork and vegetables | วุ้นเส้น | *wúhn•sêhn* |
|     fish balls | ลูกชิ้นปลา | *lôok•chíhn bplar* |
|     pickled vegetables | เกี้ยมฉ่าย | *géam•chìe* |
|     seaweed | สาหร่ายทะเล | *săr•rìe tah•le* |
|     tofu and ground pork | เต้าหู้หมูสับ | *dtôu•hôo mŏo sàhp* |
| clear soup with mixed vegetables, pumpkin and shrimp [prawn] | แกงเลียง | *gaeng•leang* |

| clear soup with pork ribs and mixed vegetable | ต้มจับฉ่าย dtôm jàhp•chìe |
| clear soup with tofu and napa cabbage | แกงจืดเต้าหู้กับผักกาดขาว gaeng•jùeet dtôu•hôo gàhp pàhk•gàrt•kŏw |
| egg noodle soup | บะหมี่น้ำ bàh•mèe nárm |
| hot and sour soup | ต้มยำ dtôm•yahm |
| hot and sour soup with dried fish and spices | ต้มโคล้งปลาย่าง dtôm•klóeng bplar•yârng |
| mushroom soup | ซุปเห็ด súhp hèht |

## Fish & Seafood

| baby clam | หอยลาย hŏry•lie |
| black-banded kingfish (similar to mackerel) | ปลาสำลี bplar săhm•lee |
| catfish | ปลาดุก bplar•dùhk |
| clam | หอยกาบ hŏry•garp |
| crab | ปู bpoo |
| deep-fried, spicy fishcake | ทอดมันปลา tôrt•mahn bplar |

| featherback (freshwater fish) | ปลากราย *bplar grie* |
| fried fish topped with sweet, sour and spicy sauce | ปลาสามรส *bplar sǎrm•rót* |
| gourami (freshwater fish) | ปลาสลิด *bplar sah•liht* |
| grouper | ปลาเก๋า *bplar gǒu* |
| lobster | กุ้งมังกร *gûhng mahng•gorn* |
| mackerel | ปลาทู *bplar too* |
| mussels | หอยแมลงภู่ *hǒry mah•laeng pôo* |
| octopus | ปลาหมึกยักษ์ *bplar•mùek yáhk* |
| oyster | หอยนางรม *hǒry narng•rom* |
| pomfret (a deep-sea fish) | ปลาจาระเม็ด *bplar jar•ráh•méht* |
| red snapper | ปลากะพงแดง *bplar grah•pong daeng* |
| rock lobster | กั้ง *gâhng* |
| salmon | ปลาแซลมอน *bplar san•môrn* |
| sea bass | ปลากะพงขาว *bplar grah•pong kǒw* |
| seafood | อาหารทะเล *ar•hǎrn tah•le* |
| snakehead (a freshwater fish) | ปลาช่อน *bplar chôrn* |
| shrimp [prawn] | กุ้ง *gûhng* |
| squid | ปลาหมึก *bplar•mùek* |

Thai food is highly regional, however น้ำปลา *náhm•bplar* (fish sauce) is one ingredient common to dishes across the country. Lemongrass, curry, cilantro and chili, the latter being responsible for a good deal of the spiciness of Thai cuisine, are also quite common.

| | | |
|---|---|---|
| steamed pomfret with plum pickles | ปลาจาระเม็ดนึ่งบ๊วย | *bplar jar•ráh•méht nûeng bóary* |
| steamed seafood curry | ห่อหมกทะเล | *hòr mòk tah•le* |
| sweet and sour fish | ปลาเปรี้ยวหวาน | *bplar bprêaw•wǎrn* |
| tuna | ปลาทูน่า | *bplar too•nâr* |

## Meat & Poultry

| | | |
|---|---|---|
| beef | เนื้อวัว | *núea woar* |
| capon | ไก่ตอน | *gì dtorn* |
| chicken | ไก่ | *gì* |
| crispy roast pork | หมูกรอบ | *mǒo gròrp* |
| duck | เป็ด | *bpèht* |
| (smoked) ham | หมูแฮม (รมควัน) | *mǒo•ham (rom•kwahn)* |
| liver | ตับ | *dtàhp* |
| meatballs | ลูกชิ้นเนื้อ | *look•chíhn núea* |
| oxtail | หางวัว | *hǎrng woar* |
| pork | เนื้อหมู | *núea mǒo* |
| red roast pork | หมูแดง | *mǒo•daeng* |
| roast beef | เนื้ออบ | *núea òp* |
| sausage | ไส้กรอก | *sî gròrk* |
| sirloin | เนื้อสันนอก | *núea sǎhn nôrk* |
| steak | สเต็ก | *sah•dték* |
| suckling pig | หมูหัน | *mǒo•hǎhn* |
| tenderloin | เนื้อสันใน | *núea sǎhn ni* |
| tongue | ลิ้น | *líhn* |

## Vegetables & Staples

| | | |
|---|---|---|
| aniseed | โป๊ยกั๊ก | *bpóey•gáhk* |
| aromatic ginger | กระชาย | *grah•chie* |
| asparagus (tip) | (ยอด) หน่อไม้ฝรั่ง | *(yôrt) nòr•mí fah•ràhng* |
| baby corn | ข้าวโพดอ่อน | *kôw pôet òrn* |
| bay leaf | ใบกระวาน | *bi grah•warn* |

| | |
|---|---|
| bean | ถั่ว *tòar* |
| beansprout | ถั่วงอก *tòar•ngôrk* |
| bitter gourd | มะระ *mah•ráh* |
| broccoli | บร็อคโคลี่ *bróhk•koe•lêe* |
| cabbage | กะหล่ำปลี *gah•làhm bplee* |
| caraway | ยี่หร่า *yêe•ràr* |
| carrot | แคร็อท *kae•ròht* |
| cauliflower | กะหล่ำดอก *gah•làhm dòrk* |
| celery | คื่นช่ายฝรั่ง *kûen•chîe fah•ràhng* |
| chili | พริก *príhk* |
| cashew nut | เม็ดมะม่วงหิมพานต์ *méht máh•môarng•hĭhm•mah•parn* |
| cilantro [coriander] | ผักชี *pàhk•chee* |
| corn | ข้าวโพด *kôw•pôet* |
| cucumber | แตงกวา *dtaeng•gwar* |
| deep-fried, battered vegetables | ผักชุบแป้งทอด *pàhk chúhp•bpâeng tôrt* |
| deep-fried bean curd | เต้าหู้ทอด *dtôu•hôo tôrt* |
| eggplant [aubergine] | มะเขือยาว *mah•kŭea yow* |
| fresh salad with peanut sauce | สลัดแขก *sah•làht kàek* |
| galanga | ข่า *kàr* |
| garlic | กระเทียม *grah•team* |

Thailand is the largest exporter of rice in the world, so it is no surprise that rice is a staple at every meal. Jasmine rice is the most common type of rice grown in Thailand. Sticky rice, a particularly starchy variety, is commonly eaten in the North and Northeast, an area heavily influenced by the cuisine and culture of Laos. Though rice is generally the accompaniment to a dish, noodles comprise a dish on their own. Pad Thai is a popular stir-fried noodle recipe. For Noodle dishes, see On The Menu on page 82.

| | | |
|---|---|---|
| ginger | ขิง | *kǐhng* |
| green bean | ถั่วแขก | *tòar kàek* |
| green onion | ต้นหอม | *dtôn•hǒrm* |
| holy basil | กะเพรา | *grah•prou* |
| lemongrass | ตะไคร้ | *dtah•krí* |
| lentils | ถั่วแขก | *tòar kàek* |
| lettuce | ผักกาดหอม | *pàhk•gàrt hǒrm* |
| long bean | ถั่วฝักยาว | *tòar fàhk•yow* |
| mint | สะระแหน่ | *sah•rah•nàe* |
| mushroom | เห็ด | *hèht* |
| napa cabbage | ผักกาดขาว | *pàhk•gàrt kǒw* |
| nutmeg | ลูกจันทน์ | *lôok•jahn* |
| okra [ladies' fingers] | กระเจี๊ยบ | *grah•jéap* |
| olive | มะกอก | *mah•gòrk* |
| onion | หอมหัวใหญ่ | *hǒrm hǒar yì* |
| parsley | ผักชีฝรั่ง | *pahk•chee fah•ràhng* |
| peanut | ถั่วลิสง | *tòar•lih•sǒng* |
| pepper (seasoning) | พริกไทย | *príhk•ti* |
| (green/red) pepper | พริกหยวก (เขียว/แดง) | *príhk•yòark (kěaw/daeng)* |
| potato | มันฝรั่ง | *mahn fah•rahng* |

| | | |
|---|---|---|
| pumpkin | ฟักทอง | *fáhk•torng* |
| red vegetable curry | แกงเผ็ดเจ | *gaeng•pèht je* |
| rice | ข้าว | *kôw* |
| sesame | งา | *ngar* |
| shallot | หอมแดง | *hŏrm•daeng* |
| snow pea | ถั่วลันเตา | *tòar lahn•dtou* |
| spicy noodle salad | ยำวุ้นเส้นเจ | *yahm wúhn•sêhn je* |
| spicy salad of ground [minced] mushrooms | ลาบเห็ด | *lârp•hèht* |
| spinach | ผักโขม | *pàhk•kŏem* |
| stir-fried eggplant | ผัดมะเขือยาว | *pàht mah•kŭea•yow* |
| stir-fried mixed vegetables | ผัดผักรวมมิตรเจ | *pàht pàk roarm•míht je* |
| stir-fried mushrooms, basil and baby corn | ผัดกะเพราเห็ดกับข้าวโพดอ่อน | *pàht grah•prou hèht gàhp kôw•pôet•òrn* |
| stir-fried rice noodle in soy sauce with Chinese kale | ผัดซีอิ๊วเจ | *pàht see•íhw je* |
| stir-fried rice noodle with peanut, bean curd and radish | ผัดไทยเจ | *pàht•ti je* |

| | |
|---|---|
| stir-fried snow peas with baby corn | ผัดถั่วลันเตากับข้าวโพดอ่อน *pàht tòar lahn•dtou gàhp kôw•pôet•òrn* |
| stir-fried water spinach leaves | ผัดผักบุ้ง *pàht pàhk•bûhng* |
| sweet and sour fried vegetables | ผัดเปรี้ยวหวานเจ *pàht bprêaw•wǎrn je* |
| sweet basil | โหระพา *hǒe•rah•par* |
| sweet corn | ข้าวโพดหวาน *kôw•pôet wǎrn* |
| sweet potato | มันเทศ *mahn•têt* |
| tofu | เต้าหู้ *dtôu•hôo* |
| tomato | มะเขือเทศ *mah•kǔea•têt* |
| vegetable | ผัก *pàhk* |
| vegetarian spring rolls | เปาะเปี๊ยะเจ *bpòr•bpéa je* |
| water mimosa | ผักกระเฉด *pàhk grah•chèt* |
| water spinach | ผักบุ้ง *pàhk•bûhng* |

## Fruit

| | |
|---|---|
| apple | แอปเปิ้ล *áep•bpêrn* |
| banana | กล้วย *glôary* |
| blueberry | บลูเบอรี่ *bloo•ber•rêe* |
| cherry | เชอรี่ *cher•rêe* |
| coconut | มะพร้าว *mah•prrów* |

Exotic, tropical fruit is abundant all year-round in Thailand. Some, like durian – a large fruit with a soft, yellow flesh – are available fresh, frozen, dried and even as fruit chips. Jackfruit is a sweet, golden fruit, frequently served with fruit punch or ice cream. Langsat and longan grow in bunches, and the fruit can be enjoyed by pressing or peeling off the skin. Mangosteen, with its reddish-purple skin, is often enjoyed fresh or as a juice. The pomelo is a large, grapefruit-like treat, peeled and eaten like an orange. Rambutan is a red fruit with a prickly exterior. Sapodilla, an oval-shaped fruit with yellow-brown skin, is peeled and eaten fresh.

| | | |
|---|---|---|
| custard apple | น้อยหน่า | *nóry·nàr* |
| date | อินทผาลัม | *ihn·tah·pǎr·lahm* |
| dragon fruit | แก้วมังกร | *gâew·mahng·gorn* |
| dried fruit | ผลไม้แห้ง | *pǒn·lah·mí hâeng* |
| durian | ทุเรียน | *túh·rean* |
| fruit | ผลไม้ | *pǒn·lah·mie* |
| grape | องุ่น | *ah·ngùhn* |
| guava | ฝรั่ง | *fah·ràhng* |
| jackfruit | ขนุน | *kah·nǔhn* |
| langsat | ลางสาด | *larng·sàrt* |
| lemon | มะนาวเหลือง | *mah·now lǔeang* |
| lime | มะนาว | *mah·now* |
| longan | ลำไย | *lahm·yi* |
| lychee | ลิ้นจี่ | *líhn·jèe* |
| mango | มะม่วง | *mah·môarng* |
| mangosteen | มังคุด | *mahng·kúht* |
| melon | แตงไทย | *dtaeng·ti* |
| orange | ส้ม | *sôm* |

| papaya | มะละกอ *mah•lah•gor* |
|---|---|
| peach | ลูกท้อ *lôok•tór* |
| pear | สาลี่ *săr•lêe* |
| pineapple | สับปะรด *sàhp•bpah•rót* |
| plums | ลูกไหน *lôok•nĭ* |
| pomelo | ส้มโอ *sôm•oe* |
| prunes | ลูกพรุน *lôok•pruhn* |
| raisins | ลูกเกด *lôok•gèt* |
| rambutan | เงาะ *ngóh* |
| rose apple | ชมพู่ *chom•pôo* |
| sapodilla | ละมุด *lah•múht* |
| strawberry | สตรอเบอร์รี่ *sah•dtror•ber•rêe* |
| tangerine | ส้มจีน *sôm•jeen* |
| watermelon | แตงโม *dtaeng•moe* |

## Dessert

| bananas in coconut milk | กล้วยบวชชี *glôary bòart•chee* |
|---|---|
| caramelized bananas | กล้วยเชื่อม *glôary chûeam* |
| egg custard | สังขยา *săhng•kah•yăr* |
| egg yolks with flour and syrup | ทองหยิบ *torng•yìhp* |
| jellied water chestnuts in coconut milk | ทับทิมกรอบ *táhp•tihm•gròrp* |
| layered sweet coconut cream pancakes | ขนมชั้น *kah•nŏm•cháhn* |
| mixed fresh fruit | ผลไม้รวม *pŏn•lah•mí roarm* |
| mung bean coconut custard | ขนมหม้อแกง *kah•nŏm môr•gaeng* |
| mung bean rice crepe | ถั่วแปบ *tòar•bpàep* |

| | | |
|---|---|---|
| pandanus-scented rice noodles in coconut milk | ลอดช่องน้ำกะทิ | *lôrt•chôhng náhm•gah•tí* |
| pumpkin/taro stewed in coconut milk | ฟักทอง/เผือก บวด | *fáhk•torng/pèuak bòart* |
| sticky rice in coconut milk | ข้าวเหนียวเปียก | *kôw•něaw bpèak* |
| sticky rice with banana or taro in banana leaves | ข้าวต้มมัด | *kôw•dtôm•máht* |
| sticky rice with coconut cream and egg custard/mango | ข้าวเหนียวสังขยา/มะม่วง | *kôw•něaw sǎhng•kah•yǎr/ mah•môarng* |
| sweet bean threads in coconut milk | ซ่าหริ่ม | *sâr•rìhm* |
| sweet coconut milk jelly | วุ้นกะทิ | *wúhn gah•tí* |
| tapioca and beans in coconut milk | สาคูถั่วดำ | *sǎr•koo tòar•dahm* |
| taro balls and eggs in coconut milk | บัวลอยไข่หวาน | *boar•lory kì•wǎrn* |
| thread of egg yolk dropped in syrup | ฝอยทอง | *fǒry•torng* |

## Sauces & Condiments

| | | |
|---|---|---|
| salt | เกลือ | *kluea* |
| pepper | พริกไทย | *prihk•ti* |
| mustard | มัสตาร์ด | *mahs•dtard* |
| ketchup | ซอสมะเขือเทศ | *s´ors mah•kuea•ted* |

## At the Market

| | |
|---|---|
| Where are the carts [trolleys]/baskets? | รถเข็น/ตะกร้า อยู่ที่ไหน? *rót kěhn/dtah•grâr yòo têe•nî* |
| Where is…? | …อยู่ที่ไหน? …*yòo têe•nî* |
| I'd like some of that/this. | ผม *m* /ฉัน *f* ขอ อันนี้/อันนั้น *pǒm/chán kǒr ahn née/ ahn náhn* |
| Can I taste it? | ขอชิมหน่อยได้ไหม *kǒr chihm nòhy dî mí* |
| I'd like… | ผม *m* /ฉัน *f* ขอ… *pǒm/chán kǒr…* |
| a kilo/half-kilo of… | …หนึ่งกิโล/ครึ่งกิโล …*nùeng gih•loe/krûeng gih•loe* |
| a liter of… | …หนึ่งลิตร …*nùeng líht* |
| a piece of… | …หนึ่งชิ้น …*nùeng chíhn* |
| a slice of… | …หนึ่งชิ้น …*nùeng chíhn* |
| More/Less. | มากกว่า/น้อยกว่า *mârk gwàr/nóry gwàr* |
| How much? | เท่าไหร่? *tôu•rî* |
| Where do I pay? | ผม *m* /ฉัน *f* จะจ่ายเงิน ได้ที่ไหน? *pǒm/chán jah jìe ngern dîe têe•nî* |
| A bag, please. | ขอถุงหน่อย *kǒr tǔhng nòhy* |
| I'm being helped. | ผม *m* /ฉัน *f* มีคนช่วยแล้ว *pǒm/chán mee kon chôary láew* |

For Conversion Tables, see page 163.

Measurements in Thailand are generally metric - and that applies to the weight of food too. If you tend to think in pounds and ounces, it's worth brushing up on what the metric equivalent is before you go shopping for fruit and veg in markets and supermarkets. Five hundred grams, or half a kilo, is a common quantity to order, and that converts to just over a pound (17.65 ounces, to be precise).

In Thailand, there are several large, international supermarkets as well as Thai chains. You will also find many small shops and, of course, markets. Seafood is typically fresh and abundant. The meat selection is quality controlled by the government.

## YOU MAY HEAR...

| | | |
|---|---|---|
| มีอะไรให้ช่วยไหม? | *mee ah•ri hî chôary mí* | Can I help you? |
| คุณต้องการอะไร? | *kun dtôhng•garn ah•ri* | What would you like? |
| รับอะไรอีกไหม? | *ráhp ah•ri èek mí* | Anything else? |
| อันนั้น...บาท | *ahn náhn...bàrt* | That's...baht. |

## In the Kitchen

| | |
|---|---|
| bottle opener | ที่เปิดขวด *têe bpèrt kòart* |
| bowl | ชาม *charm* |
| can opener | ที่เปิดกระป๋อง *têe bpèrt grah•bpŏhng* |
| corkscrew | ที่เปิดจุกก๊อก *têe bpèrt jùhk•góhk* |
| cup | ถ้วย *tôary* |
| fork | ส้อม *sôhm* |
| frying pan | กระทะ *grah•táh* |
| glass | แก้วน้ำ *gâew nárm* |
| (steak) knife | มีด (สเต็ก) *mêet (sah•dték)* |
| measuring cup/spoon | ถ้วย/ช้อน ตวง *tôary/chórn dtoarng* |
| napkin | กระดาษเช็ดปาก *grah•dàrt chéht bpàrk* |
| plate | จาน *jarn* |
| pot | หม้อ *môr* |
| spatula | ตะหลิว *dtah•lĭhw* |
| spoon | ช้อน *chórn* |

## YOU MAY SEE...

| | |
|---|---|
| ควรรับประทานก่อน... *koarn ráh•bprah•tarn bprah•tarn gòrn...* | best if used by... |
| เก็บไว้ในตู้เย็น *gèhp wí ni dtôo•yehn* | keep refrigerated |
| จำหน่ายภายใน... *jahm•nìe pie ni...* | sell by... |
| สำหรับคนที่กินมังสวิรัติ *săhm•ràhp kon têe gihn mahng• sàh•wíh•ráht* | suitable for vegetarians |

## Drinks

### ESSENTIAL

| | |
|---|---|
| The wine list/drink menu, please. | ขอเมนูไวน์/เครื่องดื่ม หน่อย *kŏr me•noo wie/krûeang dùeem nòhy* |
| What do you recommend? | มีอะไรแนะนำบ้าง? *mee ah•ri ná•nahm bârng* |
| I'd like a bottle/glass of white/red wine. | ผม *m* /ฉัน *f* ขอไวน์ ขาว/แดง หนึ่งขวด/แก้ว *pŏm/cháhn kŏr wie kŏw/daeng nùeng kòart/gâew* |
| The house wine, please. | ขอเฮ้าส์ไวน์ *kŏr hóus•wie* |
| Another bottle/glass, please. | ขอเพิ่มอีก ขวด/แก้ว *kŏr pérm èek kòart/gâew* |
| I'd like a local beer. | ผม *m* /ฉัน *f* ขอเบียร์ไทย *pŏm/cháhn kŏr bea ti* |
| Can I buy you a drink? | ผม *m* /ฉัน *f* ขอเลี้ยงเครื่องดื่มคุณ ได้ไหม? *pŏm/cháhn kŏr léang krûeang•dùeem kuhn dî mí* |
| A coffee/tea, please. | ขอ กาแฟ/ชา หนึ่งที่ *kŏr gar•fae/char nùeng têe* |
| Black. | ดำ *dahm* |
| With... | ใส่... *sì...* |
| milk | นม *nom* |
| sugar | น้ำตาล *náhm•dtarn* |

| | |
|---|---|
| artificial sweetener | น้ำตาลเทียม *náhm•dtarn team* |
| ..., please. | ขอ... *kŏr...* |
| Juice | น้ำผลไม้ *nárm pŏn•lah•mí* |
| Soda | น้ำอัดลม *nárm àht•lom* |
| Sparkling/Still water | น้ำ โซดา/เปล่า *nárm soe•dar/bplòw* |
| Is the water safe to drink? | น้ำนี้ดื่ม ได้ไหม? *nárm née dùeem dîe mí* |

## Non-alcoholic Drinks

| | |
|---|---|
| apple juice | น้ำแอปเปิ้ล *nárm áp•bpêrn* |
| boiled water | น้ำต้มสุก *nárm dtôm sùhk* |
| chrysanthemum tea | น้ำเก็กฮวย *nárm géhk•hoary* |
| Chinese tea | ชาจีน *char jeen* |
| (hot/iced) chocolate | ช็อกโกแล็ต (ร้อน/เย็น) *chóhk•goe•lát (rórn/yehn)* |
| (hot/iced) coffee | กาแฟ (ร้อน/เย็น) *gar•fae (rórn/yehn)* |
| fruit juice | น้ำผลไม้ *nárm pŏn•lah•míe* |
| ginger tea | น้ำขิง *nárm•kǐhng* |
| herbal tea | ชาสมุนไพร *char sah•mǔhn•pri* |
| juice | น้ำผลไม้ *nárm pŏn•lah•míe* |

Curiously enough, Red Bull energy drinks are originally Thai. The Thai version, กระทิงแดง *grah•tihng•daeng* (Red Bull), however, is very sweet and non-carbonated. It is even more caffeinated than the western Red Bull, so watch out, and is also sold in bottles rather than cans. Another typical drink is Thai iced tea. The use of tamarind seed lends the drink its distinctive orange color. Strong, but sweet, it is usually served with condensed milk. As a general rule, do not drink the tap water in Thailand.

| | |
|---|---|
| longan tea | น้ำลำไย *nárm lahm•yi* |
| lemonade | น้ำมะนาว *nárm mah•now* |
| lemongrass tea | น้ำตะไคร้ *nárm dtah•krí* |
| lime juice | น้ำมะนาว *nárm mah•now* |
| milk | นม *nom* |
| milkshake | มิลค์เชก *míw•chék* |
| mineral water | น้ำแร่ *nárm râe* |
| mocha | ม็อคค่า *móhk•kâr* |
| orange juice | น้ำส้ม *nárm sôm* |
| roselle tea | น้ำกระเจี๊ยบ *nárm grah•jéap* |
| smoothie (drink) | น้ำ (ผลไม้) ปั่น *nárm (pǒn•lah•mí) bpàhn* |
| soda | น้ำอัดลม *nárm àht•lom* |
| (hot /iced) tea | ชา (ร้อน/เย็น) *char (rórn/yehn)* |
| tomato juice | น้ำมะเขือเทศ *nárm mah•kǔea•têt* |
| tonic water | น้ำโทนิค *nárm toe•nìhk* |
| water | น้ำ *nárm* |
| young coconut juice | น้ำมะพร้าวอ่อน *nárm mah•prów•òrn* |

## YOU MAY HEAR...

| | |
|---|---|
| คุณจะดื่มอะไรไหม? *kuhn jah dùeem ah•ri mí* | Can I get you a drink? |
| ใส่นมหรือน้ำตาลไหม? *sì nom rǔee náhm•dtarn mí* | With milk or sugar? |
| น้ำโซดา หรือ น้ำเปล่า? *nárm soe•dar rǔee nárm bplòw* | Sparkling or still water? |

## Aperitifs, Cocktails & Liqueurs

| brandy | บรั่นดี *bah•ràhn•dee* |
|---|---|
| cognac | คอนยัค *korn•yàhk* |
| gin | ยิน *yihn* |
| liqueur | เหล้าหวาน *lôu wǎrn* |
| rum | เหล้ารัม *lôu rahm* |
| scotch | เหล้าสก็อตช์ *lôu sah•góht* |
| tequila | เตกีล่า *dte•gee•lâr* |
| vermouth | เวอมัธ *wer•máht* |
| vodka | ว็อดก้า *wóht•gâr* |
| whisky | วิสกี้ *wíht•sah•gêe* |

## Beer

| | |
|---|---|
| beer | เบียร์ *bea* |
| canned/bottled | กระป๋อง/ขวด *grah•bpŏhng/kòart* |
| dark/light | ดำ/ไลท์ *dahm/lí* |
| draft [draught] | สด *sòt* |
| local/imported | ไทย/นำเข้า *ti/nahm•kôu* |
| non-alcoholic | ไม่มีแอลกอฮอล์ *mî mee ael•gor•hor* |

## Wine

| | |
|---|---|
| champagne | แชมเปญ *chaem•bpen* |
| dessert wine | ดิเสิร์ทไวน์ *dìh•sèrt wie* |
| dry/sweet | ดราย/สวีท *drie/sah•wèet* |
| house/table | เฮ้าส์ไวน์/เทเบิลไวน์ *hóus•wie/te•bêrn wie* |
| red/white | แดง/ขาว *daeng/kŏw* |
| sparkling wine | สปาร์กลิ่งไวน์ *sah•bpárk•lîhng wie* |
| wine | ไวน์ *wie* |
| I'd like... | ผม *m*/ฉัน *f* ขอ... *pŏm/cháhn kŏr...* |
| Another..., please. | ขอ...อีกขวดหนึ่ง *kŏr...èek kòart nùeng* |
| A local..., please. | ขอ...ไทย *kŏr...ti* |

# On the Menu

| | |
|---|---|
| American fried rice | ข้าวผัดอเมริกัน *kôw•pàht ah•me•rih•gahn* |
| aniseed | โป๊ยกั๊ก *bpóey•gáhk* |
| apple | แอ็ปเปิ้ล *áp•bpêrn* |
| apple juice | น้ำแอ็ปเปิ้ล *nárm áp•bpêrn* |
| aromatic ginger | กระชาย *grah•chie* |
| asparagus (tip) | (ยอด) หน่อไม้ฝรั่ง *(yôrt) nòr•míe fah•ràhng* |
| baby clam | หอยลาย *hŏry•lie* |
| baby corn | ข้าวโพดอ่อน *kôw•poet•òrn* |
| bacon | เบคอน *be•kôhn* |

| | |
|---|---|
| banana | กล้วย *glôary* |
| bananas stewed in coconut milk | กล้วยบวชชี *glôary bòart•chee* |
| bay leaf | ใบกระวาน *bi grah•warn* |
| bean | ถั่ว *tòar* |
| bean sprout | ถั่วงอก *tòar•ngôrk* |
| beef | เนื้อวัว *núea woar* |
| beef satay | สะเต๊ะเนื้อ *sah•dtéh núea* |
| beer | เบียร์ *bea* |
| bitter gourd | มะระ *mah•ráh* |
| black-banded kingfish | ปลาสำลี *bplar săhm•lee* |
| blueberry | บลูเบอรี่ *bloo•ber•rêe* |
| boiled sticky rice in coconut milk | ข้าวเหนียวเปียก *kôw•něaw bpèak* |
| brandy | บรั่นดี *bah•ràhn•dee* |
| bread | ขนมปัง *kah•nŏm•bpahng* |
| broccoli | บร็อคโคลี่ *bróhk•koe lêe* |
| butter | เนย *nery* |
| cabbage | กะหล่ำปลี *grah•làhm•bplee* |
| capon | ไก่ตอน *gì dtorn* |
| caramelized bananas | กล้วยเชื่อม *glôary•chûeem* |
| caraway | ยี่หร่า *yêe•ràr* |
| carrot | แครอท *kae•ròht* |
| cashew nut | เม็ดมะม่วงหิมพานต์ *méht mah•môarng•hĭhm•mah•parn* |
| catfish | ปลาดุก *bplar•dùhk* |
| cauliflower | กะหล่ำดอก *grah•làhm dòrk* |
| celery | คื่นช่ายฝรั่ง *kûen•chîe fah•ràhng* |
| (cold/hot) cereal | ซีเรียล (เย็น/ร้อน) *see•rêan (yehn/rórn)* |
| champagne | แชมเปญ *chaem•bpen* |
| cherry | เชอรี่ *cher•rêe* |
| chicken | ไก่ *gì* |

| | |
|---|---|
| chicken and coconut milk soup flavored with galanga | ต้มข่าไก่ *dtôm•kàr gì* |
| chicken cooked in pandanus leaves | ไก่ห่อใบเตย *gì hòr bi•dtery* |
| chicken satay | สะเต๊ะไก่ *sah•dtéh gì* |
| chicken soup | ซุปไก่ *súhp gì* |
| chicken stew with soy sauce | ไก่ต้มเค็ม *gì dtôm•kehm* |
| chilli | พริก *príhk* |
| Chinese glass noodle | วุ้นเส้น *wúhn•sêhn* |
| Chinese tea | ชาจีน *char•jeen* |
| (hot/iced) chocolate | ช็อกโกแล็ต (ร้อน/เย็น) *chóhk•goe•lát (rórn/yehn)* |
| chrysanthemum tea | น้ำเก็กฮวย *nárm géhk•hoary* |
| cilantro [coriander] | ผักชี *pàhk•chee* |
| clam | หอยกาบ *hŏry•gàrp* |
| clear soup | แกงจืด *gaeng•jùeet* |
| clear soup with fish balls | แกงจืดลูกชิ้นปลา *gaeng•jùeet lôok•chíhn bplar* |
| clear soup with mixed vegetables, pumpkin and shrimp [prawn] | แกงเลียง *gaeng•leang* |
| clear soup with noodles, pork and vegetables | แกงจืดวุ้นเส้น *gaeng•jùeet wúhn•sêhn* |
| clear soup with pickled vegetables | แกงจืดเกี๊ยมฉ่าย *gaeng•jùeet géam•chìe* |
| clear soup with pork ribs and vegetables | ต้มจับฉ่าย *dtôm jàhp•chìe* |
| clear soup with seaweed | แกงจืดสาหร่ายทะเล *gaeng•jùeet sǎr•rìe tah•le* |

| | |
|---|---|
| clear soup with tofu and ground pork | แกงจืดเต้าหู้หมูสับ *gaeng•jùeet dtôu•hôo mŏo•sàhp* |
| clear soup with tofu and napa cabbage | แกงจืดเต้าหู้กับผักกาดขาว *gaeng•jùeet dtôu•hôo gàhp pàhk•gart•kŏw* |
| coconut | มะพร้าว *mah•prów* |
| coconut milk | กะทิ *gah•tíh* |
| (hot/iced) coffee | กาแฟ (ร้อน/เย็น) *gar•fae (rórn/yehn)* |
| cognac | คอนยัค *kohn•yàhk* |
| corn | ข้าวโพด *kôw•pôet* |
| crab | ปู *bpoo* |
| crab fried with curry powder | ปูผัดผงกะหรี่ *bpoo pàht pŏng•gah•rèe* |
| crab roasted in a clay pot | ปูอบหม้อดิน *bpoo òp môr•dihn* |
| crispy roast pork | หมูกรอบ *mŏo•gròrp* |
| crispy, deep-fried gourami fish | ปลาสลิดทอดกรอบ *bplar sah•lìht tôrt gròrp* |
| cucumber | แตงกวา *dtaeng•gwar* |
| hot and sour curry with snakehead (fish) and mixed vegetables | แกงส้มปลาช่อน *gaeng•sôm bplar•chôrn* |

| | |
|---|---|
| hot and sour curry with fish and water mimosa (type of watercress) | แกงส้มผักกระเฉด gaeng•sôm pàhk•grah•chèt |
| green curry with. . . | แกงเขียวหวาน. . . gaeng kĕaw•wărn. . . |
| Indian-style curry with. . . | แกงมัสมั่น. . . gaeng máht•sah•màhn. . . |
| mild red curry with. . . | พะแนง. . . pah•naeng. . . |
| spicy red curry with. . . | แกงเผ็ด. . . gaeng•pèht. . . |
|    beef | เนื้อ núea |
|    chicken | ไก่ gì |
|    pork | หมู mŏo |
| custard apple | น้อยหน่า nóry•nàr |
| date | อินทผาลัม ihn•tah•păr•lahm |
| deep-fried, battered vegetables | ผักชุบแป้งทอด pàhk chúhp bpaeng tôrt |
| deep-fried bean curd | เต้าหู้ทอด dtôu•hôo tôrt |
| deep-fried beef | เนื้อทอด núea tôrt |
| deep-fried chicken | ไก่ทอด gì tôrt |
| deep-fried, crispy wanton | เกี๊ยวทอด géaw tôrt |
| deep-fried pastry cups with ground [minced] pork | กระทงทอง grah•tong torng |
| deep-fried, spicy fishcakes | ทอดมันปลา tôrt•mahn bplar |
| deep-fried spring roll | เปาะเปี๊ยะ bpor•bpéa tôrt |
| draft [draught] beer | เบียร์สด bea sòt |
| dragon fruit | แก้วมังกร gâew•mahng•gorn |
| dried fruit | ผลไม้แห้ง pŏn•lah•míe hâeng |
| duck | เป็ด bpèht |
| durian | ทุเรียน túh•rean |

| | |
|---|---|
| egg custard | สังขยา *săhng•kah•yăr* |
| egg noodle | บะหมี่ *bah•mèe* |
| egg noodle in spicy curry with chicken/ beef | ข้าวซอย ไก่/เนื้อ *kôw•sory gì/núea* |
| egg noodle soup | บะหมี่น้ำ *bah•mèe nárm* |
| Chinese glass noodle | วุ้นเส้น *wúhn•sêhn* |
| egg noodle | บะหมี่ *bàh•mèe* |
| egg noodle in spicy curry with chicken/ beef | ข้าวซอย ไก่/เนื้อ *kôw•sory gì/núea* |
| fermented rice noodle | เส้นขนมจีน *sêhn kah•nŏm•jeen* |
| fried noodles topped with thickened sauce and vegetables | ก๋วยเตี๋ยวราดหน้า *gŏary•tĕaw rârt nâr* |
| fried rice... | ข้าวผัด... *kôw•pàht...* |
|     American-style | อเมริกัน *ah•me•rih•gahn* |
|     with crab | ปู *bpoo* |
|     with pork | หมู *mŏo* |
|     with shrimp [prawn] | กุ้ง *gûhng* |
| pasta | เส้นพาสต้า *sêhn párs•dtâr* |
| rice vermicelli | เส้นหมี่ *sêhn•mèe* |
| rice with... | ข้าว... *kôw...* |
|     curry | ราดแกง *rârt gaeng* |
|     fermented shrimp paste | คลุกกะปิ *klúhk gah•bpìh* |
|     roast duck | หน้าเป็ด *nâr bpèht* |
|     roast pork | หมูแดง *mŏo•daeng* |
|     steamed chicken | มันไก่ *mahn gì* |
|     stewed leg of pork | ขาหมู *kăr•mŏo* |

| | |
|---|---|
| stir-fried rice noodle in soy sauce with Chinese kale and chicken/pork | ผัดซีอิ๊ว ไก่/หมู *pàht•see•íhw gì/mŏo* |
| stir-fried rice noodle with shrimp, tofu, peanuts (pad thai) | ผัดไทย *pàht•ti* |
| short, clear noodle | เส้นเซี่ยงไฮ้ *sêhn sêang•hí* |
| short, rolled rice noodle | เส้นก๋วยจั๊บ *sêhn gŏary•jáhp* |
| egg yolk mixed with flour and dropped in syrup | ทองหยิบ *torng•yìhp* |
| eggplant [aubergine] | มะเขือยาว *mah•kŭea yow* |
| featherback (fish) | ปลากราย *bplar grie* |
| fermented rice noodle | เส้นขนมจีน *sêhn kah•nŏm•jeen* |
| fermented rice noodle with red curry/sweet sauce | ขนมจีน น้ำยา/น้ำพริก *kah•nŏm•jeen náhm•yar/náhm príhk* |
| fish stew with soy sauce | ปลาต้มเค็ม *bplar dtôm•kehm* |
| fresh salad with peanut sauce | สลัดแขก *sah•làht kàek* |
| fresh spring roll | เปาะเปี๊ยะสด *bpor•bpéa sòt* |
| fried bread with ground [minced] pork/shrimp [prawn] | ขนมปังหน้า หมู/กุ้ง *kah•nŏm•bpahng nâr mŏo/gûhng* |
| fried egg | ไข่ดาว *kì dow* |
| fried egg noodle with chicken | โกยซีหมี่ *goey•see•mèe* |

| | |
|---|---|
| fried fish with sweet, sour and spicy sauce | ปลาสามรส *bplar sărm•rót* |
| fried noodles with sauce and vegetables | ก๋วยเตี๋ยวราดหน้า *gŏary•tĕaw rârt nâr* |
| fried rice mixed with fermented shrimp paste | ข้าวคลุกกะปิ *kôw klúhk gah•bpìh* |
| fried rice with pork/ shrimp [prawn] | ข้าวผัด หมู/กุ้ง *kôw pàht mŏo/gûhng* |
| fruit | ผลไม้ *pŏn•lah•mí* |
| galanga (spice) | ข่า *kàr* |
| garlic | กระเทียม *grah•team* |
| gin | ยิน *yihn* |
| ginger | ขิง *kĭhng* |
| ginger tea | น้ำขิง *nárm•kĭhng* |
| gourami (freshwater fish) | ปลาสลิด *bplar sah•lìht* |
| grape | องุ่น *ah•ngùhn* |
| green bean | ถั่วแขก *tòar kàek* |
| green curry | แกงเขียวหวาน *gaeng kĕaw•wărn* |
| green onion | ต้นหอม *dtôn•hŏrm* |
| grilled black-banded kingfish, wrapped in banana leaves | ปลาสำลีเผา *bplar săhm•lee pŏu* |
| grilled catfish | ปลาดุกย่าง *bplar•dùhk yârng* |
| grilled chicken | ไก่ย่าง *gì yârng* |
| grilled duck | เป็ดย่าง *bpèht yârng* |
| grilled pork | หมูย่าง *mŏo yârng* |
| grilled squid | ปลาหมึกย่าง *bplar•mùek yârng* |
| grouper | ปลาเก๋า *bplar gŏu* |
| guava | ฝรั่ง *fah•ràhng* |

| (smoked) ham | หมูแฮม (รมควัน) *mŏo•haem (rom•kwahn)* |
|---|---|
| hard-boiled egg | ไข่ต้ม *kì dtôm* |
| herbal tea | ชาสมุนไพร *char sah•mŭhn•pri* |
| holy basil | กะเพรา *ga•prou* |
| hot and sour curry with dried fish and spices | ต้มโคล้งปลาย่าง *dtôm•klóeng bplar•yârng* |
| hot and sour curry with fish and water mimosa | แกงส้มผักกระเฉด *gaeng•sôm pàhk•grah•chèt* |
| hot and sour curry with snakehead (fish) and mixed vegetables | แกงส้มปลาช่อน *gaeng•sôm bplar•chôrn* |
| hot and sour soup | ต้มยำ *dtôm•yahm* |
| hot red vegetable curry | แกงเผ็ดเจ *gaeng•pèht je* |
| house wine | เฮ้าส์ไวน์ *hóus wie* |
| imported beer | เบียร์นำเข้า *bea nahm kôu* |
| Indian-style curry with beef/chicken | แกงมัสมั่น เนื้อ/ไก่ *gaeng máht•sah•màhn núea/gì* |
| jackfruit | ขนุน *kah•nŭhn* |
| jam | แยม *yaem* |

| | | |
|---|---|---|
| jellied water chestnuts in coconut milk | ทับทิมกรอบ | *táhp•tihm•gròrp* |
| jelly | เยลลี่ | *yen•lêe* |
| juice | น้ำผลไม้ | *nárm pŏn•lah•míe* |
| langsat (fruit) | ลางสาด | *larng•sàrt* |
| large thread rice noodle | ก๋วยเตี๋ยวเส้นใหญ่ | *gŏary•tĕaw sêhn•yì* |
| layered sweet coconut cream pancakes | ขนมชั้น | *kah•nŏm cháhn* |
| lemon | มะนาว | *mah•now* |
| lemonade | น้ำมะนาว | *nárm mah•now* |
| lemongrass | ตะไคร้ | *dtah•krí* |
| lemongrass tea | น้ำตะไคร้ | *nárm dtah•krí* |
| lentils | ถั่วแขก | *tòar•kàek* |
| lettuce | ผักกาดหอม | *pàhk•gàrt hŏrm* |
| light beer | ไลท์เบียร์ | *lí•bea* |
| lime | มะนาว | *mah•now* |
| lime juice | น้ำมะนาว | *nárm mah•now* |
| liqueur | เหล้า | *lôu* |
| liver | ตับ | *dtàhp* |
| lobster | กุ้งมังกร | *gûhng•mahng•gorn* |
| long bean | ถั่วฝักยาว | *tòar•fàhk•yow* |
| longan (fruit) | ลำไย | *lahm•yi* |
| longan tea | น้ำลำไย | *nárm lahm•yi* |
| lychee (fruit) | ลิ้นจี่ | *lihn•jèe* |
| mackerel | ปลาทู | *bplar too* |
| mango | มะม่วง | *mah•môarng* |
| mangosteen | มังคุด | *mahng•kúht* |
| mashed mung beans with coconut milk and egg yolk | เม็ดขนุน | *méht•kah•nŭhn* |

| | |
|---|---|
| meatballs | ลูกชิ้นเนื้อ *lôok•chíhn núea* |
| medium thread rice noodle | ก๋วยเตี๋ยวเส้นเล็ก *gŏary•tĕaw sêhn•léhk* |
| melon | แตงไทย *dtaeng•ti* |
| mild red curry | พะแนง *pah•naeng* |
| milk | นม *nom* |
| milkshake | มิลค์เชค *míw•chék* |
| mineral water | น้ำแร่ *nárm râe* |
| mint | สะระแหน่ *sah•rah•nàe* |
| mung bean coconut custard | ขนมหม้อแกง *kah•nŏm môr•gaeng* |
| mung bean rice crepe | ถั่วแปบ *tòar•bpàep* |
| mushroom | เห็ด *hèht* |
| mushroom soup | ซุปเห็ด *súhp hèht* |
| mushroom soup cooked in coconut milk and galanga | ต้มข่าเห็ด *dtôm•kàr hèht* |
| mussels | หอยแมลงภู่ *hŏry mah•laeng•pôo* |
| napa cabbage | ผักกาดขาว *pàhk•gàrt kŏw* |
| non-alcoholic beer | เบียร์ไม่มีแอลกอฮอล์ *bea mî mee aen•gor•hor* |
| noodle soup | ก๋วยเตี๋ยวน้ำ *gŏary•tĕaw nárm* |
| nutmeg | ลูกจันทน์ *lôok•jahn* |
| oatmeal | ข้าวโอ๊ต *kôw•óet* |
| octopus | ปลาหมึกยักษ์ *bplar•mùek yáhk* |
| okra [ladies' fingers] | กระเจี๊ยบ *grah•jéap* |
| olive | มะกอก *mah•gòrk* |
| omelet | ไข่เจียว *kì jeaw* |
| onion | หอมหัวใหญ่ *hŏrm hŏar yì* |
| orange | ส้ม *sôm* |
| orange juice | น้ำส้ม *nárm sôm* |
| oxtail | หางวัว *hărng woar* |

| | | |
|---|---|---|
| oyster | หอยนางรม | *hǒry narng•rom* |
| pandanus-scented rice noodles in coconut milk | ลอดช่องน้ำกะทิ | *lôrt•chôhng nárm•gah•tí* |
| papaya | มะละกอ | *mah•lah•gor* |
| parsley | ผักชีฝรั่ง | *pàhk•chee fah•ràhng* |
| pasta | เส้นพาสต้า | *sêhn párs•dtâr* |
| peach | ลูกท้อ | *lôok tór* |
| peanut | ถั่วลิสง | *tòar líh•sŏng* |
| pear | สาลี่ | *sǎr•lêe* |
| pepper (seasoning) | พริกไทย | *príhk•ti* |
| (green/red) pepper | พริกหยวก (เขียว/แดง) | *príhk•yòark (kĕaw/daeng)* |
| pineapple | สับปะรด | *sàhp•bpah•rót* |
| plums | ลูกไหน | *lôok nǐ* |
| pomelo (fruit) | ส้มโอ | *sôm•oe* |
| pomfret (fish) | ปลาจาระเม็ด | *bplar jar•rah•méht* |
| pork | เนื้อหมู | *núea•mŏo* |
| pork fried with garlic | หมูทอดกระเทียม | *mŏo tôrt grah•team* |
| pork fried with ginger | หมูผัดขิง | *mŏo pàht•kǐhng* |
| pork satay | สะเต๊ะหมู | *sah•dtéh mŏo* |
| pork stew in Chinese five spice sauce | หมูพะโล้ | *mŏo pah•lóe* |
| pork stew with soy sauce | หมูต้มเค็ม | *mŏo dtôm•kehm* |
| potato | มันฝรั่ง | *mahn•fah•ràhng* |
| prunes | ลูกพรุน | *lôok pruhn* |
| pumpkin | ฟักทอง | *fáhk•torng* |
| pumpkin stewed in coconut milk | ฟักทองบวด | *fáhk•torng bòart* |
| raisins | ลูกเกด | *lôok•gèt* |
| rambutan (fruit) | เงาะ | *ngóh* |

| | |
|---|---|
| red roast pork | หมูแดง *mŏo•daeng* |
| red snapper | ปลากะพงแดง *bplar grah•pong daeng* |
| red wine | ไวน์แดง *wie daeng* |
| rice | ข้าว *kôw* |
| rice porridge with chicken/pork | โจ๊ก ไก่/หมู *jóek gì/mŏo* |
| rice soup | ข้าวต้ม *kôw•dtôm* |
| rice vermicelli | เส้นหมี่ *sêhn•mèe* |
| rice with curry | ข้าวราดแกง *kôw rârt gaeng* |
| rice with roast duck | ข้าวหน้าเป็ด *kôw nâr bpèht* |
| rice with roast pork | ข้าวหมูแดง *kôw mŏo•daeng* |
| rice with steamed chicken | ข้าวมันไก่ *kôw mahn gì* |
| rice with stewed leg of pork | ข้าวขาหมู *kôw kăr•mŏo* |
| rice with stir-fried beef and chili | ข้าวราดผัดพริกเนื้อ *kôw rârt pàht•prìhk núea* |
| rice with stir-fried chicken and chili | ข้าวราดผัดพริกไก่ *kôw rârt pàht•prìhk gì* |
| rice with stir-fried pork and chili | ข้าวราดผัดพริกหมู *kôw rârt pàht•prìhk mŏo* |
| roast beef | เนื้ออบ *núea òp* |
| roasted shrimp [prawn] | กุ้งเผา *gûhng pŏu* |
| roasted shrimp [prawn] in a clay pot | กุ้งอบหม้อดิน *gûhng òp môr•dihn* |
| rock lobster | กั้ง *gâhng* |
| rose apple | ชมพู่ *chom•pôo* |
| roselle tea | น้ำกระเจี๊ยบ *nárm grah•jéap* |
| rum | เหล้ารัม *lôu rahm* |
| salmon | ปลาแซลมอน *bplar san•môrn* |

| | | |
|---|---|---|
| sapodilla (fruit) | ละมุด | *lah•múht* |
| satay | สะเต๊ะ | *sah•dtéh* |
| sausage | ไส้กรอก | *sî•gròrk* |
| scotch | เหล้าสก็อตช์ | *lôu sah•góht* |
| scrambled egg | ไข่คน | *kì kon* |
| sea bass | ปลากะพงขาว | *bplar grah•pong kŏw* |
| seafood | อาหารทะเล | *ar•hărn tah•le* |
| sesame | งา | *ngar* |
| shallot | หอมแดง | *hŏrm•daeng* |
| short, clear noodle | เส้นเซี่ยงไฮ้ | *sêhn sêang•hí* |
| short, rolled rice noodle | เส้นก๋วยจั๊บ | *sêhn gŏary•jáhp* |
| shrimp [prawn] | กุ้ง | *gûhng* |
| shrimp [prawn] rice cracker | ข้าวเกรียบกุ้ง | *kôw•grèap gûhng* |
| sirloin | เนื้อสันนอก | *núea săhn nôrk* |
| snakehead (fish) | ปลาช่อน | *bplar•chôrn* |
| snakehead (fish) with spicy herbs | ปลาช่อนแป๊ะซะ | *bplar•chôrn bpá•sáh* |
| snow pea | ถั่วลันเตา | *tòar lahn•dtou* |
| soda | น้ำอัดลม | *nárm àht•lom* |
| soft-boiled egg | ไข่ลวก | *kì•lôark* |
| sparkling wine | สปาร์กลิ่งไวน์ | *sah•bpárk•lîhng wie* |
| spicy catfish salad | ยำปลาดุกฟู | *yahm bplar•dùk foo* |
| spicy deep-fried gourami salad | ยำปลาสลิด | *yahm bplar•sah•lìht* |
| spicy grilled beef salad | ยำเนื้อย่าง | *yahm núea yârng* |
| spicy ground [minced] chicken/duck salad | ลาบไก่/เป็ด | *lârp gì/bpèht* |
| spicy northeastern sausage | ไส้กรอกอีสาน | *sî•gròrk ee•sărn* |

| | |
|---|---|
| spicy deep-fried catfish salad | ยำปลาดุกฟู *yahm bplar•dùhk foo* |
| spicy deep-fried gourami salad | ยำปลาสลิด *yahm bplar•sah•lìht* |
| spicy beef salad | ยำเนื้อย่าง *yam núea yârng* |
| spicy ground [minced] chicken/duck salad | ลาบไก่/เป็ด *lârp gì/bpèht* |
| spicy papaya salad | ส้มตำ *sôm•dtahm* |
| spicy sausage salad | ยำหมูยอ *yahm mŏo•yor* |
| spicy pork sausage salad | ยำหมูยอ *yahm mŏo•yor* |
| spicy red curry with beef/chicken | แกงเผ็ด เนื้อ/ไก่ *gaeng•pèht núea/gì* |
| spicy red curry with grilled duck | แกงเผ็ดเป็ดย่าง *gaeng•pèht bpèht•yârng* |
| spicy salad of ground [minced] mushrooms | ลาบเห็ด *lârp hèht* |
| spicy seafood salad | ยำทะเล *yahm tah•le* |
| spicy stir-fried catfish | ผัดเผ็ดปลาดุก *pàht•pèht bplar•dùhk* |
| spinach | ผักโขม *pàhk•kŏem* |
| squid | ปลาหมึก *bplar•mùek* |
| steak | สเต็ก *sah•dték* |
| steamed fish curry | ห่อหมกปลา *hòr•mòk bplar* |
| steamed pomfret (fish) with sour plums | ปลาจาระเม็ดนึ่งบ๊วย *bplar jar•rah•méht nûeng bóary* |
| steamed seafood curry | ห่อหมกทะเล *hòr•mòk tah•le* |
| steamed sticky rice with banana or taro in banana leaves | ข้าวต้มมัด *kôw•dtôm•máht* |
| stewed beef | เนื้อตุ๋น *núea dtǔhn* |
| stewed duck | เป็ดตุ๋น *bpèht dtǔhn* |

| | |
|---|---|
| sticky rice, coconut and egg custard | ข้าวเหนียวสังขยา *kôw•něaw sahng•kah•yǎr* |
| sticky rice, coconut and mango | ข้าวเหนียวมะม่วง *kôw•něaw mah•môarng* |
| stir-fried baby clams with curry powder | หอยลายผัดผงกะหรี่ *hǒry•lie pàht pǒng gah•rèe* |
| stir-fried baby clams with chili paste | หอยลายผัดน้ำพริกเผา *hǒry•lie pàht náhm•príhk•pǒu* |
| stir-fried beef with basil leaves | เนื้อผัดกะเพรา *núea pàht gah•prou* |
| stir-fried beef with chili | เนื้อผัดพริก *núea pàht príhk* |
| stir-fried beef with oyster sauce | เนื้อผัดน้ำมันหอย *núea pàht náhm•mahn•hǒry* |
| stir-fried chicken with basil leaves | ไก่ผัดกะเพรา *gì pàht gah•prou* |
| stir-fried chicken with cashew nuts | ไก่ผัดเม็ดมะม่วงหิมพานต์ *gì pàht méht•mah•môarng•hǐhm•mah•parn* |
| stir-fried chicken with chili | ไก่ผัดพริก *gì pàht príhk* |
| stir-fried chicken/ pork with ginger | ไก่/หมู ผัดขิง *gì/mǒo pàht•kǐhng* |
| stir-fried crispy pork with Chinese kale | ผัดคะน้าหมูกรอบ *pàht kah•nár mǒo•gròrp* |
| stir-fried eggplant | ผัดมะเขือยาว *pàht mah•kǔea•yow* |
| stir-fried mixed vegetables | ผัดผักรวมมิตรเจ *pàht pàk roarm•míht je* |
| stir-fried mushrooms, basil and baby corn | ผัดกะเพราเห็ดกับข้าวโพดอ่อน *pàht gah•prou hèht gàhp kôw•pôet•òrn* |
| stir-fried pork with basil | หมูผัดกะเพรา *mǒo pàht gah•prou* |

| | |
|---|---|
| stir-fried pork with chili | หมูผัดพริก *mŏo pàht príhk* |
| stir-fried rice noodles in soy sauce with Chinese kale | ผัดซีอิ๊วเจ *pàht see•íhw je* |
| stir-fried rice noodles in soy sauce with Chinese kale and chicken/pork | ผัดซีอิ๊ว ไก่/หมู *pàht see•íhw gì/mŏo* |
| stir-fried rice noodles with shrimp, tofu and peanuts (pad thai) | ผัดไทย *pàht•ti* |
| stir-fried snow peas with baby corn | ผัดถั่วลันเตากับข้าวโพดอ่อน *pàht tòar•lahn•dtou gàhp kôw•pôet•òrn* |
| stir-fried water spinach leaves | ผัดผักบุ้ง *pàht pàhk•bûhng* |
| stir-fried, spicy... with holy basil leaves | ...ผัดกะเพรา ...*pàht grah•prou* |
| stir-fried...with chili | ...ผัดพริก ...*pàht•príhk* |
| stir-fried...with ginger | ...ผัดขิง ...*pàht•kǐhng* |
| beef | เนื้อ *núea* |
| chicken | ไก่ *gì* |
| pork | หมู *mŏo* |
| stir-fried beef with oyster sauce | เนื้อผัดน้ำมันหอย *núea pàht náhm•mahn•hŏry* |
| stir-fried chicken with cashew nuts | ไก่ผัดเม็ดมะม่วงหิมพานต์ *gì pàht méht•mah•môarng•hǐhm•mah•parn* |
| stir-fried crispy pork with Chinese kale | ผัดคะน้าหมูกรอบ *pàht kah•nár mŏo•gròrp* |
| strawberry | สตรอเบอร์รี่ *sah•dtror•ber•rêe* |
| stuffed chicken wings | ปีกไก่ยัดไส้ *bpèek gì yáht sî* |

| | |
|---|---|
| suckling pig | หมูหัน *mŏo•hăhn* |
| sweet and sour fish | ปลาเปรี้ยวหวาน *bplar bprêaw•wărn* |
| sweet and sour fried vegetables | ผัดเปรี้ยวหวานเจ *pàht bprêaw•wărn je* |
| sweet basil | โหระพา *hŏe•rah•par* |
| sweet bean thread in coconut milk | ซ่าหริ่ม *sâr•rìhm* |
| sweet coconut milk jelly | วุ้นกะทิ *wúhn gah•tí* |
| sweet corn | ข้าวโพดหวาน *kôw•pôet•wărn* |
| sweet potato | มันเทศ *mahn•têt* |
| tamarind | มะขาม *mah•kărm* |
| tangerine | ส้มจีน *sôm•jeen* |
| tapioca and beans in coconut milk | สาคูถั่วดำ *săr•koo tòar•dahm* |
| taro balls and sweet eggs in coconut milk | บัวลอยไข่หวาน *boar•lory kì wărn* |
| taro stewed in coconut milk | เผือกบวด *pèuak bòart* |
| (hot/iced) tea | ชา (ร้อน/เย็น) *char (rórn/yehn)* |
| tequila | เตกีล่า *dte•gee•lâr* |
| thread of egg yolk dropped in syrup | ฝอยทอง *fŏry•torng* |
| toast | ขนมปังปิ้ง *kah•nŏm•bpahng bpîhng* |
| tofu | เต้าหู้ *dtôu•hôo* |
| tomato | มะเขือเทศ *mah•kŭea•têt* |
| tomato juice | น้ำมะเขือเทศ *nárm mah•kŭea•têt* |
| tonic water | น้ำโทนิค *nárm toe•nìhk* |
| tuna | ปลาทูน่า *bplar too•nâr* |
| turkey | ไก่งวง *gì ngoarng* |
| vegetable | ผัก *pàhk* |

| | | |
|---|---|---|
| vegetarian spring rolls | เปาะเปี๊ยะเจ | *bpor•bpéa je* |
| vegetarian stir-fried rice noodle with peanut, bean curd and radish | ผัดไทยเจ | *pàht•ti je* |
| vermouth | เวอมัธ | *wer•máht* |
| vodka | ว็อดก้า | *wóht•gâr* |
| water | น้ำ | *nárm* |
| water mimosa | ผักกระเฉด | *pàhk grah•chèt* |
| water spinach | ผักบุ้ง | *pàhk•bûng* |
| watermelon | แตงโม | *dtaeng•moe* |
| whisky | วิสกี้ | *wíht•sah•gêe* |
| white wine | ไวน์ขาว | *wie kŏw* |
| wine | ไวน์ | *wie* |
| yogurt | โยเกิร์ต | *yoe•gèrt* |
| young coconut juice | น้ำมะพร้าวอ่อน | *nárm mah•prów•òrn* |

# People

## ESSENTIAL

| | |
|---|---|
| Hello! | สวัสดี! *sah•wàht•dee* |
| How are you? | เป็นยังไง *bpehn yahng•ngi* |
| Fine, thanks. | สบายดี ขอบคุณ *sah•bie dee kòrp•kuhn* |
| Excuse me! | ขอโทษ! *kǒr•tôet* |
| Do you speak English? | คุณพูดภาษาอังกฤษได้ไหม? *kuhn pôot par•sǎr ahng•grìht dîe mí* |
| What's your name? | คุณชื่ออะไร? *kuhn chûee ah•ri* |
| My name is... | ผม *m* /ฉัน *f* ชื่อ... *pǒm/cháhn chûee...* |
| Nice to meet you. | ยินดีที่ได้รู้จัก *yihn dee têe dîe róo•jàhk* |
| Where are you from? | คุณมาจากไหน? *kuhn mar jàrk nǐ* |
| I'm from the U.S./U.K. | ผม *m* /ฉัน *f* มาจาก อเมริกา/อังกฤษ *pǒm/cháhn mar jàrk ah•me•rih•gar/ahng•grìht* |
| What do you do? | คุณทำงานอะไร? *kuhn tahm•ngarn ah•ri* |
| I work for... | ผม *m* /ฉัน *f* ทำงานที่... *pǒm/cháhn tahm•ngarn têe...* |
| I'm a student. | ผม *m* /ฉัน *f* เป็นนักศึกษา *pǒm/cháhn bpehn náhk•sùek•sǎr* |
| I'm retired. | ผม *m* /ฉัน *f* เกษียณแล้ว *pǒm/cháhn gah•sěan láew* |
| Do you like...? | คุณชอบ...ไหม? *kuhn chôrp...mí* |
| Goodbye. | สวัสดี *sah•wàht•dee* |
| See you later. | แล้วเจอกัน *láew jer gahn* |

---

In Thai, an all-purpose form for greeting at any time of the day and for saying goodbye is สวัสดี *sah•wàht•dee*.

Standard Thai, sometimes called Central Thai or Siamese, part
of the Tai family of languages, is a tonal language with a highly
complex orthographic system. Written Thai does not use space to
mark word boundary: 'thaileavesnospacebetweenwords'. And, though
punctuation marks exist, they are generally not used in writing.

## Language Difficulties

| | |
|---|---|
| Do you speak English? | คุณพูดภาษาอังกฤษได้ไหม? *kuhn pôot par•săr ahng•grìht dîe mí* |
| Does anyone here speak English? | ที่นี่มีใครพูดภาษาอังกฤษได้บ้าง? *têe•nêe mee kri pôot par•săr ahng•grìht dîe bârng* |
| I don't speak/speak a little Thai. | ผม *m* /ฉัน *f* พูดภาษาไทย ไม่ได้/ได้นิดหน่อย *pŏm/cháhn pôot par•săr ti mî dîe/dîe nít•nòhy* |
| Can you speak more slowly? | พูดช้าลงหน่อยได้ไหม? *pôot chár long nòhy dî mí* |
| Can you repeat that? | พูดอีกทีได้ไหม? *pôot èek tee dî mí* |
| Excuse me? | อะไรนะ? *ah•ri náh* |
| What was that? | นั่นอะไร? *nâhn ah•ri* |
| Can you spell it? | คุณช่วยสะกดให้ดูหน่อยได้ไหม? *kuhn chôary sah•gòt hî doo nòhy dî mí* |

## YOU MAY HEAR...

ผม *m* /ฉัน *f* พูดภาษาอังกฤษได้ นิดหน่อย *pŏm/ cháhn pôot par•săr ahng•grìht dîe níht•nòhy*
ผม *m* /ฉัน *f* พูดภาษาอังกฤษไม่ได้ *pŏm/cháhn pôot par•săr ahng•grìht mî dîe*

I only speak a little English.
I don't speak English.

Thai has various registers appropriate for certain social contexts. For example, different ways of speaking are appropriate for official use, on the street, in religious settings, when addressing the monarchy, etc. Thais who address you are more likely to use your first name rather than your last name. If you hear the word คุณ *kuhn* (Mr., Mrs., Miss) before your name, know that it is a polite form of address.

| | |
|---|---|
| Please write it down. | ช่วยเขียนให้ดูหน่อย *chôary kĕan hî doo nòhy* |
| Can you translate this into English for me? | คุณช่วยแปลอันนี้ให้ ผม *m* /ฉัน *f* หน่อย ได้ไหม? *kuhn chôary bplae ahn née hî pŏm/cháhn nòhy dî mí* |
| What does this/that mean? | นี่/นั่น หมายความว่าอะไร? *nêe/nân mĭe•kwarm wâr ah•ri* |
| I understand. | ผม *m* /ฉัน *f* เข้าใจ *pŏm/cháhn kôu•ji* |
| I don't understand. | ผม *m* /ฉัน *f* ไม่เข้าใจ *pŏm/cháhn mî kôu•ji* |
| Do you understand? | คุณเข้าใจไหม? *kuhn kôu•ji mí* |

## Making Friends

| | |
|---|---|
| Hello! | สวัสดี! *sah•wàht•dee* |
| My name is… | ผม *m* /ฉัน *f* ชื่อ… *pŏm/cháhn chûee…* |

In Thailand it is polite to greet people with ไหว้ *wie* (wai, Thai gesture of greeting). To perform a wai, put your palms together, in a prayer-like gesture, and bow slightly. The higher the hands are held and the deeper the bow, the more reverent the greeting.

| | |
|---|---|
| What's your name? | คุณชื่ออะไร? *kuhn chûee ah•ri* |
| I'd like to introduce you to... | ผม *m* /ฉัน *f* อยากแนะนำให้คุณรู้จักกับ... *pǒm/cháhn yàrk ná•nahm hî kuhn róo•jàhk gàhp...* |
| Nice to meet you. | ยินดีที่ได้รู้จัก *yihn dee têe dîe róo•jàhk* |
| How are you? | เป็นยังไง *bpehn yahng•ngi* |
| Fine, thanks. And you? | สบายดี ขอบคุณ แล้วคุณล่ะ? *sah•bie dee kòrp•kuhn láew kuhn lài* |

## Travel Talk

| | |
|---|---|
| I'm here... | ผม *m* /ฉัน *f* มาที่นี่เพื่อ... *pǒm/cháhn mar têe•nêe pûea...* |
| on business | ทำธุรกิจ *tahm túh•ráh•gìht* |
| on vacation [holiday] | พักผ่อน *páhk•pòhn* |
| studying | เรียนหนังสือ *rean nǎhng•sǔee* |
| I'm staying for... | ผม *m* /ฉัน *f* จะอยู่ที่นี่... *pǒm/cháhn jah yòo têe•nêe...* |
| I've been here... | ผม *m* /ฉัน *f* มาที่นี่ได้...แล้ว *pǒm/cháhn mar têe•nêe dîe...láew* |
| a day | หนึ่งวัน *nùeng wahn* |
| a week | หนึ่งสัปดาห์ *nùeng sàhp•dar* |
| a month | หนึ่งเดือน *nùeng duean* |
| Where are you from? | คุณมาจากไหน? *kuhn mar jàrk nǐ* |
| I'm from... | ผม *m* /ฉัน *f* มาจาก... *pǒm/cháhn mar jàrk...* |

For Numbers, see page 158.

## Personal

| | |
|---|---|
| Who are you with? | คุณมากับใคร? *kuhn mar gàhp kri* |
| I'm here alone. | ผม *m* /ฉัน *f* มาคนเดียว *pŏm/cháhn mar kon deaw* |
| I'm with my... | ผม *m* /ฉัน *f* มากับ...ของผม *m* /ฉัน *f pŏm/ |
| | *cháhn mar gàhp... kŏhng pŏm/cháhn* |
| husband/wife | สามี/ภรรยา *săr•mee/pahn•rah•yar* |
| boyfriend/girlfriend | แฟน *faen* |
| father/mother | พ่อ/แม่ *pôr/mâe* |
| friend/colleague | เพื่อน/เพื่อนร่วมงาน *pûean/pûean•rôarm•ngarn* |
| colleagues | เพื่อนร่วมงาน *pûean ro˝arm•ngarn* |
| older/younger brother | พี่ชาย/น้องชาย *pêe chie/nórng chie* |
| older/younger sister | พี่สาว/น้องสาว *pêe sŏw/nórng sŏw* |
| When's your birthday? | วันเกิดของคุณเมื่อไหร่? *wahn gèrt kŏhng kuhn mûea•rì* |
| How old are you? | คุณอายุเท่าไหร่? *kuhn ar•yúh tôu•rì* |
| I'm... | ผม *m* /ฉัน *f* อายุ... *pŏm/cháhn ar•yúh...* |
| Are you married? | คุณแต่งงานแล้วหรือยัง? *kuhn dtàng•ngarn láew rúe yahng* |
| I'm... | ผม *m* /ฉัน *f* ... *pŏm/cháhn...* |
| single/in a relationship | ยังโสด/มีแฟนแล้ว *yahng sòet/mee faen láew* |

| | |
|---|---|
| engaged/married | มีคู่หมั้นแล้ว/แต่งงานแล้ว *mee kôo•mâhn láew/* *dtàng•ngarn láew* |
| divorced/separated | หย่าแล้ว/แยกกันอยู่ *yàr láew/yâek gahn yòo* |
| widowed | เป็นหม้าย *bpehn mîe* |
| Do you have children/ grandchildren? | คุณมี ลูก/หลาน ไหม? *kuhn mee lôok/lăhn mí* |

For Numbers, see page 158.

## Work & School

| | |
|---|---|
| What do you do? | คุณทำงานอะไร? *kuhn tahm•ngarn ah•ri* |
| What are you studying? | คุณกำลังเรียนอะไรอยู่? *kuhn gahm•lahng rean ah•ri yòo* |
| I'm studying Thai. | ผม *m* /ฉัน *f* กำลังเรียนภาษาไทย *pŏm/chán gahm•lahng rean par•săr ti* |
| Who do you work for? | คุณทำงานที่ไหน? *kuhn tahm•ngarn têe•ní* |
| I work for... | ผม *m* /ฉัน *f* ทำงานที่... *pŏm/chán tahm•ngarn têe...* |
| Here's my business card. | นี่นามบัตรของผม *m* /ฉัน *f nêe narm•bàht kŏhng pŏm/ chán* |

## Weather

| | |
|---|---|
| What's the forecast? | พยากรณ์อากาศ เป็นยังไง? *pah•yar•gorn ar•gàrt bpehn yahng•ngi* |
| What beautiful/ terrible weather! | อากาศ ดี/แย่ จัง! *ar•gàrt dee/yâe jahng* |
| Will it be...tomorrow? | พรุ่งนี้... ไหม? *prûhng•née... mí* |
| cool/warm | เย็น/อุ่น *yehn/ùhn* |
| cold/hot | หนาว/ร้อน *nŏw/rórn* |
| rainy/sunny | ฝนตก/แดดออก *fŏn dtòk/dàet òrk* |
| Do I need a jacket/ an umbrella? | ผม *m* /ฉัน *f* ต้องใช้ เสื้อแจ็กเก็ต/ร่ม ไหม? *pŏm/chán dtôhng chî sûea•ják•géht/rôm mí* |

## ESSENTIAL

| | |
|---|---|
| Would you like to go out for a drink/dinner? | คุณอยากไป ดื่ม/ทานอาหารเย็น ข้างนอกไหม? *kuhn yàrk bpi dùeem/tarn ar•hǎrn yehn kâhng•nôrk mí* |
| What are your plans for tonight/tomorrow? | คืนนี้/พรุ่งนี้ คุณมีแผนอะไรไหม? *kuen née/ prûhng• née kuhn mee pǎen ah•ri mí* |
| Can I have your number? | ผม *m* /ฉัน *f* ขอเบอร์โทรศัพท์ของคุณหน่อยได้ไหม? *pǒm/chán kǒrber toe•rah•sàhp kǒng kuhn nòhy dîmí* |
| Can I join you? | ผม *m* /ฉัน *f* ขอนั่งด้วยได้ไหม? *pǒm/chán kǒr nâhng dôary dî mí* |
| Can I get you a drink? | คุณจะดื่มอะไรไหม? *kuhn jah dùeem ah•ri mí* |
| I like/love you. | ผม *m* /ฉัน *f* ชอบ/รัก คุณ *pǒm/chán chôrp/ráhk kuhn* |

## The Dating Game

| | |
|---|---|
| Would you like to go out for...? | คุณอยากออกไปหา...ทานไหม? *kuhn yàrk òrk bpi hǎr... tarn mí* |
| coffee | กาแฟ *gar•fae* |
| a drink | เครื่องดื่ม *krûeang•dùeem* |
| dinner | อาหารเย็น *ar•hǎrn yehn* |
| What are your plans for...? | คุณมีแผนอะไรสำหรับ...ไหม? *kuhn mee pǎen ah•ri sǎhm•ràhp...mí* |
| today | วันนี้ *wahn•née* |
| tonight | คืนนี้ *kuen née* |
| tomorrow | พรุ่งนี้ *prûhng•née* |
| this weekend | สุดสัปดาห์นี้ *sùht sàhp•dar née* |
| Where would you like to go? | คุณอยากจะไปไหน? *kuhn yàrk•jah bpi nǐ* |

| | |
|---|---|
| Can I have your number/e-mail? | ผม *m* /ฉัน *f* ขอ เบอร์โทรศัพท์/อีเมล์ ของคุณหน่อยได้ ไหม? *pǒm/chán kǒr ber toe·rah·sàhp/ee·mew kǒhng kuhn nòhy dî mí* |
| Are you on Facebook/Twitter? | คุณเล่นเฟซบุ๊ค/ทวิตเตอร์ไหม? *kuhn l`ehn fes·buhk/ tah·wiht·ter mí?* |
| Can I join you? | ผม *m* /ฉัน *f* ขอนั่งด้วยได้ ไหม? *pǒm/chán kǒr nâhng dôary dî mí* |
| You're very attractive. | คุณมีเสน่ห์มาก *kuhn mee sah·nè mârk* |
| Let's go somewhere quieter. | ไปหาที่ที่เงียบกว่านี้ดีกว่า *bpi hǎr têe têe ngêap gwàr née dee gwàr* |

For Communications, see page 48.

## Accepting & Rejecting

| | |
|---|---|
| I'd love to. | ผม *m* /ฉัน *f* สนใจมาก *pǒm/chán sǒn·ji mârk* |
| Where should we meet? | เราจะเจอกันที่ไหนดีล่ะ? *rou jah jer gahn têe·nǐ dee làh* |
| I'll meet you at the bar/your hotel. | ผม *m* /ฉัน *f* จะไปเจอคุณที่ บาร์/โรงแรมของคุณ *pǒm/ chán jah bpi jer kuhn têe bar/roeng·raem kǒhng kuhn* |
| I'll come by at… | ผม *m* /ฉัน *f* จะไปถึงตอน… *pǒm/chán jah bpi tǔeng dtorn…* |
| I'm busy. | ขอบคุณ แต่ว่าผม *m* /ฉัน *f* ยุ่งมาก *kòrp·kuhn dtàe·wâr pǒm/chán yûhng mârk* |
| I'm not interested. | ผม *m* /ฉัน *f* ไม่สนใจ *pǒm/chán mî sǒn·ji* |
| Leave me alone. | ขอร้อง อย่ายุ่งกับผม *m* /ฉัน *f* ได้ ไหม *kǒr·rórng yàr yûhng gàhp pǒm/chán dî mí* |
| Stop bothering me! | เลิกมากวนใจผม *m* /ฉัน *f* ชะที! *lêrk mar goarn·ji pǒm/ chán sáh tee* |

For Time, see page 160.

## Getting Intimate

| | |
|---|---|
| Can I hug/kiss you? | ผม *m*/ฉัน *f* ขอ กอด/จูบ คุณ ได้ ไหม? *pŏm/cháhn kŏr gòrt/jòop kuhn dîe mí* |
| Yes. | ครับ *m*/ค่ะ *f* *kráhp/kâh* |
| No. | ไม่ได้ *mî dîe* |
| Stop! | หยุดนะ! *yùht náh* |
| I like/love you. | ผม *m*/ฉัน *f* ชอบ/รัก คุณ *pŏm/cháhn chôrp/ráhk kuhn* |

## Sexual Preferences

| | |
|---|---|
| Are you gay? | คุณเป็นเกย์หรือเปล่า? *kuhn bpehn ge rúe•bplòw* |
| I'm... | ผม *m*/ฉัน *f*... *pŏm/cháhn...* |
| heterosexual | ไม่ได้เป็นเกย์ *mî dîe bpehn ge* |
| homosexual | เป็นเกย์ *bpehn ge* |
| bisexual | เป็นไบเซ็กช่วล *bpehn bi séhk•chôarn* |
| Do you like men/ women? | คุณชอบผู้ชายหรือผู้หญิง? *kuhn chorb poo•chĭe rúe poo•yĭhng* |

# Leisure Time

## Sightseeing

### ESSENTIAL

| | |
|---|---|
| Where's the tourist information office? | สำนักงานท่องเที่ยวอยู่ที่ไหน? *săhm•náhk•ngarn tôhng•têaw yòo têe•nĭ* |
| What are the main attractions? | มีอะไรที่น่าสนใจบ้าง? *mee ah•ri têe nâr•sŏn•ji bârng* |
| Do you have tours in English? | คุณมีทัวร์ที่เป็นภาษาอังกฤษไหม? *kuhn mee toar têe bpehn par•săr ahng•grìht mí* |
| Can I have a map/ guide? | ผม *m*/ฉัน *f* ขอ แผนที่/หนังสือแนะนำการท่องเที่ยว ได้ไหม? *pŏm/cháhn kŏr păen•têe/năhng•sŭee ná•nahm garn tôhng•têaw dî mí* |

### Tourist Information

| | |
|---|---|
| Do you have information on...? | คุณมีข้อมูลเกี่ยวกับ... ไหม? *kuhn mee kôr•moon gèaw gàhp...mí* |
| How do we get there? | ผม *m*/ฉัน *f* จะไปที่นั่นได้ยังไง? *pŏm/cháhn jah bpi têe nâhn dî yahng•ngi* |

The Tourism Authority of Thailand (TAT) has offices throughout Thailand. The main office is located in Bangkok. TAT information counters are open daily, 8:30 a.m. to 4:30 p.m.

| | | |
|---|---|---|
| Can you recommend...? | ช่วยแนะนำ...ให้หน่อยได้ไหม? | *chôary ná•nahm...hî nòhy dî mí* |
| a boat trip | ทัวร์ทางเรือ | *toar tarng ruea* |
| a bus tour | ทัวร์ทางรถ | *toar tarng rót* |
| an excursion to... | ทัวร์ระยะสั้น... | *toar rah•yáh sâhn...* |
| a sightseeing tour | ทัวร์ชมเมือง | *toar chom mueang* |

## On Tour

| | | |
|---|---|---|
| I'd like to go on the tour to... | ผม *m* /ฉัน *f* ต้องการทัวร์ไป... | *pǒm/cháhn dtôhng•garn toar bpi...* |
| When's the next tour? | ทัวร์กรุ๊ปต่อไปออกเมื่อไหร่? | *toar grúhp dtòr•bpi òrk mûea•rì* |
| Are there tours in English? | มีทัวร์ที่เป็นภาษาอังกฤษไหม? | *mee toar têe bpehn par•săr ahng•grìht mí* |
| Is there an English guide book/audio guide? | มี หนังสือนำเที่ยว/เทปนำเที่ยว เป็นภาษาอังกฤษไหม? | *mee năhng•sŭee nahm•têaw/tép nahm•têaw bpehn par•săr ahng•grìht mí* |
| What time do we leave/return? | เราจะออกเดินทาง/กลับกันกี่โมง? | *rou jah òrk dern•tarng/glahb gahn kêe moeng* |
| I'd like to see... | ผม *m* /ฉัน *f* อยากไปดู... | *pǒm/cháhn yàrk bpi doo...* |
| Can we stop here...? | เราขอหยุดตรงนี้เพื่อ...ได้ไหม? | *rou kŏr yùht dtrong•née pûea...dî mí* |
| to take photos | ถ่ายรูป | *tìe rôop* |
| for souvenirs | ซื้อของที่ระลึก | *sûee krng têe•rah•lúek* |
| for the toilets | เข้าห้องน้ำ | *kôu hôhng•nárm* |

| Can we look around? | เราขอดูรอบ ๆ หน่อยได้ไหม? *rou kŏr doo rôrp•rôrp nòry dî mí* |
| Is it disabled-accessible? | มีทางเข้าออกสำหรับคนพิการไหม? *mee tarng kôu òrk săhm•ràhp kon píh•garn mí* |

## Seeing the Sights

| Where's...? | ...อยู่ที่ไหน? *...yòo têe•nĭ* |
| the battleground | สมรภูมิ *sah•mŏr•rah•poom* |
| the botanical garden | สวนพฤกษศาสตร์ *sŏarn prúek•sah•sârt* |
| Where's...? | ...อยู่ที่ไหน? *...yòo têe•nĭ* |
| the downtown area | ย่านใจกลางเมือง *yârn ji•glarng mueang* |
| the fountain | น้ำพุ *náhm•púh* |
| the library | ห้องสมุด *hôhng sah•mùht* |
| the market | ตลาด *dtah•làrt* |
| the (war) memorial | อนุสาวรีย์ (สงคราม) *ah•nùh•săr•wah•ree (sŏng•krarm)* |
| the museum | พิพิธภัณฑ์ *píh•píht•tah•pahn* |
| the old town | เมืองเก่า *mueang gòu* |
| the palace | วัง *wahng* |
| the park | สวนสาธารณะ *sŏarn săr•tar•rah•náh* |
| the ruins | ซากปรักหักพัง *sark•pah•r ̂ahk•h ̂ahk•p ̂ahng* |
| the shopping area | ย่านช็อปปิ้ง *yârn chóhp•bpîhng* |
| Can you show me on the map? | คุณช่วยชี้ในแผนที่ให้หน่อยได้ไหม? *kuhn chôary chée ni păen•têe hî nòhy dî mí* |
| It's... | มัน... *mahn...* |
| beautiful | สวย *sŏary* |
| interesting | น่าสนใจ *nâr•sŏn•ji* |
| romantic | โรแมนติก *roe•maen•dtìhk* |
| strange | แปลก *plàek* |
| stunning | น่าตกตะลึง *nâr dtòk•dtàh•lueng* |
| terrible | แย่สุดๆ *yâe sùht•sùht* |
| I (don't) like it. | ผม *m* /ฉัน *f* (ไม่) ชอบ *pŏm/cháhn (mî) chôrp* |

## Religious Sites

| | |
|---|---|
| Where's…? | …อยู่ที่ไหน? …yòo têe•nî |
| the Catholic/ | โบสถ์ คาทอลิก/โปรเตสแตนต์ bòet kar•tor•lìhk/ |
| Protestant church | proe•dtés•dtáen |
| the mosque | มัสยิด/สุเหร่า máht•sah•yìht/suh•ròu |
| the shrine | ศาลเจ้า sărn•jârw |
| the synagogue | โบสถ์ยิว bòet yihw |
| the temple | วัด wáht |
| What time is mass/ | เวลาทำมิสซา/สวดมนต์ กี่โมง? we•lar tahm míht•sar/ |
| the service? | sòart•mon gèe moeng |

# Shopping

## ESSENTIAL

| | |
|---|---|
| Where's the market/ | ตลาด/ศูนย์การค้า อยู่ที่ไหน? dtah•làrt/sŏon•garn•kár |
| mall [shopping centre]? | yòo têe•nî |
| I'm just looking. | ผม m/ฉัน f แค่ดูเฉยๆ pŏm/cháhn kâe doo chŏey•chŏey |
| Can you help me? | ช่วยผม m/ฉัน f หน่อยได้ไหม? chôary pŏm/cháhn |
| | nòhy dî mí |
| I'm being helped. | ผม m/ฉัน f มีคนช่วยแล้ว pŏm/cháhn mee kon chôary |
| | láew |
| How much? | เท่าไหร่? tôu•rì |
| That one, please. | ขออันนั้นหน่อย kŏr ahn náhn nòhy |
| That's all. | แค่นี้แหละ kâe née là |
| Where can I pay? | ผม m/ฉัน f จะจ่ายเงินที่ไหน? pŏm/cháhn jah jìe ngern |
| | dîe têe•nî |
| I'll pay in cash/by | ผม m/ฉัน f จะจ่ายด้วย เงินสด/บัตรเครดิต pŏm/cháhn |
| credit card. | jah jìe dôary ngern•sòt/bàht•kre•dìht |
| A receipt, please. | ขอใบเสร็จด้วย kŏr bi•sèht dôary |

There are countless malls and markets in Thailand. During your stay, be sure to visit one of the many night markets. The largest are located in Bangkok and Chiang Mai. Night markets offer the opportunity to buy many designer and unique goods that are not available in regular shopping malls or day markets.

## At the Shops

| | | |
|---|---|---|
| Where's...? | ...อยู่ที่ไหน? | ...yòo têe•nî |
| the antiques store | ร้านขายของเก่า | rárn kǐe kǒrng•gòu |
| the bakery | ร้านเบเกอรี่ | rárn be•ger•rêe |
| the bank | ธนาคาร | tah•nar•karn |
| the bookstore | ร้านหนังสือ | rárn nǎhng•sǔee |
| the camera store | ร้านขายกล้องถ่ายรูป | rárn kie glôhng•tìe•rôop |
| the clothing store | ร้านขายเสื้อผ้า | rárn kie sûea•pâr |
| the department store | ห้างสรรพสินค้า | hârng sàhp•pah•sǐhn•kár |
| the gift shop | ร้านกิฟต์ช็อป | rárn gíhp•chòhp |
| the health food store | ร้านขายอาหารสุขภาพ | rárn kie ar•hǎrn sùhk•kah•pârp |
| the jeweler | ร้านขายเครื่องประดับ | rárn kǐe krûeang•bprah•dàhp |
| the liquor store [off licence] | ร้านขายเหล้า | rárn kie lôu |
| the market | ตลาด | dtah•làrt |
| the music store | ร้านขายซีดีเพลง | rárn kie see•dee pleng |
| the pharmacy [chemist] | ร้านขายยา | rárn kǐe yar |
| the produce [grocery] store | ร้านขายของชำ | rárn kǐe kǒrng•chahm |
| the shoe store | ร้านขายรองเท้า | rárn kǐe rorng•tów |

| | | |
|---|---|---|
| the shopping mall [shopping centre] | ศูนย์การค้า | *sŏon•garn•kár* |
| the souvenir store | ร้านขายของที่ระลึก | *rárn kĭe kŏrng•têe•rah•lúehk* |
| the supermarket | ซุปเปอร์มาร์เก็ต | *súhp•bpêr mar•gêht* |
| the toy store | ร้านขายของเล่น | *rárn kĭe kŏrng•lên* |

## Ask an Assistant

| | | |
|---|---|---|
| When do you open/ close? | คุณ เปิด/ปิด เมื่อไหร่? | *kuhn bpèrt/bpìht mûea•rì* |
| Where's...? | ...อยู่ที่ไหน? | *...yòo têe•nĭ* |
| the cashier | แคชเชียร์ | *káet•chea* |
| the escalator | บันไดเลื่อน | *bahn•di lûean* |
| the elevator [lift] | ลิฟต์ | *líhp* |
| the fitting room | ห้องลองเสื้อผ้า | *hôhng lorng sûea•pâr* |
| the store directory | รายการร้านค้า | *rie•garn rárn•kár* |
| Can you help me? | ช่วยผม **m** /ฉัน **f** หน่อยได้ไหม? | *chôary pŏm/cháhn nòhy dî mí* |
| I'm just looking. | ผม **m** /ฉัน **f** แค่ดูเฉยๆ | *pŏm/cháhn kâe doo chŏey•chŏey* |
| I'm being helped. | ผม **m** /ฉัน **f** มีคนช่วยแล้ว | *pŏm/cháhn mee kon chôary láew* |
| Do you have...? | คุณมี...ไหม? | *kuhn mee...mí* |

## YOU MAY SEE...

| | |
|---|---|
| เปิด/ปิด *bpèrt/bpìht* | open/closed |
| เวลาเปิดทำการ *we•la bperd tahm garn* | opening hours |
| ห้องลองเสื้อผ้า *hôhng lorng sûea•pâr* | fitting room |
| แคชเชียร์ *káet•chea* | cashier |
| จ่ายเงินที่นี่ *jary ngern têe•nee* | pay here |
| รับเฉพาะเงินสด *ráhp chah•póh ngern•sòt* | cash only |
| ยินดีรับบัตรเครดิต *yihn•dee ráhp bàht•kre•dìht* | credit cards accepted |
| ทางเข้า/ทางออก *tarng kôu/tarng òrk* | entrance/exit |

| | | |
|---|---|---|
| Can you show me...? | ขอดู...หน่อยได้ไหม? *kŏr doo...nòhy dî mí* | |
| Can you ship/wrap it? | ช่วย ส่ง/ห่อ ให้หน่อยได้ไหม? *chôary sòng/hòr hî nòhy dî mí* | |
| How much? | เท่าไหร่? *tôu•rì* | |
| That's all. | แค่นี้แหละ *kâe née là* | |

## Personal Preferences

| | | |
|---|---|---|
| I'd like something... | ผม *m* /ฉัน *f* อยากได้อะไรที่... *pŏm/cháhn yàrk•die ah•ri têe...* | |
|    cheap/expensive | ถูก/แพง *tòok/paeng* | |
|    nicer | สวยกว่านี้ *sŏary gwàr née* | |
|    from this region | เป็นของในท้องถิ่น *bpehn kŏrng ni tórng•tìn* | |
| Around...baht. | ประมาณ...บาท *bprah•marn...bàrt* | |
| Is it real? | ของแท้หรือเปล่า? *kŏrng táe rúe•bplòw* | |
| Can you show me this/that? | ขอดู อันนี้/อันนั้น หน่อยได้ไหม? *kŏr doo ahn née/ahn náhn nòhy dî mí* | |
| That's not quite what I want. | มันไม่ใช่สิ่งที่ผม *m* /ฉัน *f* ต้องการซะทีเดียว *mahn mî chî sìhng têe pŏm/cháhn dtôhng•garn sáh tee deaw* | |
| No, I don't like it. | ไม่ ผม *m* /ฉัน *f* ไม่ชอบอันนี้ *mî pŏm/cháhn mî chôrp ahn née* | |

I have to think about it. ผม *m* /ฉัน *f* ขอคิดดูก่อน *pǒm/cháhn kǒr kíht doo gòrn*

I'll take it. ผม *m* /ฉัน *f* เอาอันนี้แหละ *pǒm/cháhn ou ahn née là*

## Paying & Bargaining

| | |
|---|---|
| How much? | เท่าไหร่? *tôu•rì* |
| I'll pay... | ผม *m* /ฉัน *f* จะจ่าย... *pǒm/cháhn jah jàry...* |
| in cash | เป็นเงินสด *bpehn ngern•sòt* |
| by credit card | ด้วยบัตรเครดิต *dôary bàht•kre•dìht* |
| by traveler's check [cheque] | ด้วยเช็คเดินทาง *dôary chéhk dern•tarng* |
| A receipt, please. | ขอใบเสร็จด้วย *kǒr bi•sèht dôary* |
| That's too much. | แพงไป *paeng bpi* |
| I'll give you...baht. | ตกลง...บาทก็แล้วกัน *dtòk•long...bàrt gôr•láew•gahn* |
| Is that your best price? | ราคาต่ำสุดแล้วหรือ? *rar•kar dtàhm sùht láew rěr* |
| Can you give me a discount? | ลดให้ผม *m* /ฉัน *f* หน่อยได้ไหม? *lót hî pǒm/cháhn nòhy dîe mí* |

For Numbers, see page 158.

## Making a Complaint

| | |
|---|---|
| I'd like... | ผม *m* /ฉัน *f* อยากจะ... *pǒm/cháhn yàrk jah...* |
| to exchange this | เปลี่ยนของชิ้นนี้ *bplèan kǒrng chíhn née* |

## YOU MAY HEAR...

| | |
|---|---|
| มีอะไรให้ช่วยไหม? *mee ah•ri hî chôary mí* | Can I help you? |
| จะรับอะไรดี? *jah ráhp ah•ri dee* | What would you like? |
| รับอะไรอีกไหม? *ráhp ah•ri èek mí* | Anything else? |
| บัตรเครดิตของคุณใช้ไม่ได้ *bàht cre•dit korng kuhn chi mî di* | Your credit card has been declined. |
| ขอตรวจบัตรหน่อยค่ะ *ko ˇr bàht tro ˇard nòhy kâh* | ID, please. |
| เราไม่รับบัตรเครดิต *rou mî rahb bàht cre•dit* | We don't accept credit cards. |
| รับเฉพาะเงินสดเท่านั้นค่ะ *rahb chah•poh ngern•sod kâh* | Cash only, please. |

| | | |
|---|---|---|
| a refund | ขอเงินคืน | *kǒr ngern kueen* |
| to see the manager | พบผู้จัดการ | *póp pôo•jàht•garn* |

## Services

| | | |
|---|---|---|
| Can you recommend...? | คุณช่วยแนะนำ...ให้หน่อยได้ไหม? | *kuhn chôary ná•nahm...hî nòhy dî mí* |
| a barber | ร้านตัดผมผู้ชาย | *rárn dtàht•pǒm pôo•chie* |
| a dry cleaner | ร้านซักแห้ง | *rárn sáhk•hâeng* |
| a hairstylist | ร้านทำผม | *rárn tahm•pǒm* |
| a laundromat [launderette] | ร้านซักผ้า | *rárn sáhk•pâr* |
| a nail salon | ร้านทำเล็บ | *rárn tahm•léhp* |
| a spa | สปา | *sah•bpar* |
| a travel agency | บริษัททัวร์ | *bor•rih•sàht toar* |
| Can you...this? | คุณช่วย...นี่ให้หน่อยได้ไหม? | *kuhn chôary...née hî nòhy die mí* |
| alter | แก้ | *gǎe* |

## YOU MAY HEAR...

คุณจะจ่ายยังไง? *kuhn jah jàry yahng•ngi*   How are you paying?

เราไม่รับบัตรเครดิต *rou mî ráhp bàht•kre•dìht*   We don't accept credit cards.

รับเฉพาะเงินสด *ráhp chah•póh ngern•sòt*   Cash only, please.

| | | |
|---|---|---|
| clean | ทำความสะอาด | *tahm kwarm sah•àrt* |
| fix [mend] | ซ่อม | *sôhm* |
| press | รีด | *rêet* |
| When will it be ready? | จะเสร็จเมื่อไหร่? *jah sèht mûea•rì* | |

## Hair & Beauty

| | | |
|---|---|---|
| I'd like... | ผม *m*/ฉัน *f* อยากจะ... *pŏm/cháhn yàrk jah...* | |
| an appointment for today/ tomorrow | ขอนัดเวลาสำหรับ วันนี้/พรุ่งนี้ *kŏr náht we•lar săhm•ràhp wahn•née/prûhng•née* | |
| some color/ highlights | ทำสี/ทำไฮไลท์ ผม *tahm•sĕe/tahm hie•lí pŏm* | |
| my hair styled/ blow-dried | เซ็ต/เป่า ผม *séht/bpòu pŏm* | |
| a haircut | ตัดผม *dtàht•pŏm* | |

| | |
|---|---|
| Not too short. | ไม่ต้องสั้นมาก mî dtôhng sâhn mârk |
| Shorter here. | ตรงนี้สั้นอีกนิด dtrong•née sâhn èek níht |
| I'd like... | ผม *m* /ฉัน *f* อยากจะ... pŏm/cháhn yàrk jah... |
| an eyebrow/ bikini wax | แว็กซ์ ขนคิ้ว/แนวบิกินี่ wák kŏn kíhw/naew bih•gih•nêe |
| a facial | นวดหน้า nôart•nâr |
| a manicure/ pedicure | ทำ เล็บมือ/เล็บเท้า tahm léhp•muee/léhp•tów |
| a massage | นวดตัว nôart•dtoar |
| Do you have/do...? | คุณมีบริการ... ไหม? kuhn mee bor•rih•garn...mí |
| acupuncture | ฝังเข็ม făhng•kĕhm |
| aromatherapy | อโรมาเทราปี ah•roe•mâr te•rar•pêe |
| oxygen treatment | ทำทรีตเมนต์ด้วยอ็อกซิเจน tahm tréet•méhn dôary óhk•sih•jên |
| a sauna | อบซาวน่า òp sou•nâr |

## Antiques

| | |
|---|---|
| How old is it? | มันเก่าขนาดไหน? mahn gòu kah•nàrt nĭ |
| Do you have anything from the...period? | คุณมีของที่อยู่ในสมัย... ไหม? kuhn mee kŏrng têe•yòo ni sah•mĭ...mí |
| Do I have to fill out any forms? | ผม *m* /ฉัน *f* ต้องกรอกแบบฟอร์มอะ ไรหรือเปล่า? pŏm/cháhn dtôhng gròrk baep•form ah•ri rúe•bplòw |
| Is there a certificate of authenticity? | มีใบรับรองว่าเป็นของแท้หรือเปล่า? mee bi•ráhp•rorng wâr bpehn kŏrng•táe rúe•bplòw |

## Clothing

| | |
|---|---|
| I'd like... | ผม *m* /ฉัน *f* อยากจะ... pŏm/cháhn yàrk jah... |
| Can I try this on? | ขอลองหน่อยได้ไหม? kŏr lorng nòhy dî mí |
| It doesn't fit. | มันไม่พอดี mahn mî por•dee |
| It's too... | มัน...เกินไป mahn...gern bpi |
| big/small | ใหญ่/เล็ก yì/léhk |
| short/long | สั้น/ยาว sâhn/yow |

| tight/loose | คับ/หลวม káhp/lŏarm |
| Do you have this in size…? | คุณมีขนาด…ไหม? kuhn mee kah•nàrt…mí |
| Do you have this in a bigger/smaller size? | คุณมีขนาดใหญ่กว่า/เล็กกว่า นี้ไหม? kuhn mee kah•nàrt yâi gwàr/léhk gwar née mí |

For Numbers, see page 158.

## Colors

| I'd like something in… | ผม *m* /ฉัน *f* อยากได้ที่เป็น… pŏm/cháhn yàrk•dîe têe bpehn… |
| beige | สีน้ำตาลอ่อน sĕe náhm•dtarn òrn |
| black | สีดำ sĕe dahm |
| blue | สีน้ำเงิน sĕe náhm•ngern |
| brown | สีน้ำตาล sĕe náhm•dtarn |
| green | สีเขียว sĕe kĕaw |
| gray | สีเทา sĕe tou |
| orange | สีส้ม sĕe sôm |
| pink | สีชมพู sĕe chom•poo |
| purple | สีม่วง sĕe môarng |
| red | สีแดง sĕe daeng |
| white | สีขาว sĕe kŏw |
| yellow | สีเหลือง sĕe lŭeang |

## Clothes & Accessories

| backpack | เป้สะพายหลัง bpê sah•pie lăhng |
| belt | เข็มขัด kĕhm•kàht |
| bikini | บิกินี่ bih•gih•nêe |
| blouse | เสื้อผู้หญิง sûea pôo•yĭhng |
| bra | ยกทรง yók•song |
| briefs [underpants] | กางเกงใน garng•geng ni |
| coat | เสื้อโค้ท sûea kóet |
| dress | ชุดกระโปรง chúht gràh•bproeng |

123

## YOU MAY SEE…

| | |
|---|---|
| สำหรับผู้ชาย *săhm•ràhp pôo•chie* | men's |
| สำหรับผู้หญิง *săhm•ràhp pôo•yĭng* | women's |
| สำหรับเด็ก *săhm•ràhp dèhk* | children's |

| | |
|---|---|
| hat | หมวก *mòark* |
| jacket | เสื้อแจ็กเก็ต *sûea jáek•gèht* |
| jeans | กางเกงยีนส์ *garng•geng yeen* |
| pajamas | ชุดนอน *chúht norn* |
| panties | กางเกงใน *garng•geng ni* |
| pants [trousers] | กางเกงขายาว *garng•geng kăr yow* |
| pantyhose [tights] | ถุงน่อง *tŭhng•nôhng* |
| purse [handbag] | กระเป๋าถือ *grah•bpŏu tŭee* |
| raincoat | เสื้อกันฝน *sûea gahn fŏn* |
| scarf | ผ้าพันคอ *pâr•pahn•kor* |
| shirt | เสื้อเชิร์ต *sûea•chért* |
| shorts | กางเกงขาสั้น *garng•geng kăr sâhn* |
| skirt | กระโปรง *grah•bproeng* |
| socks | ถุงเท้า *tŭhng•tóu* |
| suit | ชุดสูท *chúht•sòot* |
| sunglasses | แว่นกันแดด *wân gahn dàet* |
| sweater | เสื้อสเว็ตเตอร์ *sûea sah•wéht•dtêr* |
| sweatshirt | เสื้อสเว็ตเชิร์ต *sûea sah•wéht•chért* |
| swimsuit | ชุดว่ายน้ำ *chúht wîe•nárm* |
| T-shirt | เสื้อยืด *sûea•yûeet* |
| tie | เนคไท *néhk•ti* |
| underwear | ชุดชั้นใน *chúht cháhn ni* |

## Fabric

| | |
|---|---|
| I'd like… | ผม *m*/ฉัน *f* อยากได้… *pŏm/cháhn yàrk•dîe…* |
| cotton | ผ้าฝ้าย *pâr fîe* |

| denim | ผ้ายีนส์ *pâr yeen* |
|---|---|
| lace | ผ้าลูกไม *pâr lôok•mí* |
| leather | หนัง *năhng* |
| linen | ผ้าลินิน *pâr lih•nihn* |
| silk | ผ้าไหม *pâr mĭ* |
| wool | ผ้าวูล *pâr woon* |
| Is it machine washable? | อันนี้ซักด้วยเครื่องซักผ้าได้ไหม? *ahn née sáhk dôary krûeang•sáhk•pâr dîe mí* |

## Shoes

| I'd like... | ผม *m* /ฉัน *f* อยากได้... *pŏm/cháhn yàrk•dîe...* |
|---|---|
| high-heels/flats | รองเท้าส้นสูง/รองเท้าส้นแบน *rorng•tów sôn sŏong/ rorng•tów sôn baen* |
| boots | รองเท้าบู๊ท *rorng•tów bóot* |
| flip-flops | รองเท้าแตะ *rorng•tów dtà* |
| hiking boots | รองเท้าเดินเขา *rorng•tów dern•kŏu* |
| loafers | รองเท้าสวม *rorng•tów sŏarm* |
| sandals | รองเท้าแตะ *rorng•tów dtà* |
| shoes | รองเท้า *rorng•tów* |
| slippers | รองเท้าแตะ *rorng•tów dtà* |
| sneakers | รองเท้าผ้าใบ *rorng•tów pâr•bi* |
| Size... | ไซส์... *sí...* |

For Numbers, see page 158.

## Sizes

| small | เล็ก *léhk* |
|---|---|
| medium | กลาง *glarng* |
| large | ใหญ่ *yì* |
| extra large | ใหญ่พิเศษ *yì píh•sèt* |
| petite | สำหรับคนตัวเล็ก *săhm•ràhp kon dtoar léhk* |

## Newsagent & Tobacconist

| Do you sell English-language newspapers? | คุณมีหนังสือพิมพ์ภาษาอังกฤษขายไหม? *kuhn mee nǎhng•sǔee•pihm par•sǎr ahng•grìht kǐe mí* |
|---|---|
| I'd like... | ผม *m* /ฉัน *f* อยากได้... *pǒm/chán yàrk•dîe...* |
| chewing gum | หมากฝรั่ง *mark•fah•ràhng* |
| a cigar | ซิการ์ *síh•gâr* |
| a pack/carton of cigarettes | บุหรี่หนึ่ง ซอง/ห่อ *buh•rèe nùeng sorng/hòr* |
| a lighter | ไฟแช็ก *fi•chák* |
| a magazine | นิตยสาร *níht•tah•yah•sǎrn* |
| matches | ไม้ขีด *mí•kèet* |
| I'd like... | ผม *m* /ฉัน *f* อยากได้... *pǒm/chán yàrk•dîe...* |
| a newspaper | หนังสือพิมพ์ *nǎhng•sǔee•pihm* |
| a postcard | โปสการ์ด *bpóet•sah•gárt* |
| a road/town map of... | แผนที่ ถนน/เมือง ของ... *pǎen•têe tah•nǒn/mueang kǒrng...* |
| stamps | แสตมป์ *sah•dtaem* |

## Photography

| I'd like...camera. | ผม *m* /ฉัน *f* อยากได้กล้อง... *pǒm/chán yàrk•dîe glôhng...* |
|---|---|
| an automatic | อัตโนมัติ *àht•tah•noe•máht* |
| a digital | ดิจิตอล *dih•jih•dtôhn* |
| a disposable | ใช้แล้วทิ้ง *chí láew tíhng* |
| I'd like... | ผม *m* /ฉัน *f* อยากได้... *pǒm/chán yàrk•dîe...* |
| a battery | แบ็ตเตอรี่ *bàt•dter•rêe* |
| digital prints | ภาพดิจิตอล *pârp dih•jih•dtôhn* |
| a memory card | เมมโมรี่การ์ด *mem•moe•rêe gárt* |
| Can I print digital photos here? | ที่นี่มีบริการอัดภาพดิจิตอลไหม? *têe•nêe mee bor•rih•garn àht pârp dih•jih•dtôhn mí* |

# Souvenirs

| | | |
|---|---|---|
| Buddha image | พระพุทธรูป | *práh•púht•tah•rôop* |
| ceramics | เซรามิค | *se•rar•mìhk* |
| doll | ตุ๊กตา | *dtúhk•gah•dtar* |
| handmade flowers | ดอกไม้ประดิษฐ์ | *dòrk•mí bprah•dìht* |
| hill tribe clothes | ชุดชาวเขา | *chúht chow kǒu* |
| jewelry | เครื่องประดับ | *krûeang•bprah•dàhp* |
| key ring | พวงกุญแจ | *poarng guhn•jae* |
| kite | ว่าว | *wôw* |
| lacquerware | เครื่องเขิน | *krûeang kěrn* |
| nielloware | เครื่องถม | *krûeang tǒm* |
| postcard | โปสการ์ด | *bpóet•sah•gárt* |
| pottery | เครื่องปั้นดินเผา | *krûeang bpâhn dihn•pǒu* |
| silk | ผ้าไหม | *pâr mǐ* |
| silverware | เครื่องเงิน | *krûeang ngern* |
| T-shirt | เสื้อยืด | *sûea•yûeet* |
| wooden elephant | ช้างไม้ | *chárng•míe* |
| Can I see this/that? | ผม *m* /ฉัน *f* ขอดู อันนี้/อันนั้น หน่อยได้ไหม? *pǒm/cháhn kǒr doo ahn née/ahn náhn nòhy dî mǐ* |  |
| It's in the window/ display case. | มันอยู่ใน ที่จัดโชว์/ตู้โชว์ *mahn yòo ni têe jàht choe/ dtôo•choe* |  |
| I'd like... | ผม *m* /ฉัน *f* อยากได้... *pǒm/cháhn yàrk•dîe...* |  |
| a battery | แบ็ตเตอรี่ | *bàt•dter•rêe* |
| a bracelet | สร้อยข้อมือ | *sôry kôr•muee* |
| a brooch | เข็มกลัด | *kěhm•glàht* |
| a clock | นาฬิกา | *nar•lih•gar* |
| earrings | ตุ้มหู | *dtûm•hǒo* |
| a necklace | สร้อยคอ | *sôry•kor* |
| a ring | แหวน | *wǎen* |
| a watch | นาฬิกาข้อมือ | *nar•líh•gar kôr•muee* |

| | |
|---|---|
| I'd like… | ผม *m* /ฉัน *f* อยากได้ที่เป็น… *pŏm/cháhn yàrk•die têe bpehn…* |
| copper | ทองแดง *torng•daeng* |
| crystal | คริสตัล *kríhs•dtâhn* |
| cut glass | แก้วเจียระไน *gâew jea•rah•ni* |
| diamonds | เพชร *péht* |
| enamel | ลงยา/เคลือบ *long•yar/klûeap* |
| gold | ทองคำ *torng•kahm* |
| pearls | ไข่มุก *kì•múhk* |
| pewter | พิวเตอร์ *pihw•dtêr* |
| platinum | ทองขาว *torng•kǎrw* |
| sterling silver | เงินสเตอร์ลิง *ngern sah•dter•lihng* |
| Is this real? | นี่ของแท้หรือเปล่า? *nêe kǒrng táe rúe•bplòw* |
| Is there a certificate for it? | มีใบรับรองหรือเปล่า? *mee bi•ráhp•rorng rúe•bplòw* |
| Can you engrave it? | ช่วยสลักตัวอักษรให้ด้วยได้ไหม? *chôary sàh•làhk dtoar•àhk•sǒrn hî dôary dî mí* |

# Sport & Leisure

## ESSENTIAL

| | |
|---|---|
| When's the game? | เริ่มแข่งกี่โมง? *rêrm kàng gèe moeng* |
| Where's...? | ...อยู่ที่ไหน? *...yòo têe•nĭ* |
| the beach | ชายหาด *chie•hàrt* |
| the park | สวนสาธารณะ *sŏarn săr•tar•rah•náh* |
| the pool | สระว่ายน้ำ *sàh wîe•nárm* |
| Is it safe to swim here? | ที่นี่ปลอดภัยพอที่จะ ว่ายน้ำไหม? *têe•nêe bplòrt•pi por têe jah wîe•nárm mí* |
| Can I rent [hire] golf clubs? | ผม *m*/ฉัน *f* ขอเช่าไม้กอล์ฟได้ไหม? *pŏm/cháhn kŏr chôu mí•górf dîe mí* |
| How much per hour? | ชั่วโมงละเท่าไหร่? *chôar•moeng lah tôu•rì* |
| How far is it to...? | ไป...ไกลไหม? *bpi...gli mí* |
| Show me on the map, please. | ช่วยชี้ในแผนที่ให้หน่อย *chôary chée ni păen•têe hî nòhy* |

## Watching Sport

| | |
|---|---|
| When's...game/ match/tournament? | ...นัด นี้เริ่มแข่งกี่โมง? *...nát née rêrm kàng gèe moeng* |
| the badminton | แบดมินตัน *bàt•mihn•tâhn* |
| the basketball | บาสเก็ตบอล *bárt•sah•gêht bohn* |
| the boxing | มวย *moary* |
| the golf | กอล์ฟ *górf* |
| the soccer [football] | ฟุตบอล *fúht•bohn* |
| the table tennis | ปิงปอง *bpihng•bpohng* |
| the takraw | ตะกร้อ *dtah•grôr* |
| the tennis | เทนนิส *ten•níht* |
| the volleyball | วอลเล่ย์บอล *wohn•lê•bohn* |
| Who's playing? | ใครแข่งกับใคร? *kri kàng gàhp kri* |

| | |
|---|---|
| Where's the racetrack/ stadium? | สนามแข่ง/สนามกีฬา อยู่ที่ไหน? *sah•nărm kàng/ sah•nărm geel•ar yòo têe•nĭ* |

For Tickets, see page 20.

The national sport in Thailand is Muay Thai or Thai boxing. It differs from other martial arts in that it allows eight points of contact: the two hands, shins, elbows and knees compared to just the fists and feet. Another popular game is takraw; it's similar to volleyball but one's head and feet are used to play.

## Playing Sport

| | |
|---|---|
| Where is/are…? | …อยู่ที่ไหน? *…yòo têe•nĭ* |
| the golf course | สนามกอล์ฟ *sah•nărm górf* |
| the gym | โรงยิม *roeng yihm* |
| the park | สวนสาธารณะ *sŏarn săr•tar•rah•náh* |
| the tennis courts | สนามเทนนิส *sah•nărm ten•níht* |
| How much per…? | …ละเท่าไหร่? *…lah tôu•rì* |
| day | วัน *wahn* |
| hour | ชั่วโมง *chôar•moeng* |
| game | เกม *gem* |
| round | รอบ *rôrp* |

## At the Beach/Pool

| | | |
|---|---|---|
| Where's the beach/pool? | ชายหาด/สระว่ายน้ำอยู่ที่ไหน? | chie•hàrt/sàh wîe•nárm yòo têe•nî |
| Is there…? | มี…ไหม? | mee…mí |
| a kiddie [paddling] pool | สระเด็ก | sàh dèhk |
| an indoor/outdoor pool | สระในร่ม/กลางแจ้ง | sàh ni•rôm/glarng•jâeng |
| a lifeguard | ยามไลฟ์การ์ด | yarm lí•gàrt |
| Is it safe…? | ปลอดภัย…ไหม? | bplòrt•pi…mí |
| to swim | ที่จะว่ายน้ำ | têe jah wîe•nárm |
| to dive | ที่จะดำน้ำ | têe jah dahm•nárm |
| for children | สำหรับเด็ก | sǎhm•ràhp dèhk |
| I'd like to rent [hire]… | ผม m /ฉัน f อยากเช่า… | pǒm/cháhn yàrk chôu… |
| diving equipment | อุปกรณ์ดำน้ำ | ùhp•bpah•gorn dahm•nárm |
| a jet ski | เจ็ทสกี | jéht sah•gee |
| a motorboat | เรือยนต์ | ruea yon |
| a rowboat | เรือพาย | ruea pie |
| snorkeling equipment | อุปกรณ์สนอร์กเกิ้ล | ùhp•bpah•gorn sah•nórk•gêrn |
| a surfboard | กระดานโต้คลื่น | grah•darn dtôe•klûeen |
| an umbrella | ร่ม | rôm |
| water skis | สกีน้ำ | sah•gee nárm |
| a windsurfer | วินด์เซิร์ฟ | wihn•sérp |
| For…hours. | สำหรับ…ชั่วโมง | sǎhm•ràhp… chôar•moeng |

## Out in the Country

| | | |
|---|---|---|
| A map of…, please. | ขอแผนที่ของ…หน่อย | kǒr pǎen•têe kǒhng…nòhy |
| this region | แถวนี้ | tǎew•née |
| the walking routes | เส้นทางเดินเท้า | sên•tarng dern•tóu |
| the bike routes | เส้นทางจักรยาน | sên•tarng jàhk•grah•yarn |

| | |
|---|---|
| the trails | เส้นทางเดินป่า *sên•tarng dern•bpàr* |
| Is it…? | อันนี้…หรือเปล่า? *ahn née…rúe•bplòw* |
| easy | ง่าย *ngîe* |
| difficult | ยาก *yârk* |
| far | ไกล *gli* |
| steep | ชัน *chahn* |
| How far is it to…? | ไป…ไกลไหม? *bpi…gli mí* |
| Show me on the map, please. | ช่วยชี้ในแผนที่ให้ หน่อย *chôary chée ni pǎen•têe hî nòhy* |
| I'm lost. | ผม **m** /ฉัน **f** หลงทาง *pǒm/cháhn lǒng•tarng* |
| Where's…? | …อยู่ที่ไหน? *…yòo têe•nǐ* |
| the cave | ถ้ำ *tâhm* |
| the forest | ป่า *bpàr* |
| the lake | ทะเลสาบ *tah•le•sàrp* |
| the mountain | ภูเขา *poo•kǒu* |
| the nature preserve | เขตอนุรักษ์ธรรมชาติ *kèt àh•núh•ráhk tahm•mah•chárt* |
| the overlook [viewpoint] | จุดชมวิว *jùht chom wihw* |
| the park | สวนสาธารณะ *sǒarn sǎr•tar•rah•náh* |
| the picnic area | ที่ปิกนิก *têe bpíhk•níhk* |
| the rainforest | ป่าดิบชื้น *bpàr•dìhp chúeen* |
| the river | แม่น้ำ *mâe•nárm* |
| the sea | ทะเล *tah•le* |
| the hot spring | บ่อน้ำร้อน *bòr•nárm•rórn* |
| the waterfall | น้ำตก *náhm•dtòk* |

# Going Out

## ESSENTIAL

| | |
|---|---|
| What's there to do at night? | ที่นี่มีอะไรให้ทำตอนกลางคืนบ้าง? *têe nêe mee ah•ri hî tahm dtorn glarng•kueen bârng* |
| Do you have a program of events? | คุณมีโปรแกรมกิจกรรมไหม? *kuhn mee bproe•graem gìht•jah•gahm mí* |
| Where's...? | ...อยู่ที่ไหน? *...yòo têe•nî* |
| the downtown area | ย่านใจกลางเมือง *yârn ji•glarng mueang* |
| the bar | บาร์ *bar* |
| the dance club | คลับเต้นรำ *klàhp dtên•rahm* |
| Is there a cover charge? | มีค่าเข้าไหม? *mee kâr•kôu mí* |

## Entertainment

| | |
|---|---|
| Can you recommend...? | คุณช่วยแนะนำ...ให้หน่อยได้ไหม? *kuhn chôary ná•nahm... hî nòhy dî mí* |
| a ballet | บัลเล่ต์ *bahn•lê* |
| a concert | คอนเสิร์ต *kohn•sèrt* |
| a movie | ภาพยนตร์ *pârp•pah•yon* |
| a play | ละครเวที *lah•korn we•tee* |
| When does it start/end? | มันเริ่ม/เลิกเมื่อไหร่? *mahn rêrm/lêrk mûee•rì* |
| Where's...? | ...อยู่ที่ไหน? *...yòo têe•nî* |
| the concert hall | โรงคอนเสิร์ต *roeng kohn•sèrt* |
| the movie theater [cinema] | โรงหนัง *roeng năng* |
| the theater | โรงละคร *roeng lah•korn* |
| What's the dress code? | ต้องใส่เสื้อผ้าแบบไหน? *dtôrng sì sêua•pâr bàep nî* |

For Tickets, see page 20.

## Nightlife

| | |
|---|---|
| What's there to do at night? | ที่นี่มีอะไรให้ทำตอนกลางคืนบ้าง? *têe nêe mee ah•ri hî tahm dtorn glarng•kueen bârng* |
| Can you recommend...? | คุณช่วยแนะนำ...ให้หน่อยได้ไหม? *kuhn chôary ná•nahm...hî nòhy dî mí* |
| a bar | บาร์ *bar* |
| a cabaret | คาบาเร่ต์ *kar•bar•re* |
| a dance club | คลับเต้นรำ *klàhp dtên•rahm* |
| a jazz club | คลับที่เล่นเพลงแจ๊ซ *klàhp têe lên pleng jáet* |
| a club with.... Music | ไนท์คลับที่มีดนตรี... *ni•klahb têe mee don•dtree...* |
| a club with Thai music | คลับที่เล่นเพลงไทย *klàhp têe lên pleng ti* |
| Is there live music? | มีดนตรีเล่นสดไหม? *mee don•dtree lên sòt mí* |
| How do I get there? | ผม *m* /ฉัน *f* จะไปที่นั่นได้ยังไง? *pǒm/cháhn jah bpi têe nân dîe yahng•ngi* |
| Is there a cover charge? | มีค่าเข้าไหม? *mee kâr•kôu mí* |
| Let's go dancing. | ไปเต้นรำกันเถอะ *bpi dtên•rahm gahn tèr* |
| Is this area safe at night? | ที่นี่ตอนกลางคืนปลอดภัยใช่ไหม? *têe•nee dtorn glarng•kueen bplord•pi chî mí* |

---

### YOU MAY HEAR...

กรุณาปิดมือถือของท่านด้วย *gah•rúh•nar bpìht muee•tǔee kǒhng tâhn dôary*

Turn off your cell [mobile] phones, please.

# Special Requirements

# Business Travel

## ESSENTIAL

| | |
|---|---|
| I'm here on business. | ผม *m* /ฉัน *f* มาธุระ *pǒm/cháhn mar túh•ráh* |
| Here's my business card. | นี่นามบัตรของผม *m* /ฉัน *f* *nêe narm•bàht kǒhng pǒm/ cháhn* |
| Can I have your card? | ผม *m* /ฉัน *f* ขอนามบัตรของคุณ ได้ไหม? *pǒm/cháhn kǒr narm•bàht kǒhng kuhn dî mí* |
| I have a meeting with... | ผม *m* /ฉัน *f* มีประชุมกับ... *pǒm/cháhn mee bprah•chuhm gàhp...* |
| Where's...? | ...อยู่ที่ไหน? *...yòo têe•nǐ* |
| the business center | ศูนย์บริการทางธุรกิจ *sǒon bor•rih•garn tarng túh•ráh•gìht* |
| the convention hall | ห้องคอนเวนชั่น *hôhng kohn•wen•châhn* |
| the meeting room | ห้องประชุม *hôhng bprah•chuhm* |

In Thailand it is polite to refer to someone by the title คุณ *kuhn* (Mr., Mrs., Miss), then the first name. The traditional greeting is the wai, made by pressing the palms together under the chin and making a slight bow; shaking hands is also common in business settings. In Thai culture, age deserves respect; however, you should always be courteous: impatience and displays of anger are frowned upon. Thais are reluctant to say 'no' directly, so be alert to non-verbal communication.

## YOU MAY HEAR...

| | | |
|---|---|---|
| คุณนัดไว้หรือเปล่า? *kuhn náht wí rúe•bplòw* | | Do you have an appointment? |
| กับใคร? *gàhp kri* | | With whom? |
| กรุณารอสักครู่ *gah•rúh•nar ror sáhk krôo* | | One moment, please. |

## On Business

| | |
|---|---|
| I'm here... | ผม *m* /ฉัน *f* มาที่นี่เพื่อ... *pǒm/cháhn mar têe•nêe pûea...* |
| on business | ทำธุระ *tahm túh•ráh* |
| for a seminar | สัมมนา *sǎhm•mah•nar* |
| for a conference | ประชุมสัมมนา *bprah•chuhm sǎhm•mah•nar* |
| for a meeting | ประชุม *bprah•chuhm* |
| My name is... | ผม *m* /ฉัน *f* ชื่อ... *pǒm/cháhn chûee...* |
| May I introduce my colleague... | ผม *m* /ฉัน *f* ขอแนะนำเพื่อนร่วมงานของผม *m* /ฉัน *f*... *pǒm/cháhn kǒr ná•nahm pûean•rôarm•ngarn kǒhng pǒm/cháhn...* |
| I have a meeting/an appointment with... | ผม *m* /ฉัน *f* มีประชุม/นัดกับ... *pǒm/cháhn mee bprah•chuhm/náht gàhp...* |
| I'm sorry I'm late. | ขอโทษ ที่มาสาย *kǒr•tôet têe mar sǐe* |
| I need an interpreter. | ผม *m* /ฉัน *f* ต้องการล่าม *pǒm/cháhn dtôhng•garn lârm* |
| You can reach me at the...Hotel. | คุณติดต่อผม *m* /ฉัน *f* ได้ที่โรงแรม... *kuhn dtìht•dtòr pǒm/cháhn dîe têe roeng•raem...* |
| I'm here until... | ผม *m* /ฉัน *f* จะอยู่ที่นี่จนถึง... *pǒm/cháhn jah yòo têe•nêe jon•tǔeng...* |
| I need to... | ผม *m* /ฉัน *f* ต้องการ... *pǒm/cháhn dtôhng•garn...* |
| make a call | โทรศัพท์ *toe•rah•sàhp* |
| make a photocopy | ถ่ายเอกสาร *tìe èk•gah•sǎrn* |
| send an e-mail | ส่งอีเมล์ *sòng ee•mew* |
| send a fax | ส่งแฟกซ์ *sòng fák* |

send a package ส่งพัสดุ sòng páht•sah•dùh
It was a pleasure to ยินดีที่ได้พบคุณ yihn•dee têe dîe póp kuhn
meet you.

For Communications, see page 48.

## Traveling with Children

### ESSENTIAL

| | |
|---|---|
| Is there a discount for kids? | มีส่วนลดสำหรับเด็กไหม? mee sòarn•lót sǎhm•ràhp dèhk mí |
| Can you recommend a babysitter? | คุณช่วยแนะนำพี่เลี้ยงเด็กให้หน่อยได้ไหม? kuhn chôary ná•nahm pêe•léang dèhk hî nòhy dî mí |
| Do you have a child's seat/highchair? | คุณมีที่นั่งเด็ก/เก้าอี้เด็กไหม? kuhn mee têe•nâhng dèhk/ gôu•êe dèhk mí |
| Where can I change the baby? | ผม *m*/ฉัน *f* จะเปลี่ยนผ้าอ้อมให้เด็กได้ที่ไหน? pǒm/ cháhn jah bplèan pâr•ôrm hî dèhk dîe têe•nǐ |

### Out & About

| | |
|---|---|
| Can you recommend something for kids? | คุณมีอะไรที่จะแนะนำสำหรับเด็กไหม? kuhn mee ah•ri têe jah ná•nahm sǎhm•ràhp dèhk mí |
| Where's...? | ...อยู่ที่ไหน? ...yòo têe•nǐ |
| the amusement park | สวนสนุก sǒarn•sah•nùhk |
| the arcade | ตู้เล่นเกมอาเขต dtôo•lêhn•gem ar•kèt |
| the kiddie [paddling] pool | สระเด็ก sàh dèhk |
| the park | สวนสาธารณะ sǒarn sǎr•tar•rah•náh |
| the playground | สนามเด็กเล่น sah•nǎrm dèhk•lên |
| the zoo | สวนสัตว์ sǒarn•sàht |

| Are kids allowed? | เด็กเข้าได้ไหม? *dèhk kôu dîe mí* |
| Is it safe for kids? | ปลอดภัยสำหรับเด็กหรือเปล่า? *bplòrt•pi sǎhm•ràhp dèhk rúe•bplòw* |
| Is it suitable for... year olds? | อันนี้เหมาะสำหรับเด็กอายุ...ปีไหม? *ahn née mòh sǎhm•ràhp dèhk ar•yúh...bpee mí* |

For Numbers, see page 158.

## Baby Essentials

| Do you have...? | คุณมี...ไหม? *kuhn mee...mí* |
| a baby bottle | ขวดนมเด็ก *kòart•nom dèhk* |
| baby food | อาหารเด็ก *ar•hǎrn dèhk* |
| baby wipes | กระดาษเช็ดก้นเด็ก *grah•dàrt chéht gôn dèhk* |
| a car seat | ที่นั่งในรถสำหรับเด็ก *têe•nâhng ni rót sǎhm•ràhp dèhk* |
| a children's menu/ portion | เมนู/ขนาด สำหรับเด็ก *me•noo/kah•nàrt sǎhm•ràhp dèhk* |
| Do you have...? | คุณมี...ไหม? *kuhn mee...mí* |
| a child's seat/ highchair | ที่นั่งเด็ก/เก้าอี้เด็ก *têe•nâhng dèhk/gôu•êe dèhk* |
| a crib/cot | เปล/อู่นอน *bple/òo•norn* |
| diapers [nappies] | ผ้าอ้อม *pâr•ôrm* |
| formula [baby food] | นมผงเด็ก/อาหารเด็ก *nom•pǒng•dèhk/ar•hǎrn dèhk* |
| a pacifier [dummy] | จุกนม *jùhk nom* |
| a playpen | คอกเด็กเล่น *kôrk dèhk lêhn* |
| a stroller [pushchair] | รถเข็นเด็ก *rót kěhn dèhk* |
| Can I breastfeed the baby here? | ฉันให้นมลูกตรงนี้ได้ไหม? *cháhn hî nom lôok dtrong•née dîe mí* |
| Where can I breastfeed/change the baby? | ฉันจะ ให้นม/เปลี่ยนผ้าอ้อม เด็ก ได้ที่ไหน? *cháhn jah hî nom/bplèan pâr•ôrm dèhk dîe têe•nǐ* |

For Dining with Children, see page 61.

## Babysitting

| | |
|---|---|
| Can you recommend a babysitter? | คุณช่วยแนะนำพี่เลี้ยงเด็กให้หน่อยได้ไหม? *kuhn chôary ná•nahm pêe léang dèhk hî nòhy dî mí* |
| What's the charge? | คิดเท่าไหร่? *kíht tôu•rì* |
| Is there constant supervision? | มีการดูแลตลอดหรือเปล่า? *mee garn doo•lae dtah•lòrt rúe•bplòw* |
| I'll be back by... | ผม *m* /ฉัน *f* จะกลับมาเวลา... *pŏm/cháhn jah glàhp mar we•lar...* |
| I can be reached at... | คุณติดต่อผม *m* /ฉัน *f* ได้ที่... *kuhn dtìht•dtòr pŏm/cháhn dîe têe...* |
| If you need to contact me, call... | หากคุณต้องการติดต่อฉัน กรุณาโทร... *hark kuhn tong•garn dtihd•dtor cháhn gah•ruh•nar troe...* |

For Time, see page 160.

## Health & Emergency

| | |
|---|---|
| Can you recommend a pediatrician? | คุณช่วยแนะนำหมอเด็กให้หน่อยได้ไหม? *kuhn chôary ná•nahm mŏr•dèhk hî nòhy dîe mí* |
| My child is allergic to... | ลูกของผม *m* /ฉัน *f* แพ้... *lôok kŏhng pŏm/cháhn páe...* |
| My child is missing. | ลูกของผม *m* /ฉัน *f* หาย *lôok kŏhng pŏm/cháhn hĭe* |
| Have you seen a boy/girl? | คุณเห็นเด็กผู้ชาย/เด็กผู้หญิง ไหม? *kuhn hěhn dèhk pôo•chie/dèhk pôo•yǐhng mí* |

For Police, see page 145.

## ESSENTIAL

| | |
|---|---|
| Is there…? | มี…ไหม? *mee…mí* |
| access for the disabled | ทางเข้าออกสำหรับคนพิการ *tarng kôu òrk săhm•ràhp kon píh•garn* |
| a wheelchair ramp | ทางขึ้นสำหรับรถเข็นคนพิการ *tarng kûen săhm•ràhp rót•kĕhn kon píh•garn* |
| a handicapped-[disabled-] accessible toilet | ห้องน้ำสำหรับคนพิการ *hôhng•nárm săhm•ràhp kon píh•garn* |
| I need… | ผม *m*/ฉัน *f* ต้องการ… *pŏm/cháhn dtôhng•garn…* |
| assistance | ความช่วยเหลือ *kwarm chôary•lŭea* |
| an elevator [a lift] | ลิฟต์ *líhp* |
| a ground-floor room | ห้องชั้นล่าง *hôhng cháhn lârng* |

## Asking for Assistance

| | |
|---|---|
| I'm… | ผม *m*/ฉัน *f*… *pŏm/cháhn…* |
| disabled | พิการ *píh•garn* |
| visually impaired | พิการทางสายตา *píh•garn tarng săry•dtar* |
| hearing impaired/ deaf | พิการทางหู/หูหนวก *píh•garn tarng hŏo/hŏo•nòark* |
| unable to walk far/ use the stairs | เดินไกล/ใช้บันไดไม่ได้ *dern gli/chí bahn•di mî die* |
| Please speak louder. | กรุณาพูดดังขึ้นหน่อย *gah•rúh•nar pôot dahng kûeen nòhy* |

| Can I bring my wheelchair? | ผม *m* /ฉัน *f* เอารถเข็นไปด้วยได้ไหม? *pŏm/cháhn ou rót•kĕhn bpi dôary dîe mí* |
| Are guide dogs permitted? | อนุญาตให้นำสุนัขนำทางไปด้วยไหม? *àh•núh•yârt hî nahm sùh•náhk nahm•tarng bpi dôary mí* |
| Can you help me? | คุณช่วยผม *m* /ฉัน *f* หน่อยได้ไหม? *kuhn chôary pŏm/ cháhn nòhy dî mí* |
| Please open/hold the door. | ช่วย เปิด/ดึง ประตูให้หน่อย *chôary bpèrt/dueng bprah•dtoo hî nòhy* |

# In an Emergency

# Emergencies

## ESSENTIAL

| | |
|---|---|
| Help! | ช่วยด้วย! *chôary dôary* |
| Go away! | ไปให้พ้น! *bpi hî pón* |
| Stop, thief! | หยุดนะ ขโมย! *yùht náh kah•moey* |
| Get a doctor! | เรียกหมอให้หน่อย! *rêak mŏr hî nòhy* |
| Fire! | ไฟไหม้! *fi mî* |
| I'm lost. | ผม *m* /ฉัน *f* หลงทาง *pŏm/cháhn lŏng tarng* |
| Can you help me? | คุณช่วยผม *m* /ฉัน *f* หน่อยได้ไหม? *kuhn chôary pŏm/ cháhn nòhy dî mí* |

In an emergency, dial: **191** for the police
**1155** for the tourist police
**199** for the fire brigade
**1554** for the ambulance

## YOU MAY HEAR...

| | |
|---|---|
| กรอกแบบฟอร์มนี้ *gròrk bàep•form née* | Fill out this form. |
| ขอบัตรประจำตัวของคุณหน่อย *kŏr bàht•bprah•jahm•dtoar kŏhng kuhn nòhy* | Your identification, please. |
| เกิดขึ้น เมื่อไหร่/ที่ไหน? *gerd kuen muea•rì/têe•nì* | When/Where did it happen? |
| เขา *m* /เธอ หน้าตาท่าทางอย่างไร ฯ? *kŏu/ ter nar•dtar tar•tarng yarng•rì* | What does he/she look like? |

## ESSENTIAL

| | |
|---|---|
| Call the police! | ช่วยเรียกตำรวจให้หน่อย! *chôary rêak dtahm•ròart hî nòhy* |
| Where's the police station? | สถานีตำรวจอยู่ที่ไหน? *sah•tăr•nee dtahm•ròart yòo têe•nǐ* |
| There was an accident/attack. | มี อุบัติเหตุ/คนถูกทำร้าย *mee uh•bàht•dtih•hèt/kon tòok tahm•ríe* |
| My child is missing. | ลูกของผม *m* /ฉัน *f* หาย *lôok kŏhng pŏm/cháhn hǐe* |
| I need... | ผม *m* /ฉัน *f* ต้องการ... *pŏm/cháhn dtôhng•garn...* |
| an interpreter | ล่าม *lârm* |
| I need... | ผม *m* /ฉัน *f* ต้องการ... *pŏm/cháhn dtôhng•garn...* |
| to contact my lawyer | ติดต่อทนายของผม *m* /ฉัน *f* *dtìht•dtòr tah•nie kŏhng pŏm/cháhn* |
| to make a phone call | โทรศัพท์ *toe•rah•sàhp* |
| to contact the consulate | ติดต่อสถานกงสุล *dtìht•dtòr sah•tǎrn gong•sǔhn* |
| I'm innocent. | ผม *m* /ฉัน *f* บริสุทธิ์ *pŏm/cháhn bor•rih•sùht* |

## Crime & Lost Property

| | |
|---|---|
| I want to report... | ผม *m* /ฉัน *f* มาแจ้งความเรื่อง... *pŏm/cháhn mar jâeng•kwarm rûeang...* |
| a mugging | การจี้ *garn jêe* |
| a rape | การข่มขืน *garn kòm•kǔeen* |
| a theft | ขโมยของ *kah•moey kŏrng* |
| I was mugged/robbed. | ผม *m* /ฉัน *f* ถูก จี้/ปล้น *pŏm/cháhn tòok jêe/bplôn* |
| I lost my... | ...ของผม *m* /ฉัน *f* หาย *...kŏhng pom/cháhn hǐe* |

| | | |
|---|---|---|
| **My...was/were stolen.** | | ....ของผม *m* /ฉัน *f* ถูกขโมย ... *kŏhng pŏm/cháhn tòok kah•moey* |
| | backpack | เป้สะพายหลัง *bpê sah•pie•lǎhng* |
| | bicycle | จักรยาน *jàhk•grah•yarn* |
| | camera | กล้องถ่ายรูป *glôhng tìe•rôop* |
| | (rental [hire]) car | รถ (เช่า) *rót (chôu)* |
| | computer | คอมพิวเตอร์ *kohm•pihw•dtêr* |
| | credit card | บัตรเครดิต *bàht•kre•dìht* |
| | jewelry | เครื่องประดับ *krûeang bprah•dàhp* |
| | money | เงิน *ngern* |
| | passport | หนังสือเดินทาง *nǎhng•sǔee dern•tarng* |
| | purse [handbag] | กระเป๋าถือ *grah•bpŏu tǔee* |
| | traveler's checks [cheques] | เช็คเดินทาง *chéhk dern•tarng* |
| | wallet | กระเป๋าสตางค์ *grah•bpŏu sah•dtarng* |
| **I need a police report.** | | ผม *m* /ฉัน *f* ต้องการ ใบแจ้งความ *pŏm/cháhn dtôhng•garn bi•jâeng•kwarm* |
| **Where is the British/ American/Irish embassy?** | | สถานทูตของ อังกฤษ/อเมริกา/ไอริช อยู่ที่ไหน? *sah•tarn•tood korng ahng•grìht/ah•me•rih•gar/i•rihsh yoo têe•ni* |

## ESSENTIAL

| | |
|---|---|
| I'm sick [ill]. | ผม *m* /ฉัน *f* ไม่สบาย *pŏm/cháhn mî sah·bie* |
| I need an English-speaking doctor. | ผม *m* /ฉัน *f* ต้องการหมอที่พูดภาษาอังกฤษได้ *pŏm/ cháhn dtôhng·garn mŏr têe pôot par·săr ahng·grìht dîe* |
| It hurts here. | มันเจ็บตรงนี้ *mahn jèhp dtrong·née* |
| I have a stomachache. | ผม *m* /ฉัน *f* ปวดท้อง *pŏm/cháhn bpòart tórng* |

147

## Finding a Doctor

| | |
|---|---|
| Can you recommend a doctor/dentist? | คุณช่วยแนะนำ หมอ/หมอฟัน ให้หน่อยได้ไหม? *kuhn chôary ná·nahm mŏr/mŏr fahn hî nòhy dî mí* |
| Can you recommend a doctor/dentist? | คุณช่วยแนะนำ หมอ/หมอฟัน ให้หน่อยได้ไหม? *kuhn chôary ná·nahm mŏr/mŏr fahn hî nòhy dî mí* |
| Can the doctor come here? | ให้หมอมาที่นี่ได้ไหม? *hî mŏr mar têe·nêe dî mí* |
| I need an English-speaking doctor. | ผม *m* /ฉัน *f* ต้องการหมอที่พูดภาษาอังกฤษได้ *pŏm/cháhn dtôhng·garn mŏr têe pôot par·săr ahng·grìht dîe* |
| What are the office hours? | เวลาทำการกี่โมง? *we·lar tahm·garn gèe moeng* |
| I'd like an appointment for... | ผม *m* /ฉัน *f* จะขอนัด... *pŏm/cháhn jah kŏr náht...* |
| today | วันนี้ *wahn·née* |
| tomorrow | พรุ่งนี้ *prûhng·née* |
| as soon as possible | เร็วที่สุดเท่าที่จะเร็วได้ *rehw têe·sùht tôu têe jah rehw dîe* |
| It's urgent. | มันด่วนมาก *mahn dòarn mârk* |

| I have an appointment with Doctor... | ผม **m** /ฉัน **f** นัดหมอ...ไว้ *pŏm/cháhn náht mŏr... wí* |

## Symptoms

| I'm... | ผม **m** /ฉัน **f**... *pŏm/cháhn...* |
| bleeding | เลือดออก *lûeat òrk* |
| constipated | ท้องผูก *tórng•pòok* |
| dizzy | เวียนหัว *wean•hŏar* |
| nauseous | คลื่นไส้ *klueen•si* |
| vomiting | อาเจียน *ar•jean* |
| It hurts here. | มันเจ็บตรงนี้ *mahn jèhp dtrong•née* |
| I have... | ผม **m** /ฉัน **f** มีอาการ... *pŏm/cháhn mee ar•garn...* |
| an allergic reaction | ภูมิแพ้ *poom•páe* |
| chest pain | เจ็บหน้าอก *jèhp nâr•òk* |
| cramps | เป็นตะคริว *bpehn dtah•krihw* |
| diarrhea | ท้องร่วง *tórng rôarng* |
| an earache | ปวดหู *bpòart hŏo* |
| a fever | ไข้ *kî* |
| pain | เจ็บ *jèhp* |
| a rash | ผื่นคัน *bpehn pùeen•kahn* |
| a sprain | แพลง *plaeng* |
| I have... | ผม **m** /ฉัน **f** มีอาการ... *pŏm/cháhn mee ar•garn...* |
| some swelling | บวม *boarm* |
| a sore throat | เจ็บคอ *jèhp kor* |
| a stomachache | ปวดท้อง *bpòart tórng* |
| sunstroke | เป็นลมแดด *bpehn lom•dàet* |
| I've been sick [ill] for ...days. | ผม **m** /ฉัน **f** ไม่สบายมา...วันแล้ว *pŏm/cháhn mî sah•bie mar... wahn láew* |

For Numbers, see page 158.

## Conditions

| | |
|---|---|
| I'm... | ผม **m**/ฉัน **f** เป็น... *pŏm/cháhn bpehn...* |
| anemic | โรคโลหิตจาง *rôek loe•hìht jarng* |
| asthmatic | โรคหอบหืด *rôek hòrp•hùeet* |
| diabetic | โรคเบาหวาน *rôek bou•wăn* |
| I'm allergic to antibiotics/penicillin. | ผม **m**/ฉัน **f** แพ้ ยาปฏิชีวนะ/เพนิซิลลิน *pŏm/cháhn páe yar bpah•dtìh•chee•wah•náh/pe•níh•sihn•lihn* |
| I have... | ผม **m**/ฉัน **f** เป็น... *pŏm/cháhn bpehn...* |
| arthritis | โรคไขข้อเสื่อม *rôek kĭ•kôr sùeam* |
| epilepsy | โรคลมบ้าหมู *roek•lom•bar•moo* |
| a heart condition | โรคหัวใจ *rôek hŏar•ji* |
| high/low blood pressure | โรคความดัน สูง/ต่ำ *rôek kwarm•dahn sŏong/dtàhm* |
| I'm on medication. | ผม **m**/ฉัน **f** กินยาอยู่ *pŏm/cháhn gihn yar yòo* |

## YOU MAY HEAR...

| | |
|---|---|
| ตรงนี้เจ็บไหม? *dtrong•née jèhp mí* | Does it hurt here? |
| คุณใช้ยาอะไรอยู่หรือเปล่า? *kuhn chí yar ah•ri yòo rúe•bplòw* | Are you on medication? |
| คุณแพ้อะไรไหม? *kuhn páe ah•ri mí* | Are you allergic to anything? |
| อ้าปากหน่อย *âr bpàrk nòhy* | Open your mouth. |
| หายใจลึกๆ *hăry•ji lúek•lúek* | Breathe deeply. |
| ไอให้ฟังหน่อย *ai hî fahng nòhy* | Cough please. |
| คุณต้องไปหาหมอเฉพาะทาง *kuhn dtôhng bpi hăr mŏr chah•póh•tarng* | See a specialist. |
| คุณต้องไปโรงพยาบาล *kuhn dtôhng bpi roeng•pah•yar•barn* | Go to the hospital. |

## Treatment

| | |
|---|---|
| Do I need a prescription/medicine? | ผม *m*/ฉัน *f* ต้องใช้ ใบสั่งยา/ยา ไหม? *pŏm/cháhn dtôhng-chí bi•sàhng•yar/yar mí* |
| Can you prescribe a generic drug [unbranded medication]? | คุณช่วยสั่งยาสามัญทั่วไปให้ได้ไหม? *kuhn chôary sàhng yar săr•mahn dtôar•bpi hî dî mí* |
| Where can I get it? | ผม *m*/ฉัน *f* จะหาซื้อ ได้ที่ไหน? *pŏm/cháhn jah hăr súee dîe têe•nĭ* |

For Pharmacy, see page 152.

## Hospital

| | |
|---|---|
| Notify my family, please. | ช่วยแจ้งให้ครอบครัว ของผม *m*/ฉัน *f* ทราบด้วย *chôary jâeng hî krôrp•kroar kŏhng pŏm/cháhn sârp dôary* |
| I'm in pain. | ผม *m*/ฉัน *f* ปวดมาก *pŏm/cháhn bpòart mârk* |
| I need a doctor/nurse. | ผม *m*/ฉัน *f* ต้องการ หมอ/พยาบาล *pŏm/cháhn dtôhng•garn mŏr/pah•yar•barn* |
| When are visiting hours? | เวลาเยี่ยมกี่โมงถึงกี่โมง? *we•lar yêam gèe moeng tŭeng gèe moeng* |
| I'm visiting... | ผม *m*/ฉัน *f* มาเยี่ยม... *pŏm/cháhn mar yêam...* |

## Dentist

| | |
|---|---|
| I have... | ผม *m*/ฉัน *f* มาเพราะ... *pŏm/cháhn mar próh...* |
| a broken tooth | ฟันบิ่น *fahn bìhn* |
| a lost filling | ที่อุดฟันหลุด *têe•ùht•fahn lùht* |
| a toothache | ปวดฟัน *bpòart fahn* |
| Can you fix this denture? | ช่วยซ่อมฟันปลอมให้หน่อยได้ไหม? *chôary sôrm fahn•bplorm hî nòhy dî mí* |

## Gynecologist

| | |
|---|---|
| I have cramps/a vaginal infection. | ฉันมีอาการ ปวดประจำเดือน/ติดเชื้อในช่องคลอด *cháhn mee ar•garn bpòart bprah•jahm•duean/dtìht chúea ni chôhng•klôrt* |
| I missed my period. | ประจำเดือนของฉันไม่มา *bprah•jahm•duean kŏhng cháhn mî mar* |
| I'm on the Pill. | ฉันกินยาคุมอยู่ *cháhn gihn yar•kuhm yòo* |
| I'm (…months) pregnant. | ฉันท้อง (…เดือน แล้ว) *cháhn tórng (… duean láew)* |
| I'm not pregnant. | ฉันไม่ได้ท้อง *cháhn mî•dî tórng* |
| I'm …months pregnant. | ฉันท้อง…เดือนแล้ว *cháhn torng...duean laew* |
| My last period was… | ประจำเดือนของฉันมาครั้งสุดท้ายเมื่อ… *bprah•jahm•duean kŏhng cháhn mar kráhng sùht•tíe mûee…* |

## Optician

| | |
|---|---|
| I lost… | ผม *m* /ฉัน *f* ทำ…หาย *pŏm/cháhn tahm…hǐe* |
| a contact lens | คอนแท็คเลนส์ *kohn•tàk•len* |
| my glasses | แว่นตาของผม *m* /ฉัน *f* *wǎen•dtar kŏhng pŏm/cháhn* |
| a lens | เลนส์ *len* |

## Payment & Insurance

| | |
|---|---|
| How much? | เท่าไหร่? *tôu•rì* |
| Can I pay by credit card? | ผม *m* /ฉัน *f* จ่ายด้วยบัตรเครดิต ได้ไหม? *pŏm/cháhn jìe dôary bàht•kre•diht dîe mí* |
| I have insurance. | ผม *m* /ฉัน *f* มีประกัน *pŏm/cháhn mee bprah•gahn* |
| I need a receipt for my insurance. | ผม *m* /ฉัน *f* ต้องการใบเสร็จสำหรับเบิกประกัน *pŏm/ cháhn dtôhng•garn bi•sèht sǎhm•ràhp bèrk bprah•gahn* |

## Pharmacy

### ESSENTIAL

| | |
|---|---|
| Where's the pharmacy [chemist]? | ร้านขายยาอยู่ที่ไหน? rárn•kǐe•yar yòo têe•nǐ |
| What time does it open/close? | ร้านขายยา เปิด/ปิด กี่โมง? rárn•kǐe•yar bpèrt/bpìht gèe moeng |
| What would you recommend for...? | คุณมียาที่แนะนำสำหรับอาการ...ไหม? kuhn mee yar têe ná•nahm sǎhm•ràhp ar•garn...mí |
| How much do I take? | ผม?/ฉัน/ต้องทานยานี้ยังไง? pǒm/cháhndtôhng tarn yar née yahng•ngi |
| Can you fill [make up] this prescription? | ช่วยจัดยาตามใบสั่งยาให้หน่อยได้ไหม? chôary jàht yar dtarm bi•sàhng•yar hî nòhy dî mí |
| I'm allergic to... | ผม m /ฉัน f แพ้... pǒm/cháhn páe... |

You'll find that pharmacies in Thailand are abundant and that many of the drugs that are sold only with a prescription in other countries are sold freely as over-the-counter drugs. If you rely on regular prescription medicine, take a supply with you.

### What to Take

| | |
|---|---|
| How much do I take? | ผม m /ฉัน f ต้องทานยังไง? pǒm/cháhn dtôhng tarn yahng•ngi |
| How often? | บ่อยแค่ไหน? bòhy kâe nǐ |
| Is it safe for children? | ปลอดภัยสำหรับเด็กหรือเปล่า? bplòrt•pi sǎhm•rahp dèhk rúe•bplòw |
| I'm taking... | ผม m /ฉัน f ทานยา...อยู่ pǒm/cháhn tarn yar...yòo |

| Are there side effects? | มีผลข้างเคียงไหม? | *mee pŏn•kârng•keang mí* |
| I need something for... | ผม *m* /ฉัน/ อยากได้ยาแก้... | *pŏm/cháhn yàrk•dîe yar gâe...* |
| a cold | หวัด | *wàht* |
| a cough | ไอ | *i* |
| diarrhea | ท้องร่วง | *tórng rôarng* |
| a headache | ปวดหัว | *bpoard hoar* |
| insect bites | แมลงกัดต่อย | *mah•laeng gàht•dtòry* |
| motion sickness | เมารถ | *mou rót* |
| seasickness | เมาเรือ | *mou ruea* |
| a sore throat | เจ็บคอ | *jèhp kor* |
| sunburn | แดดเผา | *dàet pŏu* |
| a toothache | ปวดฟัน | *bpoard fahn* |
| an upset stomach | ท้องเสีย | *tórng sĕa* |

## Basic Supplies

| I'd like... | ผม *m* /ฉัน *f* อยากได้... | *pŏm/cháhn yàrk•dîe...* |
| acetaminophen [paracetamol] | พาราเซตตามอล | *par•rar•séht•dtar•môhn* |
| aftershave | โลชั่นทาหลังโกนหนวด | *loe•châhn tar lăhng goen•nòart* |
| antiseptic cream | ครีมแก้อักเสบ | *kreem gâe àhk•sèp* |
| aspirin | แอสไพริน | *àet•sah•pi•rihn* |
| bandages [plasters] | ผ้าพันแผล | *pâr pahn plăe* |
| a comb | หวี | *wĕe* |
| condoms | ถุงยางอนามัย | *tŭhng•yarng ah•nar•mi* |
| contact lens solution | น้ำยาแช่คอนแท็คเลนส์ | *náhm•yar châe kohn•tàk•len* |
| deodorant | ยาระงับกลิ่นตัว | *yar rah•ngáhp glìhn•dtoar* |
| a hairbrush | แปรงแปรงผม | *bpraeng•pŏm* |
| hair gel | เจลใส่ผม | *jel si pŏm* |
| hairspray | สเปรย์ฉีดผม | *sah•bpre cheed pŏm* |

## YOU MAY SEE...

| | |
|---|---|
| วันละ หนึ่ง/สาม ครั้ง *wahn lah nùeng/sǎrm krǎhng* | once/three times a day |
| หลัง/ก่อน/พร้อม อาหาร *lǎhng/gòrn/prórm ar•hǎrn* | after/before/with meals |
| ตอนท้องว่าง *dtorn tórng•wârng* | on an empty stomach |
| อาจจะทำให้ง่วง *àrt•jah tahm•hî ngôarng* | may cause drowsiness |
| สำหรับใช้ภายนอกเท่านั้น *sǎhm•ràhp chí pie•nôrk tôu•náhn* | for external use only |

| | |
|---|---|
| I'd like... | ผม *m*/ฉัน *f* อยากได้... *pǒm/cháhn yàrk•dîe...* |
| ibuprofen | อีบูโปรเฟน *ee•boo•bproe•fen* |
| insect repellent | ยาทากันแมลง *yar tar gahn mah•laeng* |
| lotion | โลชั่น *loe•châhn* |
| a nail file | ตะไบเล็บ *dtah•bi léhp* |
| a pain killer | ยาแก้ปวด *yar•gâe•bpòart* |
| a (disposable) razor | มีดโกน (ใช้แล้วทิ้ง) *mêet•goen (chí láew tíhng)* |
| razor blades | ใบมีดโกน *bi mêet•goen* |
| sanitary napkins [pads] | ผ้าอนามัย *pâr ah•nar•mi* |
| shampoo/ conditioner | แชมพู/ครีมนวดผม *chaem•poo/kreem nôart pǒm* |
| soap | สบู่ *sah•bòo* |
| sunscreen | ครีมกันแดด *kreem gahn dàet* |
| tampons | ผ้าอนามัยแบบสอด *pâr ah•nar•mi bàep•sòrt* |
| tissues | กระดาษทิชชู่ *grah•dàrt tíht•chôo* |
| toilet paper | กระดาษชำระ *grah•dàrt chahm•ráh* |
| a toothbrush | แปรงสีฟัน *bpraeng sěe fahn* |
| toothpaste | ยาสีฟัน *yar sěe fahn* |

154

# The Basics

## Grammar

### Gender

In Thai, the first person pronoun 'I' varies by gender: A man would refer to himself as ผม *pŏm*, a female speaker would say ฉัน *cháhn* (or in very formal situation ดิฉัน *dih•cháhn*). A similar gender distinction applies when ending a statement politely or to say 'yes': A man uses ครับ *kráhp*, while a woman uses ค่ะ *kâh*.

Most of the time, the subject pronoun – I, *pŏm* m /*cháhn* f; you, *kuhn*; we, *rou*, etc. – can be omitted from the sentence.

## Verbs

Verbs are not conjugated in Thai, nor is there a change in tense (present, past, future, etc.). Instead, distinctions between tenses are marked by adverbs and expressions of time, or by the context of the sentence.

A past event can be indicated by the addition of either แล้ว *láew* (already) after the verb, or of ได้ *dî* (to get or receive) immediately in front of the verb, to emphasize that the event is completed. However, these are used only sparingly and are not necessary if the past tense is implicit in the context. Sentences beginning with the time expression เมื่อ *mûea* (when), for example, are automatically considered a past event.

A future or hypothetical event is indicated by the addition of จะ *jah* (immediately) in front of the verb.

## Nouns

Instead of articles, Thai nouns have classifiers. Common classifiers include:

| | | |
|---|---|---|
| คน | *kon* | for people |
| ตัว | *dtoar* | for animals, tables, chairs and items of clothing |
| ลูก | *lôok* | for fruit, eggs and other round objects |

| ชิ้น | chíhn | meaning a 'piece', can be used for items served or sold in pieces |
| ใบ | bi | for fruit, bags and banknotes |
| ฉบับ | chah•bàhp | for letters and newspapers |
| เล่ม | lêhm | for books, candles and knives |

Portions of food and drink are classified according to the dishes and containers in which they are served. Therefore, fried rice would be classified by the word plate, coffee by cup, soup by bowl and so forth:

| ข้าวผัดจานหนึ่ง | kôw•pàht jarn nueng | one plate of fried rice |
| ก๋วยเตี๋ยวชามหนึ่ง | gǒary•těaw charm nueng | one bowl of noodles |

When the number of a certain noun is to be specified, the word order is as follows: noun + number + classifier:

| รถ+สอง+คัน | rót+sǒrng+kahn | two cars |
| ขวด+สาม+ขวด | kòart+sǎrm+kòart | three bottles |

## Word Order

Like English, Thai is a subject-verb-object language. For example:
เธอซื้อหนังสือ *ter súee nǎhng•sǔee* She buys books.

Questions can be formed by putting question words at the end of the affirmative sentences. For example:
1. หรือ *rǔee*
เธอซื้อหนังสือหรือ *ter súee nǎhng•sǔee rǔee* Did she buy books?
2. ใช่ไหม *chî•mí*
เธอซื้อหนังสือใช่ไหม *ter súee nǎhng•sǔee chî•mí* She buys books, doesn't she?

To negate, place ไม่ได้ *mî•dîe* before the verb.
เธอไม่ได้ซื้อหนังสือ *ter mî•dîe súee nǎhng•sǔee* She doesn't buy books.

# Pronouns

Pronouns in Thai can be complicated, as that they can indicate hierarchy, relationship, gender, etc. The pronouns shown in the following table are the most frequently used in normal situations.

| I | ผม *m*/ฉัน *f* pŏm/cháhn |
| you | คุณ kuhn |
| he | เขา kóu |
| she | เธอ ter |
| it | มัน manh |
| we | เรา rou |
| they | เขา kóu |

# Possessive Pronouns

Place ของ kŏhng before a noun or pronoun to indicate possession, for example:
ของผม *m* /ฉัน *f* kŏhng pŏm/cháhn (mine)

# Adjectives

An adjective in Thai is placed after the noun to which it refers, for example:
หมอฉลาด mŏr chah•làrt the clever doctor

To add emphasis, some adjectives in Thai can be repeated; note that the tone of the first word may change, for example:
ช้วยสวย sŏary sŏary extremely beautiful
ว้านหวาน wárn wărn incredibly sweet

# Comparative & Superlative

Use กว่า gwàr for the comparative:
ใหญ่กว่า yì gwàr bigger
เล็กกว่า léhk gwàr smaller

Use ที่สุด têe•sùht for the superlative:
ใหญ่ที่สุด yì têe•sùht biggest
เล็กที่สุด léhk têe•sùht smallest

## Adverbs & Adverbial Expressions

Where an adverb in Thai is placed depends on its function. Adverbs that describe a manner or degree are placed after the verb, for example:

เขาขับช้า *kóu kàhp chár* He drives slowly.

Adverbs of time and frequency can be placed before or after the verb, for example:

เขาจะทำงานคืนนี้ *kóu jah tahm•ngarn* kueen née He will work tonight.
คืนนี้เขาจะทำงาน kueen née *kóu jah tahm•ngarn*

Adverbs of negation precede the verb:

ผม *m* /ฉัน *f pŏm/cháhn* mî•kery I never drink alcohol.
ไม่เคยดื่มเหล้า *dùeem lôu*

## Numbers

## ESSENTIAL

| 0 | ๐ *sŏon* |
|---|---|
| 1 | ๑ *nùeng* |
| 2 | ๒ *sŏrng* |
| 3 | ๓ *sărm* |
| 4 | ๔ *sèe* |
| 5 | ๕ *hâr* |
| 6 | ๖ *hòk* |
| 7 | ๗ *jèht* |
| 8 | ๘ *bpàet* |
| 9 | ๙ *gôw* |
| 10 | ๑๐ *sìhp* |
| 11 | ๑๑ *sìhp•èht* |
| 12 | ๑๒ *sìhp sŏrng* |
| 13 | ๑๓ *sìhp sărm* |

| 14 | ๑๔ sìhp sèe |
| 15 | ๑๕ sìhp hâr |
| 16 | ๑๖ sìhp hòk |
| 17 | ๑๗ sìhp jèht |
| 18 | ๑๘ sìhp bpàet |
| 19 | ๑๙ sìhp gôw |
| 20 | ๒๐ yêe•sìhp |
| 21 | ๒๑ yêe•sìhp•èht |
| 22 | ๒๒ yêe•sìhp sŏrng |
| 30 | ๓๐ sărm sìhp |
| 31 | ๓๑ sărm sìhp èht |
| 40 | ๔๐ sèe sìhp |
| 50 | ๕๐ hâr sìhp |
| 60 | ๖๐ hòk sìhp |
| 70 | ๗๐ jèht sìhp |
| 80 | ๘๐ bpàet sìhp |
| 90 | ๙๐ gôw sìhp |
| 100 | ๑๐๐ nùehng róry |
| 101 | ๑๐๑ róry•èht/nùehng róry nùehng |
| 200 | ๒๐๐ sŏrng róry |
| 500 | ๕๐๐ hâr róry |
| 1,000 | ๑๐๐๐ nùeng pahn |
| 10,000 | ๑๐,๐๐๐ nùeng mùeen |
| 1,000,000 | ๑๐๐,๐๐๐ nùeng săen |

Thai numbers are mostly used in formal writing. Otherwise,
Arabic numbers are commonly used.

## Ordinal Numbers

### ESSENTIAL

| | |
|---|---|
| first | ที่หนึ่ง *têe nùeng* |
| second | ที่สอง *têe sŏrng* |
| third | ที่สาม *têe sărm* |
| fourth | ที่สี่ *têe sèe* |
| fifth | ที่ห้า *têe hâr* |
| once | ครั้งหนึ่ง/หนึ่งครั้ง *kráhng nùeng/nùeng kráhng* |
| twice | สองครั้ง *sŏrng kráhng* |
| three times | สามครั้ง *sărm kráhng* |

## Time

### ESSENTIAL

| | |
|---|---|
| What time is it? | ตอนนี้เวลา เท่าไหร่? *dtorn•née we•lar tôu•rì* |
| It's noon [midday]. | ตอนนี้ เที่ยงวัน *dtorn•née têang•wahn* |
| At midnight. | เที่ยงคืน *têang•kueen* |
| From one to two a.m. | ตั้งแต่ตีหนึ่งถึงตีสอง *dtâhng•dtàe dtee nùeng tŭeng dtee sŏrng* |
| From one to two p.m. | ตั้งแต่บ่ายโมงถึงบ่ายสองโมง *dtâhng•dtàe bìe moeng tŭeng bìe sŏrng moeng* |
| 3:45 a.m. | ตีสามสี่สิบห้านาที *dtee sărm sèe•sìhp•hâr nar•tee* |
| 3:45 p.m. | บ่ายสามโมงสี่สิบห้านาที *bìe sărm moeng sèe•sìhp•hâr nar•tee* |
| 5:30 a.m. | ตีห้าครึ่ง *dtee hâr krûeng* |
| 5:30 p.m. | บ่ายห้าโมงครึ่ง *bìe hâr moeng krûeng* |

# Days

## ESSENTIAL

| | |
|---|---|
| Monday | วันจันทร์ *wahn jahn* |
| Tuesday | วันอังคาร *wahn ahng•karn* |
| Wednesday | วันพุธ *wahn púht* |
| Thursday | วันพฤหัสบดี *wahn páh•rúe•hàht•sàh•bor•dee* |
| Friday | วันศุกร์ *wahn sùhk* |
| Saturday | วันเสาร์ *wahn sŏu* |
| Sunday | วันอาทิตย์ *wahn ar•tíht* |

# Dates

| | |
|---|---|
| yesterday | เมื่อวาน *mûea•warn* |
| today | วันนี้ *wahn•née* |
| tomorrow | พรุ่งนี้ *prûhng•née* |
| day | วัน *wahn* |
| week | สัปดาห์ *sàhp•dar* |
| month | เดือน *duean* |
| year | ปี *bpee* |

# Months

| | |
|---|---|
| January | มกราคม *mók•gah•rar•kom* |
| February | กุมภาพันธ์ *guhm•par•pahn* |
| March | มีนาคม *mee•nar•kom* |
| April | เมษายน *me•săr•yon* |
| May | พฤษภาคม *prúet•sah•par•kom* |
| June | มิถุนายน *míh•tuh•nar•yon* |
| July | กรกฎาคม *gàh•ráhk•gah•dar•kom* |
| August | สิงหาคม *sĭhng•hăr•kom* |
| September | กันยายน *kahn•yar•yon* |

| October | ตุลาคม *dtuh•lar•kom* |
| November | พฤศจิกายน *prúet•sah•jìh•gar•yon* |
| December | ธันวาคม *tahn•war•kom* |

## Seasons

| spring | ฤดูใบไม้ผลิ *rúe•doo bi•mí plì* |
| summer | ฤดูร้อน *rúe•doo rórn* |
| fall [autumn] | ฤดูใบไม้ร่วง *rúe•doo bi•mí rûang* |
| winter | ฤดูหนาว *rúe•doo nǒw* |
| rainy season | ฤดูฝน *rúe•doo fǒn* |

162

## Holidays

| January 1, New Year's Day | วันขึ้นปีใหม่ *wahn kûehn bpee mì* |
| April 6, Chakri Day | วันจักรี *wahn jàhk•gree* |
| April 13-15, Songkran (Thai New Year) | วันสงกรานต์ *wahn sǒng•grarn* |
| May 1, Labor Day | วันแรงงาน *wahn raeng•ngarn* |
| May 5, Coronation Day | วันฉัตรมงคล *wahn chàht•trah•mong•kon* |
| August 12, H.M. | วันเฉลิมพระชนมพรรษา สมเด็จพระบรมราชินีนาถ *wahn chah•lěrm práh chon•mah•pahn•sǎr sǒm•dèht práh bor•rom•mah•rar•chíh•nee•nârt* |
| October 23, Chulalongkorn Day | วันปิยมหาราช *wahn bpih•yáh mah•hǎr•rârt* |
| December 5, H.M. King's Birthday (National Day) | วันเฉลิมพระชนมพรรษา พระบาทสมเด็จพระเจ้าอยู่หัว *wahn chah•lěrm práh•chon•mah•pahn•sǎr práh•bàrt sǒm•dèht práh•jôw yòo•hǒar* |
| December 10, Constitution Day | วันรัฐธรรมนูญ *wahn ráht•tah•tahm•mah•noon* |

## Moveable Holidays

| | |
|---|---|
| Buddha Commemoration Day | มาฆบูชา *mar•káh boo•char* |
| Buddha's Birthday | วิสาขบูชา *wíh•sǎr•kàh boo•char* |
| Buddha's First Sermon | อาสาฬหบูชา *ar•sǎrn•hàh boo•char* |
| First Day of Buddhist Lent | เข้าพรรษา *kôu pahn•sǎr* |
| The Festival of Lights | ลอยกระทง *lory grah•tong* |

## Conversion Tables

| When you know | Multiply by | To find |
|---|---|---|
| ounces | 28.3 | grams |
| pounds | 0.45 | kilograms |
| inches | 2.54 | centimeters |
| feet | 0.3 | meters |
| miles | 1.61 | kilometers |
| square inches | 6.45 | sq. centimeters |
| square feet | 0.09 | sq. meters |
| square miles | 2.59 | sq. kilometers |
| pints (US/Brit) | 0.47/0.56 | liters |
| gallons (US/Brit) | 3.8/4.5 | liters |
| Fahrenheit | 5/9, after -32 | Centigrade |
| Centigrade | 9/5, then +32 | Fahrenheit |

### Mileage

| | |
|---|---|
| **1 km** – 0.62 miles | **50 km** – 31 miles |
| **5 km** – 3.1 miles | **100 km** – 62 miles |
| **10 km** – 6.2 miles | |

## Measurement

| 1 gram | กรัม *grahm* | 0.035 oz. |
|---|---|---|
| 1 kilogram (kg) | กิโลกรัม (ก.ก.) *gih•loe•grahm* | 2.2 lb |
| 1 liter (l) | ลิตร (ล.) *liht* | 1.06 U.S/0.88 Brit. quarts |
| 1 centimeter (cm) | เซ็นติเมตร (ซ.ม.) *sehn•dti•mét* | 0.4 inch |
| 1 meter (m) | เมตร (ม.) *mét* | 3.28 feet |
| 1 kilometer (km) | กิโลเมตร (ก.ม.) *gih•loe•mét* | 0.62 mile |

## Temperature

| | | |
|---|---|---|
| **-40° C** – -40° F | **-1° C** – 30° F | **20° C** – 68° F |
| **-30° C** – -22° F | **0° C** – 32° F | **25° C** – 77° F |
| **-20° C** – -4° F | **5° C** – 41° F | **30° C** – 86° F |
| **-10° C** – 14° F | **10° C** – 50° F | **35° C** – 95° F |
| **-5° C** – 23° F | **15° C** – 59° F | |

## Oven Temperature

| | |
|---|---|
| **100° C** – 212° F | **177° C** – 350° F |
| **121° C** – 250° F | **204° C** – 400° F |
| **149° C** – 300° F | **260° C** – 500° F |

# Dictionary

... mi paeng ...
เมื่อไร **mi mee sh-ri** nothing
สบาย **mi sah-bie** sick ป่วย
ใส่ **mi sì** without
**míe** wood (material)
กวาด **míe·gwart** broom
อล์ฟ **míe·górf** golf c
เขวนเสื้อ **míe·kwǎe**
hanger; coat hanger
**míe tǒo·pú·**

# English–Thai Dictionary

## A

**abroad** ต่างประเทศ *dtàrng-bprah-têt*

**accept** ยอมรับ *yorm-ráhp*

**access** เข้าถึง *kôu-tǔeng*

**accident** อุบัติเหตุ *uh-bàht-dtih-hèt*

**accommodation** ที่พัก *têe-páhk*

**accompany** มาด้วย *mar dôary*

**acetaminophen** พาราเซตตามอล *par-rar-séht-dtar-môhn*

**across** ตรงข้าม *dtrong-kârm*

**acupuncture** ฝังเข็ม *fǎhng-kěhm*

**adapter** ปลั๊กแปลงไฟฟ้า *bpláhk bplaeng fi-fár*

**additional** เพิ่มเติม *pêrm-dterm*

**address** ที่อยู่ *têe-yòo*

**admission charge** ค่าเข้า *kâr-kôu*

**adult** ผู้ใหญ่ *pôo-yì*

**after** หลังจาก *lǎhng-jàrk*

**afternoon** ตอนบ่าย *dtorn bìe*

**agree** เห็นด้วย *hěhn-dôary*

**air** (tire) ลม *lom*; อากาศ *ar-gàrt*

**air conditioning** แอร์ *ae*

**air mattress** ที่นอนอัดลม *têe-norn àht lom*

**airline** สายการบิน *sǐe-garn-bihn*

**airmail** ไปรษณีย์อากาศ *bpri-sah-nee ar-gàrt*

**airport** สนามบิน *sah-nǎrm-bihn*

**airsickness** เมาเครื่องบิน *mou krûeang-bihn*

**alarm clock** นาฬิกาปลุก *nar-li-gar bplùhk*

**allergy** ภูมิแพ้ *poom-páe*

**allow** อนุญาต *ah-núh-yârt*

**allowance** ค่าใช้จ่าย *kâr chí-jie*

**almost** เกือบจะ *gùeap-jah*

**alone** คนเดียว *kon-deaw*

**already** แล้ว *láew*

**alter** (a garment) แก้ *gâe*

**alternate** สลับ *sah-làhp*

**aluminum foil** กระดาษฟอยล์ *grah-dàrt fory*

**ambassador** เอกอัครราชทูต *èk-àhk-kah-rárt-chah-tôot*

**ambulance** รถพยาบาล *rót pah-yar-barn*

**American** อเมริกัน *ah-me-rih-gahn*

**amount** จำนวน *jahm-noarn*

**amusement park** สวนสนุก *sǒarn sah-nùhk*

**and** และ *lá*

**anemia** โรคโลหิตจาง *rôek loe-hìht jarng*

**anesthetic** ยาชา *yar-char*

**animal** สัตว์ *sàht*

**antacid** ยาลดกรด *yar lót gròt*

---

| **adj** adjective | **BE** British English | **prep** preposition |
|---|---|---|
| **adv** adverb | **n** noun | **v** verb |

**antibiotics** ยาปฏิชีวนะ *yar bpah•dtih•chee•wah•náh*

**antique** ของเก่า *kŏrng gòu*

**antiseptic cream** ครีมแก้อักเสบ *kreem gǎe àhk•sèp*

**any** ใด *di*

**anyone** ใคร *kri*

**anything** อะไร *ah•ri*

**apartment** อพาร์ตเมนต์ *ah•párt•méhn*

**apologize** ขอโทษ *kŏr•tôet*

**appointment** นัด *náht*

**approve** ยอมรับ *yorm•ráhp*

**approximately** ประมาณ *bprah•marn*

**area code** รหัสพื้นที่ *rah•hàht púeen•têe*

**arm** แขน *kǎen*

**aromatherapy** อโรมาเทราปี *ah•roe•mâr te•rar•pêe*

**around** รอบ ๆ *rôrp•rôrp*

**arrivals** ขาเข้า *kǎr•kôu*

**arrive** มาถึง *mar•tǔeng*

**art gallery** หอศิลป์ *hŏr•sǐhn*

**arthritis** โรคไขข้อเสื่อม *rôek kĭ•kôr sùeam*

**ashtray** ที่เขี่ยบุหรี่ *têe kèar buh•rèe*

**ask** ถาม *tǎrm*

**aspirin** แอสไพริน *áet•sah•pi•rihn*

**assistance** ความช่วยเหลือ *kwarm chôary•lǔea*

**asthma** โรคหอบหืด *rôek hòrp•hùeet*

**ATM** เอทีเอ็ม *e•tee•ehm*

**attack** v ทำร้าย *tahm•ríe;* n การทำร้าย *garn tahm•ríe*

**attractive** มีเสน่ห์ *mee sah•nè*

**audio guide** เทปนำเที่ยว *tép nahm•têaw*

**authentic** แท้ *táe*

**available** ว่าง *wârng*

**away** ห่าง *hàrng*

## B

**baby** เด็กอ่อน *dèhk òrn*

**baby bottle** ขวดนมเด็ก *kòart•nom dèhk*

**baby food** อาหารเด็ก *ar•hǎrn dèhk*

**babysitter** พี่เลี้ยงเด็ก *pêe•léarng dèhk*

**back** หลัง *lǎhng*

**backache** ปวดหลัง *bpòart lǎhng*

**backpack** เป้สะพายหลัง *bpê sah•pie lǎhng*

**bad** เลว *lew*

**bag** กระเป๋า *grah•bpǒu*

**baggage** [BE] กระเป๋า *grah•bpǒu*

**baggage claim** ที่รับกระเป๋า *têe ráhp grah•bpǒu*

**bakery** ร้านเบเกอรี่ *rárn be•ger•rêe*

**balcony** ระเบียง *rah•beang*

**ball** ลูกบอล *lôok•bohn*

**ballet** บัลเลต์ *bahn•lê*

**bandage** ผ้าพันแผล *pâr pahn plǎe*

**bank** ธนาคาร *tah•nar•karn*

**bar** บาร์ *bar*

**barber** ร้านตัดผมผู้ชาย *rárn dtàht•pǒm pôo•chie*

**bargain** ต่อราคา *tòr rar•kar*

**basement** ชั้นใต้ดิน *cháhn tí•dihn*

**basket** ตะกร้า *dtah•grâr*

**basketball** บาสเก็ตบอล *bárt•sah•gêht bohn*

**bath** อาบน้ำ *àrp•nárm*

**bathroom** ห้องน้ำ *hôhng•nárm*

**battery** แบตเตอรี่ *bàt•dter•rêe*

**be** เป็น *bpehn*

**beach** ชายหาด *chie•hàrt*

**beautiful** สวย *sǒary*

**because** เพราะว่า *próh•wâr*

**bed** เตียง *dteang*

**bedding** เครื่องนอน *krûeang•norn*

**bedroom** ห้องนอน *hôhng•norn*

**before** ก่อน *gòrn*

**begin** เริ่ม *rêrm*

**behind** หลัง *lǎhng*

**belong** เป็นของ *bpehn kǒhng*

**belt** เข็มขัด *kěhm•kàht*

**bet** พนัน *pah•nahn*

**between** ระหว่าง *rah•wàrng*

**beware** ระวัง *rah•wahng*

**bicycle** จักรยาน *jàhk•grah•yarn*

**big** ใหญ่ *yì*

**bike path** ทางจักรยาน *tarng jàhk•grah•yarn*

**bikini** บิกินี่ *bih•gih•nêe*

**bill** บิล *bihn*

**binoculars** กล้องส่องทางไกล *glôhng sòng tarng gli*

**bird** นก *nók*

**birthday** วันเกิด *wahn•gèrt*

**bite** กัด *gàht*

**blanket** ผ้าห่ม *pâr•hòm*

**bleed** เลือดออก *lûeat•òrk*

**blister** แผลพุพอง *plǎe púh•porng*

**blood** เลือด *lûeat*

**blood pressure** ความดันเลือด *kwarm•dahn lûeat*

**blouse** เสื้อผู้หญิง *sûea pôo•yǐhng*

**board** กระดาน *grah•darn*

**boarding card** ตั๋วขึ้นเครื่อง *dtǒar kûen krûeang*

**boat trip** ทัวร์ทางเรือ *toar tarng ruea*

**bone** กระดูก *grah•dòok*

**book** หนังสือ *nǎhng•sǔee*

**bookstore** ร้านหนังสือ *rárn nǎhng•sǔee*

**boots** รองเท้าบู๊ต *rorng•tów bóot*

**born** เกิด *gèrt*

**borrow** ยืม *yueem*

**botanical garden** สวนพฤกษศาสตร์ *sǒarn prúek•sah•sàrt*

**bother** รบกวน *róp•goarn*

**bottle** ขวด *kòart*

**bottle opener** ที่เปิดขวด *têe bpèrt kòart*

**bowl** ชาม *charm*

**box** กล่อง *glòhng*

**boxing** ชกมวย *chók•moary*

**boy** เด็กผู้ชาย *dèhk•pôo•chie*

**bra** ยกทรง *yók•song*

**bracelet** สร้อยข้อมือ *sôry kôr•muee*

**brake** v หยุด *yùht;* n เบรก *brèk*

**break** แตก *dtàek*

**breakfast** อาหารเช้า *ar•hǎrn chów*

**breast** หน้าอก *nâr•òk*

**breastfeed** ให้นม *hî•nom*

**breathe** หายใจ *hiě•ji*

**bridge** สะพาน *sah•parn*

**bring** เอามา *ou•mar*

**British (person)** คนอังกฤษ *kon ahng•grìht*

**brochure** แผ่นพับ *pàen•páhp*

**broken** เสีย *sěa*

**broom** ไม้กวาด *mie•gwàrt*

**browse** เปิดดู *bpèrt•doo*

**bruise** รอยฟกช้ำ *rory fók•cháhm*

**bucket** ถัง *tǎhng*

**Buddha image** พระพุทธรูป *práh•púht• tah•rôop*

**bug** แมลง *mah•laeng*

**build** สร้าง *sàrng*

**building** ตึก *dtùek*; อาคาร *ar•karn*

**burn** ไหม้ *mî*

**bus** รถเมล์ *rót•me*

**bus station** สถานีขนส่ง *sah•tǎr•nee kǒn•sòng*

**bus stop** ป้ายรถเมล์ *bpîe rót•me*

**bus ticket** ตั๋วรถเมล์ *dtǒar rót•me*

**business** ธุรกิจ *túh•ráh•gìht*

**business card** นามบัตร *narm•bàht*

**business center** ศูนย์บริการทางธุรกิจ *sǒon bor•rih•garn tarng túh•ráh•gìht*

**business class** ชั้นธุรกิจ *cháhn túh• ráh•gìht*

**business district** ย่านธุรกิจ *yârn túh•ráh•gìht*

**busy** ยุ่ง *yûhng*

**but** แต่ *dtàe*

**button (clothing)** กระดุม *grah•duhm*; **(device)** ปุ่ม *bpùhm*

**buy** ซื้อ *súee*

**by** โดย *doey*

**bye** สวัสดี *sah•wàht•dee*

## C

**cafe** ร้านกาแฟ *rárn gar•fae*

**calendar** ปฏิทิน *bpah•dtìh•tihn*

**call (phone)** โทรศัพท์ *toe•rah•sàhp*;

**(summon)** เรียก *rêak*

**camera** กล้องถ่ายรูป *glôhng tìe•rôop*

**camp** ตั้งแคมป์ *dtâhng•káem*

**campsite** ที่ตั้งแคมป์ *têe dtâhng•káem*

**can** กระป๋อง *grah•bpǒhng*

**can opener** ที่เปิดกระป๋อง *têe bpèrt grah•bpǒhng*

**canal** คลอง *klorng*

**cancel** ยกเลิก *yók•lêrk*

**cancer** มะเร็ง *mah•rehng*

**candle** เทียน *tean*

**candy store** ร้านขายขนม *rárn kǐe kah•nǒm*

**canoe** เรือแคนู *ruea kae•noo*

**car** รถยนต์ *rót•yon*

**car hire [BE]** รถเช่า *rót•chôu*

**car park [BE]** ที่จอดรถ *têe jòrt rót*

**car rental** รถเช่า *rót•chôu*

**car seat** ที่นั่งในรถสำหรับเด็ก *têe•nâhng ni rót sǎhm•ràhp dèhk*

**carafe** เหยือก *yùeak*

**card** บัตร *bàht*

**careful** ระวัง *rah•wahng*

**carpet** พรม *prom*

**carry-on luggage** กระเป๋าถือขึ้นเครื่อง *grah•bpǒu tǔee kûen krûeang*

**cart** รถเข็น *rót•kěhn*

**carton (of cigarettes)** กล่อง *glòhng*

**cash** v ขึ้นเงิน *kûen•ngern*; n เงินสด *ngern•sòt*

**cash register** เครื่องคิดเงิน *krûeang kít•ngern*

**cashier** แคชเชียร์ *káet•chea*

**casino** คาสิโน *kar•sih•noe*

**catch** จับ *jàhp*

**cathedral** โบสถ์ฝรั่ง *bòet fah•ràhng*

**caution** ระมัดระวัง *rah•máht rah•wahng*

**cave** ถ้ำ *tâhm*

**CD** ซีดี *see•dee*

**CD player** เครื่องเล่นซีดี *krûeang lêhn see•dee*

**cell phone** โทรศัพท์มือถือ *toe•rah•sàhp muee•tǔee*

**cemetery** สุสาน *sùh•sǎrn*

**ceramics** เซรามิก *se•rar•mìhk*

**certificate** ใบรับรอง *bi ráhp•rorng*

**change** v เปลี่ยน *bplèan;* (money) v แลกเงิน *lâek ngern;* n เงินทอน *ngern•torn*

**charcoal** ถ่าน *tàrn*

**charge** v คิดเงิน *kíht•ngern;* n ค่า *kâr*

**cheap** ถูก *tòok*

**check** n (bank) เช็ค *chéhk;* v ตรวจ *dtròart;* v (luggage) ฝากกระเป๋า *fàrk grah•bpǒu*

**check in** เช็คอิน *chéhk•ihn*

**check out** เช็คเอาท์ *chéhk•óu*

**check-in desk** โต๊ะเช็คอิน *dtó chéhk•ihn*

**checking account** บัญชีกระแสรายวัน *bahn•chee grah•sǎe rie•wahn*

**chemical toilet** ส้วมเคมี *sôarm ke•mee*

**chemist [BE]** ร้านขายยา *rárn kǎi yar*

**cheque [BE]** เช็ค *chéhk*

**chest** หน้าอก *nâr•òk*

**child** เด็ก *dèhk*

**child seat** ที่นั่งเด็ก *têe•nâhng dèhk*

**children's menu** เมนูสำหรับเด็ก *me•noo sǎhm•ràhp dèhk*

**children's portion** ขนาดสำหรับเด็ก *kah•nàrt sǎhm•ràhp dèhk*

**choose** เลือก *lûeak*

**church** โบสถ์ *bòet*

**cigar** ซิการ์ *síh•gàr*

**cigarette** บุหรี่ *bùh•rèe*

**cinema [BE]** โรงหนัง *roeng•nǎng*

**clean** adj สะอาด *sah•àrt;* v ทำความสะอาด *tahm kwarm sah•àrt*

**clearance (sale)** ลดราคา *lót rar•kar*

**cliff** หน้าผา *nâr•pǎr*

**cling film [BE]** ฟิล์มถนอมอาหาร *feem tah•nǒrm ar•hǎrn*

**clinic** คลีนิค *klee•nìhk*

**clock** นาฬิกา *nar•lih•gar*

**close (shut)** ปิด *bpìht;* (near) ใกล้ *glî*

**clothes shop [BE]** ร้านขายเสื้อผ้า *rárn kǐe sûea•pâr*

**clothing store** ร้านขายเสื้อผ้า *rárn kǐe sûea•pâr*

**club** คลับ *klàhp*

**coast** ชายฝั่ง *chie•fàhng*

**coat** เสื้อโค้ท *sûea•kóet*

**coat check** ที่รับฝากเสื้อโค้ท *têe ráhp fàrk sûea•kóet*

**code** รหัส *rah•hàht*

**coin** เหรียญ *rěan*

**cold (weather)** adj หนาว *nǒw;* n หวัด *wàht*

**collapse** ล้ม *lóm*

**colleague** เพื่อนร่วมงาน *pûean•rôarm•ngarn*

**collect (call)** โทรเก็บเงินปลายทาง *toe gèhp ngern bplie tarng*

**color** สี *sěe*

**comb** หวี *wěe*

**come** มา *mar*

**commission** ค่าบริการ *kâr bor·rih·garn*

**company** บริษัท *bor·rih·sàht*

**compartment** ที่ใส่ของ *têe sì kŏrng*

**computer** คอมพิวเตอร์ *kohm·pihw·dtêr*

**concert** คอนเสิร์ต *kohn·sèrt*

**conditioner (hair)** ครีมนวดผม *kreem nôart pŏm*

**condom** ถุงยางอนามัย *tŭhng·yarng ah·nar·mi*

**conductor (bus)** กระเป๋ารถ *grah·bpŏu rót*

**conference** การประชุมสัมมนา *garn bprah·chuhm săhm·mah·nar*

**confirm** ยืนยัน *yueen·yahn*

**congratulations** ขอแสดงความยินดี *kŏr sah·daeng kwarm yihn·dee*

**connect** เชื่อมต่อ *chûeam·dtòr*

**connection** การเชื่อมต่อ *garn chûeam·dtòr*

**conscious** รู้สึกตัว *róo·sùek dtoar*

**conservation area** เขตอนุรักษ์ *kèt àh·nú·ráhk*

**constant** คงที่ *kong·têe*

**constipation** อาการท้องผูก *ar·garn tórng·pòok*

**consulate** กงสุล *gong·sŭhn*

**consult** ปรึกษา *bprùek·săr*

**contact** v ติดต่อ *dtiht·dtòr*; n การติดต่อ *garn dtiht·dtòr*

**contact lens** คอนแท็คเลนส์ *korn·tàk·lehn*

**contact lens solution** น้ำยาคอนแท็คเลนส์ *náhm·yar korn·tàk·lehn*

**contraceptive** คุมกำเนิด *kuhm·gahm·nèrt*

**control** ควบคุม *kôarp·kuhm*

**convention** การประชุม *garn bprah·chuhm*

**convention hall** ห้องคอนเวนชั่น *hôhng kohn·wen·châhn*

**cook** v ทำอาหาร *tahm ar·hărn*; n คนครัว *kon·kroar*

**cool** เย็น *yehn*

**copy** ทำสำเนา *tahm săhm·nou*

**corkscrew** ที่เปิดจุกก๊อก *têe bpèrt jùhk·góhk*

**corner** มุม *muhm*

**correct** ถูกต้อง *took·dtôhng*

**cosmetic** เครื่องสำอาง *krûeang săhm·arng*

**cost** n ค่าใช้จ่าย *kâr chí·jie*; v ราคา *rar·kar*

**cot** เตียงพับ *dteang·páhp*

**cottage** กระท่อม *grah·tôhm*

**cotton** ผ้าฝ้าย *pâr fie*

**cough** ไอ *i*

**counter** เคาน์เตอร์ *kóu·dtêr*

**country** ประเทศ *bprah·têt*

**country code** รหัสประเทศ *rah·hàht bprah·têt*

**course** วิชา *wíh·char*

**cover charge** ค่าบริการต่อหัว *kâr bor·rih·garn dtòr hŭa*

**craft shop** ร้านขายงานฝีมือ *rárn kĭe ngarn·fĕe·muee*

**cramp (sports)** ตะคริว *dtah·kríhw*; **(period)** ปวดประจำเดือน *bpòart* bprah•jahm•duean

**credit card** บัตรเครดิต *bàht kre•dìht*

**crib** เปลเด็ก *bple dèhk*

**crowd** ฝูงคน *fŏong•kon*

**cruise** ล่องเรือ *lôhng•ruea*

**crutch** ไม้เท้า *mí•tów*

**crystal** คริสตัล *kríhts•dtâhn*

**cup** ถ้วย *tôary*

**currency** เงิน *ngern*

**currency exchange office**
ที่รับแลกเงิน *têe ráhp lâek ngern*

**curtain** ผ้าม่าน *pâr•mârn*

**customer service** บริการลูกค้า
*bor•rih•garn lôok•kár*

**customs** ศุลกากร *sŭhn•lah•gar•gorn*

**cut** *v* (knife) บาด *bàrt*; *n* บาดแผล
*bàrt•plăe*

**cute** น่ารัก *nâr•ráhk*

## D

**daily** รายวัน *rie•wahn*

**damage** เสียหาย *sĕa•hĭe*

**damp** ชื้น *chúeen*

**dance** เต้นรำ *dtêhn•rahm*

**dance club** คลับเต้นรำ *klàhp dtêhn•rahm*

**dangerous** อันตราย *ahn•dtah•rie*

**dark** มืด *mûeet*

**day** วัน *wahn*

**day trip** ทัวร์วันเดียว *toar wahn deaw*

**dead** ตาย *dtie*

**deaf** หูหนวก *hŏo•nòark*

**deck chair** เก้าอี้ผ้าใบ *gôu•êe pâr•bi*

**declare** แสดงรายการสิ่งของ *sah•daeng
rie•garn sìhng•kŏrng*

**decorative** ตกแต่ง *dtok•dtàng*

**deep** ลึก *lúek*

**degree** องศา *ong•săr*

**delay** ช้า *chár*

**delete** ลบ *lóp*

**delicious** อร่อย *ah•ròhy*

**deliver** ส่ง *sòng*

**delivery** การส่ง *garn•sòng*

**dental floss** ไหมขัดฟัน *mĭ kàht fahn*

**dentist** หมอฟัน *mŏr fahn*

**denture** ฟันปลอม *fahn bplorm*

**deodorant** ยาระงับกลิ่นตัว *yar
rah•ngáhp glìhn•dtoar*

**depart** จาก *jàrk*

**department store** ห้างสรรพสินค้า
*hârng sàhp•pah•sĭhn•kár*

**departure gate**
ประตูทางออกขึ้นเครื่อง *bprah•dtoo
tarng•òrk kûen krûeang*

**departures** ขาออก *kăr•òrk*

**deposit** *v* ฝากเงิน *fàrk ngern*; *n* เงินมัดจำ
*ngern máht•jahm*

**describe** อธิบาย *ah•tíh•bie*

**destination** ปลายทาง *bplie•tarng*

**detail** รายละเอียด *rie•lah•èat*

**detergent** ผงซักฟอก *pŏng•sáhk•fôrk*

**detour** ทางเบี่ยง *tarng•bèang*

**develop** พัฒนา *páht•tah•nar*

**diabetes** โรคเบาหวาน *rôek bou•wărn*

**diabetic** *adj* เบาหวาน *bou•wărn*;
*n* คนเป็นโรคเบาหวาน *kon bpehn rôek
bou•wărn*

**dial (phone)** กด *gòt*

**diaper** ผ้าอ้อม *pâr•ôrm*

**diarrhea** ท้องร่วง *tórng•rôarng*

**dice** v หั่น *hàhn;* n ลูกเต๋า *lôok•dtŏu*

**dictionary** พจนานุกรม *pót•jah•nar•núh•grom*

**diesel** ดีเซล *dee•sen*

**diet** v ควบคุมอาหาร *kôarp•kuhm ar•hǎrn*

**difficult** ยาก *yârk*

**digital** ดิจิตอล *dih•jih•dtôhn*

**dine** กินอาหาร *gihn ar•hǎrn*

**dining car** รถเสบียง *rót sah•beang*

**dining room** ห้องอาหาร *hôhng ar•hǎrn*

**dinner** อาหารเย็น *ar•hǎrn yehn*

**direct** adj ตรง *dtrong;* v กำกับ *gahm•gàhp*

**direction** ทิศ *tíht*

**director (company)** ผู้อำนวยการ *pôo•ahm•noary•garn*

**directory (phone)** สมุดโทรศัพท์ *sàh•mùht toe•rah•sàhp*

**dirty** สกปรก *sòk•grah•bpròk*

**disabled** adj พิการ *píh•garn;* n คนพิการ *kon píh•garn*

**disconnect** ตัดการเชื่อมต่อ *dtàht garn chûeam•dtòr*

**discount** ส่วนลด *sòarn•lót*

**dish** จาน *jarn*

**dishwasher** เครื่องล้างจาน *krûeang lárng jarn*

**dishwashing liquid** น้ำยาล้างจาน *náhm•yar lárng jarn*

**display case** ตู้โชว์ *tôo•choe*

**disposable** ใช้แล้วทิ้ง *chí láew tíhng*

**dissolve** ละลาย *lah•lie*

**distance** ระยะทาง *ráh•yáh•tarng*

**disturb** รบกวน *róp•goarn*

**dive** ดำน้ำ *dahm•nárm*

**diving equipment** อุปกรณ์ดำน้ำ *ùhp•bpah•gorn dahm•nárm*

**divorce** หย่า *yàr*

**dizzy** เวียนศีรษะ *wean sěe•sàh*

**do** ทำ *tahm*

**dock** อู่เรือ *òo•ruea*

**doctor** หมอ *mǒr*

**dog** สุนัข *suh•náhk*

**doll** ตุ๊กตา *dtúhk•gah•dtar*

**dollar** ดอลลาร์ *dohn•lâr*

**domestic** ในประเทศ *ni bprah•têt*

**donation** เงินบริจาค *ngern bor•rih•jàrk*

**door** ประตู *bprah•dtoo*

**dosage (medicine)** ขนาดรับประทาน *kah•nàrt ráhp•bprah•tarn*

**double** คู่ *kôo*

**double room** ห้องคู่ *hôhng kôo*

**downstairs** ชั้นล่าง *cháhn lârng*

**downtown** ย่านใจกลางเมือง *yârn ji•glarng mueang*

**dress** ชุดกระโปรง *chúht grah•bproeng*

**drink** v ดื่ม *dùeem;* n เครื่องดื่ม *krûeang•dùeem*

**drip** หยด *yòt*

**drive** ขับ *kàhp*

**driver** คนขับ *kon kàhp*

**driver's license** ใบขับขี่ *bi•kàhp•kèe*

**drown** จมน้ำ *jom nárm*

**drowsy** ง่วง *ngôarng*

**drugstore** ร้านขายยา *rárn kǐe yar*

**dry** adj แห้ง *hâeng*

**dry clean** ซักแห้ง *sáhk•hâeng*

**dry cleaner** ร้านซักแห้ง *rárn sáhk•hâeng*

**dummy [BE]** จุกนม *jùhk•nom*

**during** ระหว่าง *rah•wàrng*

**duty (tax)** ภาษี *par•sĕe*

**duty-free** ร้านค้าปลอดภาษี *rárn•kár bplòrt par•sĕe*

# E

**ear** หู *hŏo*

**earache** ปวดหู *bpòart hŏo*

**earrings** ตุ้มหู *dtûhm•hŏo*

**east** ทิศตะวันออก *tíht dtah•wahn•òrk*

**easy** ง่าย *ngîe*

**eat** กิน *gihn*

**economy class** ชั้นประหยัด *cháhn bprah•yàht*

**electrical outlet** ปลั๊กไฟ *bpláhk•fi*

**electronic** ไฟฟ้า *fi•fár*

**elevator** ลิฟต์ *líhp*

**e-mail** อีเมล์ *ee•mew*

**e-mail address** อีเมล์แอดเดรส *ee•mew áht•drét*

**embassy** สถานทูต *sah•tărn•tôot*

**emergency** ฉุกเฉิน *chùhk•chĕrn*

**emergency brake** เบรกฉุกเฉิน *brèk chùhk•chĕrn*

**emergency exit** ทางออกฉุกเฉิน *tarng•òrk chùhk•chĕrn*

**emergency service** บริการฉุกเฉิน *bor•rih•garn chùhk•chĕrn*

**empty** ว่าง *wârng*

**end** v จบ *jòp*; n ปลาย *bplie*

**engaged** หมั้น *mâhn*

**England** (ประเทศ)อังกฤษ *(bprah•têt) ahng•grìht*

**English (language)** ภาษาอังกฤษ *par•săr ahng•grìht;* **(person)** คนอังกฤษ *kon ahng•grìht*

**engrave** สลัก *sah•làhk*

**enjoy** สนุก *sah•nùhk*

**enlarge** ขยาย *kah•yĭe*

**enough** พอ *por*

**entrance** ทางเข้า *tarng•kôu*

**entry visa** วีซ่าเข้าประเทศ *wee•sâr kôu bprah•têt*

**envelope** ซองจดหมาย *sorng•jòt•mĭe*

**equipment** เครื่องมือ *krûeang•muee*

**error** ข้อผิดพลาด *kôr•piht•plârt*

**escalator** บันไดเลื่อน *bahn•di•lûean*

**essential** จำเป็น *jahm•bpehn*

**e-ticket** ตั๋วอิเล็กทรอนิกส์ *dtŏar ee•léhk•tror•nihk*

**Eurocheque** ยูโรเช็ค *yoo•roe chéhk*

**evening** ตอนเย็น *dtorn•yehn*

**event** เหตุการณ์ *hèt•garn*

**every** ทุก *túhk*

**exact** แน่นอน *nâe•norn*

**examination** การสอบ *garn•sòrp*

**example** ตัวอย่าง *dtoar•yàrng*

**except** ยกเว้น *yók•wéhn*

**excess luggage** กระเป๋าเกิน *grah•bpŏu gern*

**exchange** แลกเปลี่ยน *lâek•bplèan*

**exchange rate** อัตราแลกเปลี่ยน *àht•dtrar lâek•bplèan*

**excursion** ทัวร์ระยะสั้น *toar rah•yáh sâhn*

**exhausted** หมดแรง *mòt raeng*

**exit** v ออก *òrk*; n ทางออก *tarng•òrk*

**expensive** แพง *paeng*

**express mail** ไปรษณีย์ด่วน *bpri•sah•nee dòarn*

**extension (phone)** เบอร์ต่อ *ber dtòr*

**extra** เพิ่ม *pêrm*

**eye** ตา *dtar*

**eyebrow** คิ้ว *kíhw*

## F

**fabric** เนื้อผ้า *núea•pâr*

**face** หน้า *nâr*

**facility** สถานที่ *sah•tǎrn•têe*

**faint** เป็นลม *bpehn•lom*

**family** ครอบครัว *krôrp•kroar*

**famous** มีชื่อเสียง *mee chúee•sěang*

**fan** พัดลม *páht•lom*

**far** ไกล *gli*

**farm** ฟาร์ม *farm*

**fast** เร็ว *rehw*

**fast food** อาหารจานด่วน *ar•hǎrn jarn dòarn*

**faucet** ก๊อกน้ำ *górk•nárm*

**faulty** บกพร่อง *bòk•prôhng*

**favorite** ที่ชอบ *têe chôrp*

**fax** แฟ็กซ์ *fàk*

**fax machine** เครื่องแฟ็กซ์ *krûeang fàk*

**fax number** เบอร์แฟ็กซ์ *ber fàk*

**feature** รูปแบบ *rôop•baep*

**feed** ป้อน *bpôrn*

**feeding bottle [BE]** ขวดนม *kòart•nom*

**feel** รู้สึก *róo•sùek*

**female** เพศหญิง *pêt•yǐhng*

**ferry** เรือข้ามฟาก *ruea kârm•fârk*

**fever** ไข้ *kî*

**few** น้อย *nóry;* **(a few)** ไม่กี่ *mî•gèe*

**field** ทุ่ง *túhng*

**fight** ต่อสู้ *dtòr•sôo*

**fill** เติม *dterm*

**fill out** กรอก *gròrk*

**fill up** เติมให้เต็ม *dterm hî dtehm*

**filling (dental)** ที่อุดฟัน *têe•ùht•fahn*

**film** หนัง *nǎhng*

**find** หา *hǎr*

**fine (health)** สบายดี *sah•bie dee*

**finger** นิ้ว *níhw*

**fire** ไฟ *fi*

**fire alarm** สัญญาณไฟไหม้ *sǎhn•yarn fi•mî*

**fire escape** ทางหนีไฟ *tarng něe fi*

**fire exit** ทางหนีไฟ *tarng něe fi*

**fire extinguisher** ถังดับเพลิง *tǎhng dàhp•plerng*

**first** ที่หนึ่ง *têe nùeng*

**first class** ชั้นหนึ่ง *cháhn nùeng*

**fishing** ตกปลา *dtòk•bplar*

**fit** พอดี *por•dee*

**fitting room** ห้องลองเสื้อผ้า *hôhng lorng sûea•pâr*

**fix (repair)** ซ่อม *sôhm*

**flash (camera)** แฟลช *flàt*

**flashlight** ไฟฉาย *fi•chǐe*

**flat [BE] (apartment)** แฟลต *flàt*

**flavor** รสชาติ *rót•chârt*

**flea market** ตลาดนัด *dtah•làrt náht*

**flight** เที่ยวบิน *têaw•bihn*

**flight attendant** พนักงานต้อนรับ *pah•náhk•ngarn dtôrn•ráhp*

**flight number** เที่ยวบินที่ *têaw•bihn têe*

**floor (level)** ชั้น *cháhn*

**flower** ดอกไม้ *dòrk•míe*

**flu** ไข้หวัดใหญ่ *kî•wàt•yì*

**flush (toilet)** กดชักโครก *gòt cháhk•krôek*

**fly** บิน *bihn*

**fog** หมอก *mòrk*

**follow** ตาม *dtarm*

**food** อาหาร *ar•hǎrn*

**food poisoning** อาหารเป็นพิษ *ar•hǎrn bpehn•píht*

**foot** เท้า *tów*

**football [BE]** ฟุตบอล *fúht•bohn*

**footpath [BE]** ทางเท้า *tarng•tów*

**for** เพื่อ *pêua*

**for sale** สำหรับขาย *sǎhm•ràhp kǐe*

**foreign** ต่างชาติ *dtàrng•chârt*

**forest** ป่า *bpàr*

**forget** ลืม *lueem*

**fork** ส้อม *sôhm*

**form** แบบฟอร์ม *bàep•form*

**formal dress** ชุดเป็นทางการ *chúht bpehn tarng•garn*

**formula (baby)** นมผงเด็ก *nom•pǒng•dèhk*

**fountain** น้ำพุ *nárm•púh*

**fracture** ร้าว *rárw*

**free** ว่าง *wârng*

**freezer** ตู้แช่แข็ง *dtôo•châe•kǎeng*

**frequent** บ่อย *bòhy*

**fresh** สด *sòt*

**friend** เพื่อน *pûean*

**from** จาก *jàrk*

**front** ด้านหน้า *dârn•nâr*

**frying pan** กระทะ *grah•táh*

**fuel** น้ำมัน *náhm•mahn*

**full** เต็ม *dtehm*

**fun** สนุก *sah•nùhk*

**funny** ตลก *dtah•lòk*

**furniture** เฟอร์นิเจอร์ *fer•nih•jêr*

## G

**gallery** หอศิลป์ *hǒr•sǐn*

**game** เกม *gem*

**garage** โรงรถ *roeng•rót*

**garbage bag** ถุงใส่ขยะ *tǔhng sì kah•yàh*

**garden** สวน *sǒarn*

**gas** เบนซิน *ben•sihn*

**gas station** ปั๊มน้ำมัน *bpáhm náhm•mahn*

**gate** ประตู *bprah•dtoo*

**gauze** ผ้าก๊อซ *pâr•górt*

**gear** เกียร์ *gear*

**genuine** แท้ *táe*

**get off (bus, train, etc.)** ลง *long*

**gift** ของฝาก *kǒrng•fàrk*

**gift store** ร้านกิฟต์ช็อป *rárn gíp•chòhp*

**girl** เด็กหญิง *dèhk•yǐhng*

**give** ให้ *hî*

**glass** แก้ว *gâew*

**glasses (optical)** แว่นตา *wâen•dtar*

**gloves** ถุงมือ *tǔhng•muee*

**go** ไป *bpi*

**gold** ทอง *torng*

**golf** กอล์ฟ *górp*

**golf club** ไม้กอล์ฟ *mí•górp*

**golf course** สนามกอล์ฟ *sah•nǎrm górp*

**good** ดี *dee*

**goodbye** สวัสดี *sah•wàht•dee*

**gram** กรัม *grahm*

**grass** หญ้า *yâr*

**Great Britain** สหราชอาณาจักร *sah•hàh•rârt•chah•ar•nar•jahk*

**grocery store** ร้านขายของชำ *rárn kĭe kŏrng•chahm*

**group** กลุ่ม *glùhm*

**guarantee** รับประกัน *ráhp bprah•gahn*

**guesthouse** เกสต์เฮาส์ *gét•hóus*

**guide (person)** ไกด์ *gí*

**guide book** หนังสือนำเที่ยว *năhng•sŭee nahm•têaw*

**guide dog** สุนัขนำทาง *sùh•náhk nahm tarng*

**guided tour** ทัวร์นำเที่ยว *toar nahm•têaw*

**guided walk** ทัวร์เดินนำเที่ยว *toar dern nahm•têaw*

**guitar** กีตาร์ *gee•dtár*

**gym** โรงยิม *roeng•yihm*

**gynecologist** สูตินรีแพทย์ *sŏo•dtìh•nah•ree•pâet*

# H

**hair** ผม *pŏm*

**hairbrush** แปรงแปรงผม *bpraeng bpraeng•pŏm*

**hairdresser** ช่างทำผม *chárng tahm•pŏm*

**halal** ฮาลาล *har•larn*

**half** ครึ่ง *krûeng*

**hammer** ฆ้อน *kórn*

**hand** มือ *muee*

**hand luggage** กระเป๋าถือ *grah•bpŏu tŭee*

**handbag [BE]** กระเป๋าถือ *grah•bpŏu tŭee*

**handicapped** adj พิการ *píh•garn*; n **(person)** คนพิการ *kon píh•garn*

**handicrafts** หัตถกรรม *hàht•tah•gahm*

**hanger** ไม้แขวนเสื้อ *mí•kwăen•sûea*

**happy** มีความสุข *mee kwarm•sùhk*

**harbor** ท่าเรือ *târ•ruea*

**hard** แข็ง *kăng*

**hardware store** ร้านขายเครื่องมืออุปกรณ์ *rárn kĭe krûeang•muee ùhp•bpah•gorn*

**hat** หมวก *mòark*

**have** มี *mee*

**hay fever** โรคแพ้อากาศ *rôek páe•ar•gàrt*

**head** หัว *hŏar*

**headache** ปวดหัว *bpòart•hŏar*

**health** สุขภาพ *sùhk•kah•pârp*

**health food store** ร้านขายอาหารสุขภาพ *rárn kĭe ar•hărn sùhk•kah•pârp*

**health insurance** ประกันสุขภาพ *bprah•gahn sùhk•kah•pârp*

**hear** ได้ยิน *di•yin*

**hearing aid** เครื่องช่วยฟัง *krûeang•chŏary•fahng*

**hearing impaired** พิการทางหู *píh•garn tarng•hŏo*

**heart** หัวใจ *hŭa•ji*

**heart attack** หัวใจวาย *hŭa•ji wary*

**heart condition** โรคหัวใจ *rôek hŭa•ji*

**heat** ความร้อน *kwarm•rórn*

**heavy** หนัก *nàhk*

**heel** ส้น *sôn*

**height (person)** ความสูง *kwarm•sŏong*

**hello** สวัสดี *sah•wàht•dee*; **(phone)** ฮัลโหล *hahn•lŏe*

**helmet** หมวกนิรภัย *mòark níh•ráh•pi*

**help** n ความช่วยเหลือ *kwarm*

chôary•lŭea; v ช่วย chôary; **(request)** ช่วย
ด้วย chôary•dôary

**here** ที่นี่ têe•nêe

**high** สูง sŏong

**highchair** เก้าอี้เด็ก gôu•êe dèhk

**highway** ทางหลวง tarng•lŏarng

**hike** เดินป่า dern•bpàr

**hill** เนินเขา nern•kŏu

**hire** เช่า chôu

**hold** ถือ tŭee

**hole** รู roo

**holiday [BE]** วันหยุด wan yùht

**home** บ้าน bârn

**homemade** ทำเอง tahm•eng

**honeymoon** ฮันนีมูน hahn•nee•moon

**horn (car)** แตร dtrae

**horse** ม้า már

**horse racing** แข่งม้า kàeng már

**horseback riding** ขี่ม้า kèe•már

**horsetrack** ลู่ม้าวิ่ง lôo már wîhng

**hospital** โรงพยาบาล roeng pah•yar•barn

**hot** adj ร้อน rórn; **(spicy)** เผ็ด pèht

**hotel** โรงแรม roeng•raem

**hour** ชั่วโมง chôar•moeng

**house** บ้าน bârn

**how** ยังไง yahng•ngi

**how many** เท่าไหร่ tôu•rì

**how much** เท่าไหร่ tôu•rì

**hug** กอด gòrt

**hungry** หิว hĭhw

**hunt** ล่า lâr

**hurry** รีบ rêep

**hurt** เจ็บ jèhp

# I

**ibuprofen** อีบูโปรเฟน ee•boo•bproe•fen

**identification** บัตรประจำตัว bàht
bprah•jahm•dtoar

**ill [BE]** ไม่สบาย mî sah•bie

**illegal** ผิดกฎหมาย pìht gòt•mǐe

**imitation (fake)** ของเลียนแบบ kŏrng
lean•bàep

**important** สำคัญ sǎhm•kahn

**improve** ปรับปรุง bpràhp•bpruhng

**in** ใน ni

**include** รวม roarm

**indigestion** อาหารไม่ย่อย ar•hǎrn mî
yôhy

**indoor pool** สระว่ายน้ำในร่ม sàh
wîe•nárm ni•rôm

**inexpensive** ไม่แพง mî paeng

**infection** การติดเชื้อ garn dtìht•chúea

**inflammation** อาการอักเสบ ar•garn
àhk•sèp

**informal** ไม่เป็นทางการ mî bpehn
tarng•garn

**information** ข้อมูล kôr•moon

**information desk** ประชาสัมพันธ์
bprah•char•sǎhm•pahn

**injection** ฉีดยา chèet yar

**injure** บาดเจ็บ bàrt•jèhp

**innocent** บริสุทธิ์ bor•rih•sùht

**insect** แมลง mah•laeng

**insect bite** แมลงกัดต่อย mah•laeng
gàht dtòhy

**insect repellent** ยากันแมลง yar gahn
mah•laeng

**insert** แทรก sâek

**inside**  ข้างใน *kârng•ni*

**insist**  ยืนกราน *yueen•grarn*

**insomnia**  นอนไม่หลับ *norn•mâi•làhp*

**instant messenger**
โปรแกรมส่งข้อความ *bproe•graem sòng kôr•kwarm*

**instead**  แทนที่ *taen•têe*

**instructions**  คำสั่ง *kahm•sàhng*

**instructor**  ผู้สอน *pôo•sŏrn*

**insulin**  อินซูลิน *ihn•soo•lihn*

**insurance**  ประกันภัย *bprah•gahn•pi*

**interest (hobby)**  ความสนใจ *kwarm sŏn•ji*

**international**  ระหว่างประเทศ *rah•wàrng bprah•têt*

**International Student Card**
บัตรนักศึกษาสากล *bàht náhk•sùek•săr săr•gon*

**internet**  อินเตอร์เน็ต *ihn•dter•nèht*

**internet cafe**  อินเตอร์เน็ตคาเฟ่ *ihn•dter•nèht kar•fê*

**internet service**  บริการอินเตอร์เน็ต *bor•rih•garn ihn•dter•nèht*

**interpreter**  ล่าม *lârm*

**intersection**  สี่แยก *sèe•yâek*

**introduce**  แนะนำ *ná•nahm*

**invite**  เชิญ *chern*

**iron**  *n* เตารีด *dtou•rêet;* *v* รีด *rêet*

**itch**  คัน *kahn*

**itemized**  แยกตามรายการ *yâek dtarm rie•garn*

**J**

**jacket**  เสื้อแจ็กเก็ต *sûea ják•gèht*

**jar**  ขวด *kòart*

**jaw**  ขากรรไกร *kăr gahn•gri*

**jazz**  แจ๊ส *jáet*

**jeans**  ยีนส์ *yeen*

**jet lag**  เจ็ทแล็ก *jéht•làk*

**jet-ski**  เจ็ทสกี *jéht sah•gee*

**jeweler**  ร้านขายเครื่องประดับ *rárn kĭe krûeang bprah•dàhp*

**jewelry**  เครื่องประดับ *krûeang bprah•dàhp*

**job**  งาน *ngarn*

**join**  ต่อ *dtòr*

**joke**  เรื่องตลก *rûeang dtah•lôk*

**journey**  การเดินทาง *garn dern•tarng*

**K**

**keep**  เก็บ *gèhp*

**keep out**  ห้ามเข้า *hârm kôu*

**key**  กุญแจ *guhn•jae*

**key card**  คีย์การ์ด *kee•gárt*

**key ring**  พวงกุญแจ *poarng guhn•jae*

**kiddie pool**  สระเด็ก *sàh dèhk*

**kidney**  ไต *dti*

**kilogram**  กิโลกรัม *gih•loe grahm*

**kilometer**  กิโลเมตร *gih•loe mét*

**kind**  *adj* ใจดี *ji•dee;* **(type)** ประเภท *bprah•pêt*

**kiss**  จูบ *jòop*

**kitchen**  ห้องครัว *hôhng•kroar*

**kitchen foil [BE]**  กระดาษฟอยล์ *grah•dàrt fory*

**knee**  เข่า *kòu*

**knife** มีด *mêet*

**knock** เคาะ *kóh*

**know** รู้จัก *róo•jàhk*

**kosher** โคเชอร์ *koe•chêr*

## L

**label** ป้าย *bpîe*

**lace** ผ้าลูกไม้ *pâr lôok•míe*

**lactose intolerant** กินนมไม่ได้ *gihn nohm mî dîe*

**ladder** บันได *bahn•di*

**lake** ทะเลสาบ *tah•le•sàrp*

**lamp** โคมไฟ *koem•fi*

**land** ที่ดิน *têe•dihn*

**lane** เลน *len*

**large** ใหญ่ *yì*

**last (previous)** ที่แล้ว *têe•láew;* **(final)** สุดท้าย *sùht•tíe*

**late** สาย *síe*

**launderette [BE]** ร้านซักรีด *rárn sáhk•rêet*

**laundromat** ร้านซักรีด *rárn sáhk•rêet*

**laundry service** บริการซักรีด *bor•rih•garn sáhk•rêet*

**lawyer** ทนายความ *tah•nie•kwarm*

**laxative** ยาระบาย *yar rah•bie*

**lead** นำ *nahm*

**leader (group)** ผู้นำ *pôo•nahm*

**learn** เรียน *rean*

**leather** หนัง *năhng*

**leave** *v* ออกจาก *òrk•jàrk;* **(deposit)** ฝาก ไว้ *fàrk•wí*

**left** ซ้าย *síe*

**left-luggage office [BE]** แผนกสัมภาระ *pàh•nàek săhm•par•ráh*

**leg** ขา *kăr*

**legal** ถูกกฎหมาย *tòok gòt•mǐe*

**lend** ให้ยืม *hî•yueem*

**length** ความยาว *kwarm•yarw*

**lens** เลนส์ *lehn*

**less** น้อยกว่า *nóry gwàr*

**lesson** บทเรียน *bòt•rean*

**let** ปล่อย *bplòhy*

**letter** จดหมาย *jòt•mǐe*

**level** ระดับ *rah•dàhp*

**library** ห้องสมุด *hôhng sah•mùht*

**life** ชีวิต *chee•wíht*

**life boat** เรือชูชีพ *ruea choo•chêep*

**lifeguard** ยามไลฟ์การ์ด *yarm lí•gàrt*

**lifejacket** เสื้อชูชีพ *sûea choo•chêep*

**lift [BE]** ลิฟต์ *líhp*

**light** *adj* **(weight)** เบา *bou;* **(color)** อ่อน *òrn;* *v* จุดไฟ *jùht fi;* *n* ไฟ *fi*

**lightbulb** หลอดไฟ *lòrt•fi*

**lighter** ไฟแช็ก *fi•cháhk*

**lighthouse** ประภาคาร *bprah•par•karn*

**like** *v* **(same)** เหมือนกับ *mŭean•gàhp;* **(want)** อยากได้ *yàrk•dîe;* **(please)** ชอบ *chôrp*

**line** เส้น *sêhn*

**linen** ลินิน *lih•nihn*

**lip** ริมฝีปาก *rihm•fěe•bpàrk*

**lipstick** ลิปสติก *líhp•sah•dtìhk*

**liquor store** ร้านขายเหล้า *rárn kǐe lôu*

**liter** ลิตร *líht*

**little** น้อย *nóry*

**live** *v* อยู่ *yòo;* **(performance)** *adj* สด *sòht*

**lobby (theater, hotel)** ล็อบบี้ *lóhp•bêe*

**local** ท้องถิ่น *tórng•tìhn*

**lock** ล็อก *lóhk*

**log off** ออกจากระบบ *òrk•jark rah•bòp*

**log on** เข้าระบบ *kôu rah•bòp*

**long** ยาว *yow*

**long-distance bus** รถบัสทางไกล *rót báht tarng gli*

**look** ดู *doo*

**loose** หลวม *lŏarm*

**lorry [BE]** รถบรรทุก *rót bahn•túhk*

**lose** หาย *hĭe*

**lost** หลงทาง *lŏng•tarng*

**lost and found office** แผนกของหาย *pah•nàek kŏrng•hĭe*

**lost-property office [BE]** แผนกของหาย *pah•nàek kŏrng•hĭe*

**lottery** ล็อตเตอรี่ *lóht•dter•rêe*

**loud** ดัง *dahng*

**love** รัก *ráhk*

**low** ต่ำ *dtàhm*

**luggage** กระเป๋า *grah•bpŏu*

**luggage cart** รถเข็นกระเป๋า *rót kĕhn grah•bpŏu*

**luggage trolley [BE]** รถเข็นกระเป๋า *rót kĕhn grah•bpŏu*

**lunch** อาหารกลางวัน *ar•hărn glarng•wahn*

**lung** ปอด *bpòrt*

## M

**magazine** นิตยสาร *níht•tah•yah•sărn*

**mail** *n* จดหมาย *jòt•mĭe; v* ส่งจดหมาย *sòng jòt•mĭe*

**mailbox** ตู้จดหมาย *dtôo jòt•mĭe*

**main** สำคัญ *săhm•kahn*

**make-up** *v* แต่งหน้า *dtàng•nâr*

**male** เพศชาย *pêt•chie*

**mall** ศูนย์การค้า *sŏon garn•kár*

**man** ผู้ชาย *pôo•chie*

**manager** ผู้จัดการ *pôo•jàht•garn*

**mandatory** บังคับ *bahng•káhp*

**manicure** ทำเล็บมือ *tahm léhp•muee*

**many** หลาย *lĭe*

**map** แผนที่ *păen•têe*

**market** ตลาด *dtah•làrt*

**marry** แต่งงาน *dtàng•ngarn*

**mask** หน้ากาก *nâr•gàrk*

**mass (church)** มิสซา *míht•sar*

**massage** นวด *nôart*

**matches** ไม้ขีด *mí•kèet*

**matinée** รอบกลางวัน *rôrp glarng•wahn*

**mattress** ที่นอน *têe•norn*

**maybe** อาจจะ *àrt•jah*

**meal** อาหาร *ar•hărn*

**measure** วัดขนาด *wáht kah•nàrt*

**measurement** การวัด *garn wáht*

**mechanic** ช่าง *chárng*

**medication** การใช้ยา *garn chí yar*

**medicine** ยา *yar*

**medium** ขนาดกลาง *kah•nàrt glarng*

**meet** พบ *póp*

**meeting** การประชุม *garn bprah•chuhm*

**meeting room** ห้องประชุม *hôhng bprah•chuhm*

**member** สมาชิก *sah•mar•chíhk*

**memorial** อนุสาวรีย์ *ah•núh•săr•wah•ree*

**memory card** เมมโมรี่การ์ด

*mem•moe•rêe gárt*

**mend (clothes)** ชุน *chuhn*

**menstrual cramps** ปวดประจำเดือน *bpòart bprah•jahm•duean*

**menu** เมนู *me•noo*

**merge** รวม *roarm*

**message** ข้อความ *kôr•kwarm*

**metal** โลหะ *loe•hàh*

**microwave (oven)** (เตา)ไมโครเวฟ *(dtou) mi•kroe•wép*

**midday [BE]** เที่ยง *têang*

**midnight** เที่ยงคืน *têang•kueen*

**migraine** ไมเกรน *mi•gren*

**mini-bar** มินิบาร์ *míh•níh bar*

**minute** นาที *nar•tee*

**mirror** กระจกเงา *grah•jòk ngou*

**missing** หาย *hǐe*

**mistake** ผิดพลาด *piht•plârt*

**mobile phone [BE]** โทรศัพท์มือถือ *toe•rah•sàhp muee•tǔee*

**money** เงิน *ngern*

**money order** ธนาณัติ *tah•nar•náht*

**monsoon** มรสุม *mor•rah•sǔhm*

**month** เดือน *duean*

**mop** ไม้ถูพื้น *míe tǒo•púeen*

**moped** จักรยานมอเตอร์ไซค์ *jàhk•grah•yarn mor•dter•si*

**more** มากกว่า *mârk•gwàr*

**morning** ตอนเช้า *dtorn•chóu*

**mosque** สุเหร่า *suh•ròu*

**mosquito bite** ยุงกัด *yuhng•gàht*

**motion sickness** เมารถ *mou rót*

**motor** เครื่องยนต์ *krûeang•yon*

**motorboat** เรือยนต์ *ruea yon*

**motorcycle** มอเตอร์ไซค์ *mor•dter•si*

**motorway [BE]** ทางด่วน *tarng•dòarn*

**mountain** ภูเขา *poo•kǒu*

**mouth** ปาก *bpàrk*

**move** ขยับ *kah•yàhp*

**movie** หนัง *nǎhng*

**movie theater** โรงหนัง *roeng•nǎhng*

**Mr.** นาย *nie*

**Mrs.** นาง *narng*

**much** มาก *mârk*

**mugging** จี้ *jêe*

**muscle** กล้ามเนื้อ *glârm•núea*

**museum** พิพิธภัณฑ์ *píh•píht•tah•pahn*

**music** ดนตรี *don•dtree*

**must** ต้อง *dtôhng*

# N

**nail** เล็บ *léhp*

**nail file** ตะไบขัดเล็บ *dtah•bi kàht léhp*

**nail salon** ร้านทำเล็บ *rárn tahm•léhp*

**name** ชื่อ *chûee*

**napkin** กระดาษเช็ดปาก *grah•dàrt chéht bpàrk*

**nappy [BE]** ผ้าอ้อม *pâr•ôrm*

**nationality** สัญชาติ *sǎn•chârt*

**native** พื้นเมือง *púeen•mueang*

**nature** ธรรมชาติ *tahm•mah•chârt*

**nature trail** ทางเดินชมธรรมชาติ *tarng•dern chom tahm•mah•chârt*

**nausea** คลื่นไส้ *klûeen sî*

**near** ใกล้ *glî*

**nearby** ใกล้ๆ *glî•glî*

**necessary** จำเป็น *jahm•bpehn*

**neck** คอ *kor*

**necklace** สร้อยคอ *sôry•kor*

**need** ต้องการ *dtôhng•garn*

**network** เครือข่าย *kruea•kìe*

**never** ไม่เคย *mî•kery*

**new** ใหม่ *mì*

**news** ข่าว *kòw*

**newspaper** หนังสือพิมพ์ *năhng•sŭee•pihm*

**newsstand** แผงขายหนังสือพิมพ์ *păeng kìe năhng•sŭee•pihm*

**next** ถัดไป *tàht•bpi*

**next to** ติดกับ *dtìht•gàhp*

**nice** ดี *dee*

**night** กลางคืน *glarng•kueen*

**night club** ไนท์คลับ *ní•klàhp*

**no** ไม่ *mî*

**noisy** เสียงดัง *sĕang•dang*

**non-smoking** ห้ามสูบบุหรี่ *hârm sòob•buh•rèe*

**non-stop (flight)** เที่ยวบินตรง *têaw•bihn trong*

**noon** เที่ยง *têang*

**normal** ธรรมดา *tahm•mah•dar*

**north** เหนือ *nŭea*

**nose** จมูก *jah•mòok*

**not** ไม่ *mî*

**nothing** ไม่มีอะไร *mî mee ah•ri*

**notify** แจ้ง *jâeng*

**now** ตอนนี้ *dtorn•née*

**number** เบอร์ *ber*

**nurse** พยาบาล *pah•yar•barn*

## O

**office** ที่ทำงาน *têe tahm•ngarn*

**off-peak (ticket)** ช่วงออฟพีค *chôarng órp•péek*

**often** บ่อย *bòhy*

**OK** โอเค *oe•ke*

**old** เก่า *gòu*

**on** บน *bon*

**one-way ticket** เที่ยวเดียว *têaw•deaw*

**only** เท่านั้น *tôu•náhn*

**open** เปิด *bpèrt*

**opening hours** เวลาทำการ *we•lar tahm•garn*

**opera** โอเปร่า *oo•bpe•rár*

**operation** ผ่าตัด *pàr•dtàht*

**opposite** ตรงข้าม *dtrong•kârm*

**optician** ช่างตัดแว่น *chârng dtàht•wăen*

**or** หรือ *rŭee*

**orchestra** วงออเคสตร้า *wong or•kés•trâr*

**order** สั่ง *sàhng*

**organize** จัดระบบ *jàht rah•bòp*

**original** ดั้งเดิม *dâhng•derm*

**out** ออก *òrk*

**outdoor** กลางแจ้ง *glarng•jâeng*

**outdoor pool** สระกลางแจ้ง *sàh glarng•jâeng*

**outside** ข้างนอก *kârng•nôrk*

**oven** เตาอบ *dtou•òp*

**over (more than)** มากกว่า *mârk•gwàr*

**overcharge** คิดเงินเกิน *kíht•ngern gern*

**overlook** จุดชมวิว *jùht chom wihw*

**overnight** ข้ามคืน *kârm•kueen*

**owe** เป็นหนี้ *bpehn nêe*

**own** เป็นเจ้าของ *bpehn jôu•kŏrng*

**owner** เจ้าของ *jôu•kŏrng*

**oxygen** อ๊อกซิเจน *óhk•sih•jêhn*

## P

**pacifier** จุกนม *jùhk•nom*

**pack** ห่อ *hòr*

**package** พัสดุ *páht•sah•dùh*

**paddling pool** [BE] สระเด็ก
*sàh dèhk*

**padlock** กุญแจคล้อง *guhn•jae klórng*

**pail** ถัง *tăhng*

**pain** เจ็บ *jèhp;* (muscle) ปวด *bpòart*

**painting** (picture) ภาพวาด *pârp•wârt*

**pair** คู่ *kôo*

**pajamas** ชุดนอน *chúht•norn*

**palace** วัง *wahng*

**panorama** ภาพพาโนรามา *pârp
par•noe•rar•mâr*

**pants** กางเกงขายาว *garng•geng kăr•yow*

**panty hose** ถุงน่อง *tŭhng•nôhng*

**paper towel** *grah•dàrt chéht•muee*

**paracetamol** [BE] พาราเซตตามอล
*par•rar•séht•dtar•môhn*

**parcel** [BE] พัสดุ *páht•sah•dùh*

**park** n สวนสาธารณะ *sŏarn
săr•tar•rah•náh;* v จอดรถ *jòrt•rót*

**parking garage** อาคารจอดรถ *ar•karn
jòrt•rót*

**parking lot** ที่จอดรถ *têe jòrt•rót*

**partner** หุ้นส่วน *hûhn•sòarn*

**party** งานปาร์ตี้ *ngarn bpar•dtêe*

**passport** หนังสือเดินทาง *năhng•sŭee
dern•tarng*

**password** รหัส *rah•hàht*

**patient** คนไข้ *kon kî*

**pavement** [BE] ทางเท้า *tarng•tów*

**pay** จ่าย *jìe*

**pay phone** โทรศัพท์สาธารณะ
*toe•rah•sàhp săr•tar•rah•náh*

**payment** การจ่ายเงิน *garn jìe•ngern*

**pedestrian** คนเดินถนน *kon dern tah•nŏn*

**pediatrician** หมอเด็ก *mŏr•dèhk*

**pedicure** ทำเล็บเท้า *tahm léhp•tów*

**pen** ปากกา *bpàrk•gar*

**penicillin** เพนิซิลลิน *pe•níh•sih•lihn*

**per** ต่อ *dtòr*

**performance** การแสดง *garn sah•daeng*

**perhaps** บางที *barng•tee*

**period** (menstruation) ประจำเดือน
*bprah•jahm•duean*

**person** คน *kon*

**petrol** [BE] เบนซิน *ben•sihn*

**petrol station** [BE] ปั้มน้ำมัน *bpáhm
náhm•mahn*

**pharmacy** ร้านขายยา *rárn kĭe yar*

**phone** โทรศัพท์ *toe•rah•sàhp*

**phone call** โทรศัพท์ *toe•rah•sàhp*

**phone card** บัตรโทรศัพท์ *bàht
toe•rah•sàhp*

**phone directory** สมุดโทรศัพท์ *sah•mùht
toe•rah•sàhp*

**phone number** เบอร์โทรศัพท์ *ber
toe•rah•sàhp*

**photocopy** ถ่ายเอกสาร *tìe èk•gah•sărn*

**photograph** รูป *rôop*

**phrase** วลี *wah•lee*

**pick up** รับ *ráhp*

**picnic** ปิคนิค *bpíhk•níhk*

**picnic area** ที่ปิคนิค *têe bpíhk•níhk*

**piece** ชิ้น *chíhn*

**pill** ยา *yar*

**pillow** หมอน *mŏrn*

**PIN** รหัสพิน *rah•hàht pihn*

**place** สถานที่ *sah•tărn•têe*

**plan** แผน *păen*

**plane** เครื่องบิน *krûeang•bihn*

**plaster [BE]** เฝือก *fùeak*

**plastic** พลาสติก *plárt•sah•dtìhk*

**plastic wrap** ฟิล์มถนอมอาหาร *feem tah•nŏrm ar•hărn*

**plate** จาน *jarn*

**platform** ชานชาลา *charn•char•lar*

**play** *v* เล่น *lêhn*; (theater) ละคร *lah•korn*

**playground** สนามเด็กเล่น *sah•nărm dèhk lêhn*

**playpen** คอกเด็กเล่น *kôrk dèhk lêhn*

**please** กรุณา *gah•rúh•nar*

**plug** ปลั๊กไฟ *bplákh•fi*

**plunger** ที่ดูดส้วม *têe dòot sôarm*

**pneumonia** ปอดบวม *bpòrt•boarm*

**poison** ยาพิษ *yar•píht*

**police** ตำรวจ *dtahm•ròart*

**police report** ใบแจ้งความ *bi•jâeng•kwarm*

**police station** สถานีตำรวจ *sah•tăr•nee dtahm•ròart*

**pond** บ่อน้ำ *bòr•nárm*

**pool** สระว่ายน้ำ *sàh wîe•nárm*

**popular** เป็นที่นิยม *bpehn•têe níh•yom*

**port** ท่าเรือ *târ•ruea*

**porter** คนยกกระเป๋า *kon yók grah•bpŏu*

**portion** ขนาด *kah•nàrt*

**post [BE]** *v* ส่งจดหมาย *sòng jòt•mĭe*; *n* จดหมาย *jòt•mĭe*

**post office** ที่ทำการไปรษณีย์ *têe tahm•garn bpri•sah•nee*

**postage** ค่าแสตมป์ *kâr sah•dtaem*

**postbox [BE]** ตู้จดหมาย *dtôo jòt•mĭe*

**postcard** โปสการ์ด *bpóet•sah•gárt*

**pot** หม้อ *môr*

**pottery** เครื่องปั้นดินเผา *krûeang•bpâhn dihn•pŏu*

**pound (weight)** ปอนด์ *bporn*

**pound sterling** เงินปอนด์ *ngern•bporn*

**practice** ฝึก *fùek*

**pregnant** ท้อง *tórng*

**prepaid phone card** บัตรโทรศัพท์แบบเติมเงิน *bàht toe•rah•sàhp bàep dterm•ngern*

**prescription** ใบสั่งยา *bi sàhng•yar*

**present (time)** ปัจจุบัน *bpàht•juh•bahn*; *n* ของขวัญ *kŏrng•kwăhn*

**press** *v* กด *gòt*

**price** ราคา *rar•kar*

**print** ปรินท์ *príhn*

**prison** คุก *kúhk*

**private** ส่วนตัว *sòarn•dtoar*

**problem** ปัญหา *bpahn•hăr*

**produce store** ร้านขายผักผลไม้ *rárn kĭe pàhk pŏn•lah•mí*

**profession** อาชีพ *ar•chêep*

**program** โปรแกรม *bproe•graem*

**prohibited** ห้าม *hârm*

**pronounce** ออกเสียง *òrk•sĕang*

**public** สาธารณะ *săr•tar•rah•náh*

**pull** ดึง *dueng*

**pump** ปั๊ม *bpáhm*

**pure** แท้ *tâe*

**purpose** วัตถุประสงค์ *wáht•tùh•bprah•sŏng*

**purse** กระเป๋าสตางค์ *grah•bpŏu sah•tarng*

**push** ผลัก *plàhk*

**push-chair [BE]** รถเข็นเด็ก *rót•kêhn dèhk*

**put** ใส่ *sì*

## Q

**quality** คุณภาพ *kuhn•nah•pârp*

**queue [BE]** *v* เข้าคิว *kôu•kihw;* *n* คิว *kihw*

**quick** เร็ว *rehw*

**quiet** เงียบ *ngêap*

## R

**racetrack** ลู่แข่ง *lôo•kàeng*

**racket (tennis)** ไม้เทนนิส *mí ten•níht*

**railway station [BE]** สถานีรถไฟ *sah•tǎr•nee rót•fi*

**rain** ฝนตก *fŏn dtòk*

**raincoat** เสื้อกันฝน *sûea gahn fŏn*

**rape** ข่มขืน *kòm•kǔeen*

**rapids** แก่ง *gàeng*

**rash** เป็นผื่น *bpehn pùeen*

**razor** มีดโกน *mêet•goen*

**razor blade** ใบมีดโกน *bi mêet•goen*

**reach** เอื้อม *ûeam*

**reaction** ปฏิกิริยา *bpah•dtìh•gih•rih•yar*

**read** อ่าน *àrn*

**ready** พร้อม *prórm*

**real (genuine)** แท้ *tâe*

**receipt** ใบเสร็จ *bi•sèht*

**receive** ได้รับ *dî•ráhp*

**reception (desk)** แผนกต้อนรับ *pah•nàek dtôrn•ráhp*

**receptionist** พนักงานต้อนรับ *pah•náhk•ngarn dtôrn•ráhp*

**recommend** แนะนำ *ná•nahm*

**reduce** ลด *lót*

**reduction** ส่วนลด *sùan•lót*

**refrigerator** ตู้เย็น *dtôo•yehn*

**refund** *v* คืนเงิน *kueen•ngern;* *n* เงินคืน *ngern•kueen*

**region** เขต *kèt*

**regular** ธรรมดา *tahm•mah•dar*

**relationship** ความสัมพันธ์ *kwarm sǎhm•pahn*

**reliable** เชื่อถือได้ *chûea•tǔee die*

**religion** ศาสนา *sàrt•sa•nǎr*

**remember** จำได้ *jahm•die*

**remove** เอาออก *ou•òrk*

**renovation** ปรับปรุงใหม่ *bpràhp•bpruhng mì*

**rent** เช่า *chôu*

**rental car** รถเช่า *rót•chôu*

**repair** ซ่อม *sôhm*

**repeat** ซ้ำอีกที *sáhm èek•tee*

**replace** แทนที่ *taen•têe*

**report** แจ้งความ *jâeng•kwarm*

**reservation** การจอง *garn•jorng*

**reservation desk** แผนกรับจอง *pah•nàek ráhp•jorng*

**reserve** จอง *jorng*

**reservoir** อ่างเก็บน้ำ *àrng•gèhp nárm*

**responsibility** ความรับผิดชอบ *kwarm ráhp•pìht•chôrp*

**rest** *v* พัก *páhk*

**rest area** ที่พักริมทาง *têe•páhk rihm tarng*

**restaurant** ร้านอาหาร *rárn ar•hǎrn*

**restroom** ห้องน้ำ *hôhng•nárm*

**retired** เกษียณ *gah•sěan*

**return (come back)** กลับ *glàhp;* **(give back)** คืน *kueen*

**return ticket [BE]** ตั๋วขากลับ *dtǒar kǎr•glàhp*

**right (correct)** ถูก *tòok;* **(direction)** ขวา *kwǎr*

**ring** *v* กดกระดิ่ง *gòt grah•dìhng;* **(jewelry)** *n* แหวน *wǎen*

**river** แม่น้ำ *mâe•nárm*

**road** ถนน *tah•nǒn*

**robbery** การปล้น *karn bplôn*

**romantic** โรแมนติก *roe•maen•dtihk*

**roof** หลังคา *lǎrng•kar*

**room** ห้อง *hôhng*

**room service** รูมเซอร์วิส *room•ser•wiht*

**rope** เชือก *chûeak*

**round** *adj* กลม *glom; n* **(golf)** รอบ *rôrp*

**round-trip ticket** ตั๋วไปกลับ *dtǒar bpi•glàhp*

**route** เส้นทาง *sên•tarng*

**row** *v* พาย *pie; n* แถว *tǎew*

**rowboat** เรือพาย *ruea•pie*

**rubbish [BE]** *n* ขยะ *kah•yàh*

**rude** หยาบคาย *yàrp•kie*

**rush** เร่ง *rêng*

## S

**safe** *n* ตู้เซฟ *dtôo•séf; adj* ปลอดภัย *bplòrt•pi*

**safety** ความปลอดภัย *kwarm bplòrt•pi*

**safety pin** เข็มกลัด *kěhm•glàht*

**sale [BE]** ลดราคา *lót rar•kar*

**sales tax** ภาษีมูลค่าเพิ่ม *par•sěe moon•kâr pêrm*

**same** แบบเดียวกัน *bàep•deaw•gahn*

**sand** ทราย *sie*

**sandals** รองเท้าแตะ *rorng•tów dtà*

**sanitary napkin** ผ้าอนามัย *pâr ah•nar•mai*

**sanitary pad [BE]** ผ้าอนามัย *pâr ah•nar•mai*

**sauna** ซาวน่า *sow•nâr*

**save** เก็บรักษา *gèhp ráhk•sǎr*

**savings account** บัญชีออมทรัพย์ *bahn•chee orm•sáhp*

**say** พูด *pôot*

**scale** ตาชั่ง *dtar•châhng*

**scarf** ผ้าพันคอ *pâr pahn kor*

**schedule** ตาราง *dtar•rarng*

**scissors** กรรไกร *gahn•gri*

**screwdriver** ไขควง *kǐ•koarng*

**sea** ทะเล *tah•le*

**seafront** ติดทะเล *dtìht tah•le*

**seasickness** เมาเรือ *mou ruea*

**seat (on train, etc.)** ที่นั่ง *têe nâhng*

**seat belt** เข็มขัดนิรภัย *kěhm•kàht nìh•ráh•pi*

**sedative** ยาระงับประสาท *yar rah•ngáhp bprah•sàrt*

**see** เห็น *hěhn*

**self-service** บริการตนเอง *bor•rih•garn dton•eng*

**sell** ขาย *kĭe*

**seminar** สัมมนา *săhm•mah•nar*

**send** ส่ง *sòng*

**senior citizen** ผู้สูงอายุ *pôo sŏong ar•yúh*

**separate** แยก *yâek*

**separated** แยกกันอยู่ *yâek gahn yòo*

**serious** จริงจัง *jihng•jahng*

**serve** เสิร์ฟ *sèrp*

**service (work)** บริการ *bor•rih•garn;* **(church)** สวดมนต์ *sòart•mon*

**service charge** ค่าบริการ *kâr bor•rih•garn*

**service included** รวมค่าบริการ *roarm kâr bor•rih•garn*

**set menu** อาหารชุด *ar•hǎrn chúht*

**sew** เย็บ *yéhp*

**sex (gender)** เพศ *pêt;* **(activity)** เซ็กซ์ *séhk*

**shadow** เงา *ngou*

**shallow** ตื้น *dtûeen*

**shampoo** แชมพู *chaem•poo*

**shape** รูปร่าง *rôop•rârng*

**sharp** คม *kom*

**shave** โกนหนวด *goen•nòart*

**shaving cream** ครีมโกนหนวด *kreem goen•nòart*

**sheet (bed)** ผ้าปูที่นอน *pâr bpoo têe•norn*

**ship** เรือ *ruea*

**shock** ช็อค *chóhk*

**shoe** รองเท้า *rorng•tów*

**shoe repair** ซ่อมรองเท้า *sôhm rorng•tów*

**shoe store** ร้านขายรองเท้า *rárn kĭe rorng•tów*

**shop assistant** พนักงานขาย *pah•náhk•ngarn kĭe*

**shopping** ช็อปปิ้ง *chóhp•bpîhng*

**shopping area** ย่านช็อปปิ้ง *yârn chóhp•bpîhng*

**shopping basket** ตะกร้าช็อปปิ้ง *dtah•grâr chóhp•bpîhng*

**shopping cart** รถเข็น *rót•kĕhn*

**shopping centre [BE]** ศูนย์การค้า *sŏon•garn•kár*

**shopping mall** ศูนย์การค้า *sŏon•garn•kár*

**shopping trolley [BE]** รถเข็น *rót•kĕhn*

**short** สั้น *sâhn*

**shorts** กางเกงขาสั้น *garng•geng kǎr•sǎn*

**shoulder** ไหล่ *lì*

**show** *n* การแสดง *garn sah•daeng;* *v* แสดง *sah•daeng*

**shower** *v* อาบน้ำ *àrp•nárm;* *n* ห้องอาบน้ำ *hôhng àrp•nárm*

**shut** ปิด *bpiht*

**sick** ไม่สบาย *mî sah•bie*

**side effect** ผลข้างเคียง *pŏn kârng•keang*

**sidewalk** ทางเท้า *tarng•tów*

**sight (attraction)** สถานที่ท่องเที่ยว *sah•tǎrn•têe tôhng•têaw*

**sightseeing tour** ทัวร์ชมเมือง *toar chom mueang*

**sign** *n* ป้าย *bpîe;* *v* เซ็นชื่อ *sehn•chûee*

**single (marital status)** เป็นโสด *bpehn•sòet*

**single room** ห้องเดี่ยว *hôhng•dèaw*

**sink** อ่าง *àrng*

**sit** นั่ง *náhng*

**site** สถานที่ *sah•tǎrn•têe*

**size** ขนาด kah·nàrt

**skin** ผิวหนัง pǐhw·nǎhng

**skirt** กระโปรง grah·bproeng

**sleep** นอน norn

**sleeping bag** ถุงนอน tǔhng·norn

**sleeping car** ตู้นอน dtôo·norn

**sleeping pill** ยานอนหลับ yar norn·làhp

**sleeve** แขนเสื้อ kǎen sûea

**slice** v ฝาน fǎrn; n ชิ้น chíhn

**slippers** รองเท้าแตะ rorng·tów dtà

**slow** ช้า chár

**small** เล็ก léhk

**smell** n กลิ่น glìhn; v ได้กลิ่น dî·glìhn

**smoke** สูบบุหรี่ sòop·buh·rèe

**smoking area** บริเวณสูบบุหรี่ bor·rih·wen sòop·buh·rèe

**snack** อาหารว่าง ar·hǎrn wârng

**snack bar** สแน็คบาร์ sah·náhk bar

**sneakers** รองเท้าผ้าใบ rorng·tów pâr·bi

**snorkel** สนอร์กเกิ้ล sah·nórk·gêrn

**snow** หิมะ hìh·máh

**soap** สบู่ sah·bòo

**soccer** ฟุตบอล fúht·bohn

**sock** ถุงเท้า tǔhng·tów

**sold out** ขายหมด kǐe mòt

**some** บาง barng

**someone** บางคน barng kon

**something** บางอย่าง barng yàrng

**sometimes** บางครั้ง barng kráhng

**somewhere** บางที่ barng têe

**soon** ในไม่ช้า ni·mî·chár

**soother [BE]** จุกนม jùhk·nom

**sore** ปวด bpòart

**sore throat** เจ็บคอ jèhp·kor

**sorry** ขอโทษ kǒr·tôet

**sour** เปรี้ยว bprêaw

**south** ทิศใต้ tíht dtîe

**souvenir** ของที่ระลึก kǒrng·têe·rah·lúek

**souvenir store** ร้านขายของที่ระลึก rárn kǐe kǒrng·têe·rah·lúehk

**spa** สปา sah·bpar

**space** ที่ว่าง têe·wârng

**spare** สำรอง sǎhm·rorng

**spatula** ตะหลิว dtah·lǐhw

**speak** พูด pôot

**special** พิเศษ píh·sèt

**specialist (doctor)** หมอเฉพาะทาง mǒr chah·póh·tarng

**spell** สะกด sah·gòt

**spend (money)** ใช้จ่าย chí·jie

**sponge** ฟองน้ำ forng·nárm

**spoon** ช้อน chórn

**sport** กีฬา gee·lar

**sporting goods store** ร้านขายเครื่องกีฬา rárn kǐe krûeang·gee·lar

**sports club** สปอร์ตคลับ sah·bpòrt kláhp

**spot (place, site)** จุด jùht

**spouse** คู่สมรส kôo sǒm·rót

**sprain** แพลง plaeng

**stadium** สนามกีฬา sah·nǎrm gee·lar

**staff** พนักงาน pah·náhk·ngarn

**stair** บันได bahn·di

**stamp** แสตมป์ sah·dtam

**stand** ยืน yueen

**standard** มาตรฐาน mârt·dtah·tǎrn

**standby ticket** ตั๋วสำรอง dtǒar sǎhm·rorng

**start** เริ่ม rêrm

**statue** รูปปั้น *rôop•bpăn*

**stay** อยู่ *yòo*

**steal** ขโมย *kah•moey*

**steep** ชัน *chahn*

**stiff (muscle)** เมื่อย *mûeay*

**stolen** ถูกขโมย *tòok kah•moey*

**stomach** ท้อง *tórng*

**stomachache** ปวดท้อง *bpòart•tórng*

**stop** *v* จอด *jòrt;* (bus) *n* ป้ายรถเมล์ *bpîe rót•me*

**store** ร้านค้า *rárn•kár*

**store directory [BE]** รายการร้านค้า *rie•garn rárn•kár*

**store guide** รายการร้านค้า *rie•garn rárn•kár*

**stove** เตา *dtou*

**straight (ahead)** ตรงไป *dtrong bpi*

**stream** ลำธาร *lahm•tarn*

**street** ถนน *tah•nŏn*

**stroller** รถเข็นเด็ก *rót•kĕhn dèhk*

**strong** แข็งแรง *kăng•raeng*

**student** นักศึกษา *náhk sùek•săr*

**study** ศึกษา *sùek•săr*

**style** สไตล์ *sah•tie*

**subtitled** มีซับไตเติล *mee sáhp•dti•dtêrn*

**subway** รถไฟใต้ดิน *rót•fi tí•dihn*

**subway map** แผนที่รถไฟใต้ดิน *păen•têe rót•fi tíe•dihn*

**subway station** สถานีรถไฟใต้ดิน *sah•tăr•nee rót•fi tíe•dihn*

**suggest** แนะนำ *ná•nahm*

**suit** ชุดสูท *chúht•sòot*

**suitable** เหมาะสม *mòh•sŏm*

**suitcase** กระเป๋าเดินทาง *grah•bpŏu dern•tarng*

**sun (light)** แดด *dàet*

**sunbathe** อาบแดด *àrp•dàet*

**sunblock** ครีมกันแดด *kreem gahn•dàet*

**sunburn** แดดเผา *dàet pŏu*

**sunglasses** แว่นกันแดด *wân•gahn•dàet*

**sunscreen** ครีมกันแดด *kreem gahn•dàet*

**sunstroke** ลมแดด *lom•dàet*

**suntan lotion** โลชั่นอาบแดด *loe•cháhn àrp•dàet*

**superb** เยี่ยมมาก *yêam•mârk*

**supermarket** ซุปเปอร์มาร์เก็ต *súhp•bpêr•mar•gêht*

**supervision** การดูแล *garn doo•lae*

**supplement** *v* เสริม *sěrm*

**suppository** ยาเหน็บ *yar nèhp*

**sure** แน่นอน *nâe•norn*

**surfboard** กระดานโต้คลื่น *grah•darn dtôe•klûeen*

**swallow** กลืน *glueen*

**sweater** เสื้อกันหนาว *sûea gahn nǎrw*

**sweatshirt** เสื้อสเว็ตเชิร์ต *sûea sah•wéht•chért*

**sweep** กวาด *gwàrt*

**sweet** *adj* หวาน *wǎrn*

**swelling** บวม *boarm*

**swim** ว่ายน้ำ *wîe•nárm*

**swimming pool** สระว่ายน้ำ *sàh wîe•nárm*

**swimming trunks** กางเกงว่ายน้ำ *garng•geng wîe•nárm*

**swimsuit** ชุดว่ายน้ำ *chúht wîe•nárm*

**swollen** บวม *boarm*

**symbol** สัญลักษณ์ *săhn‑yah‑láhk*
**symptom** อาการ *ar‑garn*
**synagogue** โบสถ์ยิว *bòet‑yihw*

# T

**table** โต๊ะ *dtóh*
**take** เอา *ou*
**talk** พูด *pôot*
**tall** สูง *sŏong*
**tampon** ผ้าอนามัยแบบสอด *pâr ah‑nar‑mi bàep‑sòrt*
**taste** v ชิม *chihm*; n รสชาติ *rót‑chârt*
**taxi** แท็กซี่ *ták‑sêe*
**taxi rank [BE]** ที่จอดรถแท็กซี่ *têe jòrt‑rót ták‑sêe*
**taxi stand** ที่จอดรถแท็กซี่ *têe jòrt‑rót ták‑sêe*
**team** ทีม *teem*
**telephone** n โทรศัพท์ *toe‑rah‑sàhp*
**telephone booth** ตู้โทรศัพท์ *dtôo toe‑rah‑sàhp*
**telephone call** โทรศัพท์ *toe‑rah‑sàhp*
**telephone number** เบอร์โทรศัพท์ *ber toe‑rah‑sàhp*
**tell** บอก *bòrk*
**temperature** อุณหภูมิ *uhn‑hah‑poom*
**tennis** เทนนิส *tehn‑níht*
**tennis court** สนามเทนนิส *sah‑nărm tehn‑nít*
**tent** เต็นท์ *dtéhn*
**terminal** เทอร์มินอล *ter‑mih‑nôrn*
**text (SMS)** v ส่งข้อความ *sòng kôr‑kwarm*
**Thai (language)** ภาษาไทย *par‑săr ti*; (person) คนไทย *kon ti*

**Thailand** ประเทศไทย *bprah‑têt ti*
**thank** ขอบคุณ *kòrp‑kuhn*
**that** นั่น *nân*
**theater (movie)** โรงหนัง *roeng‑năhng*; (play) โรงละคร *roeng‑lah‑korn*
**theft** ขโมย *kah‑moey*
**then (afterwards)** แล้วก็ *láew‑gôr*
**there** ที่นั่น *têe‑nâhn*
**thermometer** ปรอท *bpah‑ròrt*
**thick** หนา *năr*
**thief** ขโมย *kah‑moey*
**thigh** ต้นขา *dtôn‑kăr*
**thin** บาง *barng*
**thing** สิ่งของ *sihng‑kŏrng*
**think** คิดว่า *kíht‑wâr*
**thirsty** หิวน้ำ *hĭhw‑nárm*
**this** นี่ *nêe*
**throat** คอ *kor*
**through** ผ่าน *pàrn*
**ticket** ตั๋ว *dtŏar*
**ticket inspector** คนตรวจตั๋ว *kon dtròart dtŏar*
**ticket office** แผนกจำหน่ายตั๋ว *pah‑nàek jahm‑nìe dtŏar*
**tie** เนคไท *néhk‑tie*
**tight** คับ *káhp*
**tile** กระเบื้อง *grah‑bûeang*
**time** เวลา *we‑lar*
**timetable [BE]** ตาราง *dtar‑rarng*
**tin opener [BE]** ที่เปิดกระป๋อง *têe bpèrt gra‑bpŏhng*
**tip (service)** v ทิป *tíhp*
**tire (vehicle)** ยาง *yarng*
**tired** เหนื่อย *nùeay*

**tissue** กระดาษทิชชู่ *grah•dàrt tíht•chôo*

**to (place)** ถึง *thǔeng*

**tobacco** ยาสูบ *yar•sòop*

**today** วันนี้ *wahn•née*

**toe** นิ้วเท้า *níhw•tóu*

**toilet [BE]** ห้องน้ำ *hôhng•nárm*

**toilet paper** กระดาษชำระ *grah•dàrt chahm•ráh*

**tomorrow** พรุ่งนี้ *prûhng•née*

**tongue** ลิ้น *líhn*

**tonight** คืนนี้ *kueen•née*

**too** เกินไป *gern•bpi*; **(also)** เหมือนกัน *mǔean•gahn*

**tooth** ฟัน *fahn*

**toothache** ปวดฟัน *bpòart fahn*

**toothbrush** แปรงสีฟัน *bpraeng sěe•fahn*

**toothpaste** ยาสีฟัน *yar sěe•fahn*

**torn** ฉีก *chèek*

**tough** เหนียว *něaw*

**tour** ทัวร์ *toar*

**tour guide** ไกด์ทัวร์ *gi toar*

**tourist** นักท่องเที่ยว *náhk•tôhng•têaw*

**tourist office** สำนักงานท่องเที่ยว *sǎhm•náhk•ngarn tôhng•têaw*

**tow truck** รถลาก *rót•lârk*

**towel** ผ้าเช็ดตัว *pâr•chéht•dtoar*

**tower** หอคอย *hǒr•kory*

**town** เมือง *mueang*

**toy** ของเล่น *kǒrng lên*

**toy store** ร้านขายของเล่น *rárn kǐe kǒrng•lên*

**traditional** ดั้งเดิม *dâhng•derm*

**traffic** การจราจร *garn jah•rar•jorn*

**trail** เส้นทางเดินป่า *sên tarng dern•bpàr*

**trailer** รถพ่วง *rót•pôarng*

**train** รถไฟ *rót•fi*

**train station** สถานีรถไฟ *sah•tǎr•nee rót•fi*

**tram** รถราง *rót•rarng*

**transfer (finance)** โอนเงิน *oen•ngern*

**translate** แปล *bplae*

**translation** คำแปล *kahm•bplae*

**translator** ผู้แปล *poo•bplae*

**transport** v ขนส่ง *kǒn•sòng*

**trash** ขยะ *kah•yàh*

**trash can** ถังขยะ *tǎhng kah•yàh*

**travel** ท่องเที่ยว *tôhng•têaw*

**travel agency** บริษัททัวร์ *bor•rih•sàht toar*

**travel sickness (by car)** เมารถ *mou rót*; **(by boat)** เมาเรือ *mou ruea*

**traveler's check** เช็คเดินทาง *chéhk dern•tarng*

**traveller's cheque [BE]** เช็คเดินทาง *chéhk dern•tarng*

**treatment** การรักษา *garn ráhk•sǎr*

**tree** ต้นไม้ *dtôn•mí*

**trim** เล็ม *lehm*

**trip** การเดินทาง *garn dern•tarng*

**trolley** รถเข็น *rót•kěhn*

**trousers [BE]** กางเกงขายาว *garng•geng kǎr•yow*

**truck** รถบรรทุก *rót bahn•túhk*

**true** จริง *jihng*

**T-shirt** เสื้อยืด *sûea•yûeet*

**tumor** เนื้องอก *núea•ngôrk*

**tunnel** อุโมงค์ *uh•moeng*

**turn** เลี้ยว *léaw*

**turn off** ปิด *bpìht*

**turn on** เปิด *bpèrt*

**TV** ทีวี *tee•wee*

**tweezers** แหนบ *nàep*

**twist** บิด *bìht*

**type** ชนิด *chah•níht*

**typical** ธรรมดา *tahm•mah•dar*

## U

**ugly** น่าเกลียด *nâr•glèat*

**umbrella** ร่ม *rôm*

**unconscious** หมดสติ *mòt sah•dtìh*

**under** ใต้ *dtîe*

**underground station**
[BE] สถานีรถไฟใต้ดิน *sah•tăr•nee rót•fi tîe•dihn*

**understand** เข้าใจ *kôu•ji*

**unit** หน่วย *nòary*

**United Kingdom** สหราชอาณาจักร *sah•hàh rârt•chah ar•nar•jàhk*

**United States** สหรัฐอเมริกา *sah•hàh•ráht ah•me•rih•gar*

**until** กระทั้ง *grah•tâhng*

**upstairs** ชั้นบน *cháhn•bon*

**urgent** ด่วน *dòarn*

**use** ใช้ *chí*

**username** ชื่อผู้ใช้ *chûee pôo•chí*

## V

**vacant** ว่าง *wârng*

**vacation** วันหยุด *wahn•yùht*

**vacuum cleaner** เครื่องดูดฝุ่น *krûeang dòot•fùhn*

**valet service** บริการรับจอดรถ *bor•rih•garn•ráhp jòrt•rót*

**valid** ใช้ได้ *chí•dîe*

**validate** รับรอง *ráp rorng*

**valuable** มีค่า *mee kâr*

**value** มูลค่า *moon•kâr*

**VAT [BE]** ภาษีมูลค่าเพิ่ม *par•sěe moon•kâr pêrm*

**vehicle** รถ *rót*

**very** มาก *mârk*

**view** วิว *wihw*

**viewpoint** จุดชมวิว *jùht chom wihw*

**village** หมู่บ้าน *mòo•bârn*

**vineyard** ไร่องุ่น *rî àh•ngùhn*

**visa** วีซ่า *wee•sâr*

**visit** เยี่ยม *yêam*

**visiting hours** เวลาเยี่ยม *we•lar yêam*

**visually impaired** พิการทางสายตา *píh•garn tarng săry•dtar*

**volleyball** วอลเล่ย์บอล *wohn•lê•bohn*

**vomit** อาเจียน *ar•jean*

## W

**wait** รอ *ror*

**waiter** พนักงานบริการชาย *pah•náhk•ngarn•bor•garn chie*

**waiting room** ห้องพักผู้โดยสาร *hôhng•páhk pôo•doey•sărn*

**waitress** พนักงานบริการหญิง *pah•náhk•ngarn•bor•garn•yǐng*

**wake** ปลุก *bplùhk*

**wake-up call** บริการโทรปลุก *bor•rih•garn•toe bplùhk*

**walk** เดิน *dern*

**wall** กำแพง *gahm•paeng*

**wallet** กระเป๋าเงิน *grah·bpǒu ngern*

**ward (hospital)** วอร์ดคนไข้ *wòrt kon·kî*

**warm** อุ่น *ùhn*

**warning** คำเตือน *kahm·dtuean*

**washing machine** เครื่องซักผ้า *krûeang sáhk·pâr*

**watch** นาฬิกาข้อมือ *nar·líh·gar kôr·muee*

**water** น้ำ *nárm*

**water ski** สกีน้ำ *sah·gee nárm*

**waterfall** น้ำตก *náhm·dtòk*

**waterproof** กันน้ำ *gahn·nárm*

**wave** คลื่น *klûeen*

**way** ทาง *tarng*

**wear** ใส่ *sì*

**weather** อากาศ *ar·gàrt*

**weather forecast** พยากรณ์อากาศ *pah·yar·gorn ar·gàrt*

**wedding** งานแต่งงาน *ngarn dtàng·ngarn*

**week** สัปดาห์ *sàhp·dar*

**weekday** วันธรรมดา *wahn tahm·mah·dar*

**weekend** วันเสาร์-อาทิตย์ *wahn sǒu ar·tíht*

**weigh** ชั่ง *châhng*

**weight** น้ำหนัก *náhm·nàhk*

**welcome** ยินดีต้อนรับ *yihn·dee dtôrn·ráhp*

**west** ทิศตะวันตก *tíht dtah·wahn·dtòk*

**wetsuit** เว็ทสูท *wéht·sòot*

**what** อะไร *ah·ri*

**wheelchair** รถเข็นคนพิการ *rót kěhn kon píh·garn*

**wheelchair ramp** ทางขึ้นสำหรับรถเข็น คนพิการ *tarng kûen sǎhm·ràhp rót kěhn kon píh·garn*

**when** เมื่อไหร่ *mûea·rì*

**where** ที่ไหน *têe·nǐ*

**who** ใคร *kri*

**why** ทำไม *tahm·mi*

**wide** กว้าง *gwârng*

**wildlife** สัตว์ป่า *sàht bpàr*

**wind** ลม *lom*

**windbreaker** เสื้อกันลม *sûea gahn lom*

**window** หน้าต่าง *nâr·dtàrng*

**window seat** ที่นั่งริมหน้าต่าง *têe·nâhng rihm nâr·dtàrng*

**windsurfing** เล่นวินด์เซิร์ฟ *lêhn wihn·sérp*

**windy** ลมแรง *lom raeng*

**wipe** เช็ด *chéht*

**wireless** ไร้สาย *rí·sǐe*

**wish (bless)** v อวยพร *oary·porn*

**with** กับ *gàhp*

**withdraw (bank)** ถอนเงิน *tǒrn·ngern*

**withdrawal** ถอน *tǒrn*

**without** ไม่ใส่ *mî·sì*

**witness** พยาน *pah·yarn*

**wood (material)** ไม้ *míe*

**wool** ผ้าวูล *pâr woon*

**work** ทำงาน *tahm·ngarn*

**wrap** ห่อ *hòr*

**write** เขียน *kěan*

**wrong** ผิด *pìht*

## X

**x-ray** เอ็กซเรย์ *éhk·sah·re*

## Y

**yacht**   เรือยอชท์ *ruea yórt*

**year**   ปี *bpee*

**yes**   ครับ? *kráhp?;* ค่ะ/ *kâh*

**yesterday**   เมื่อวาน *mûea•warn*

**young**   เด็ก *dèhk*

**youth**   เด็ก *dèhk*

**youth hostel**   ที่พักเยาวชน *têe páhk
  you•wah•chon*

## Z

**zipper**   ซิป *síhp*

**zoo**   สวนสัตว์ *sŏarn•sàht*

# Thai–English Dictionary

ก

กงสุล **gong‑sŭhn** consulate

กด **gòt** press; dial (phone)

กดกระดิ่ง **gòt grah‑dìhng** v ring

กดชักโครก **gòt cháhk‑krôek** flush (toilet)

กรรไกร **gahn‑gri** scissors

กรอก **gròrk** fill out (form)

กรอบแว่น **gròrp wâen** frame (glasses)

กระจกเงา **gràh‑jòk ngou** mirror

กระดาน **grah‑darn** board

กระดานโต้คลื่น **grah‑darn dtôe‑klûuen** surfboard

กระดาษชำระ **grah‑dàrt chahm‑ráh** toilet paper

กระดาษเช็ดปาก **grah‑dàrt chéht bpàrk** napkin

กระดาษเช็ดมือ **grah‑dàrt chéht muee** paper towel

กระดาษทิชชู่ **grah‑dàrt tíht‑chôo** tissue

กระดาษฟอยล์ **grah‑dàrt fory** aluminum [kitchen BE] foil

กระดุม **grah‑duhm** button

กระดูก **grah‑dòok** bone

กระท่อม **grah‑tôhm** cottage

กระทะ **grah‑táh** frying pan

กระทั่ง **grah‑tâhng** until

กระเบื้อง **grah‑bûueang** tile

กระป๋อง **grah‑bpôhng** n can

กระเป๋า **grah‑bpôu** luggage

[baggage BE]; handbag

กระเป๋าเงิน **grah‑bpôu ngern** wallet

กระเป๋าเดินทาง **grah‑bpôu dern‑tarng** suitcase

กระเป๋าถือขึ้นเครื่อง **grah‑bpôu tûee kûen krûueang** carry‑on [hand BE] luggage

กระเป๋ารถ **grah‑bpôu rót** (bus) fare collector

กระเป๋าสตางค์ **grah‑bpôu sah‑tarng** purse

กระโปรง **gràh‑bproeng** skirt

กระเพาะปัสสาวะ **grah‑póh bpàht‑sah‑wáh** bladder

กรัม **grahm** gram

กรุณา **gah‑rúh‑nar** please

กลม **glom** adj round

กล่อง **glòhng** box

กล้องถ่ายรูป **glôhng tìe‑rôop** camera

กล้องส่องทางไกล **glôhng sòhng tarng gli** binoculars

กลับ **glàhp** return (come back)

กลางคืน **glarng‑kueern** night

กลางแจ้ง **glarng‑jâeng** outdoor

กล้าม **glârm** muscle

กลิ่น **glìhn** n smell

กลืน **glueen** swallow

กลุ่ม **glùhm** group

กว้าง **gwârng** wide

กวาด **gwàrt** sweep

ก๊อกน้ำ **góhk‑nárm** faucet

กอด **gòrt** hug
ก่อน **gòrn** before
กอล์ฟ **górp** golf
กัด **gàht** bite
กันน้ำ **gahn·nárm** waterproof
กับ **gàhp** with
กางเกงขายาว **garng·geng kâr·yow** pants [trousers BE]
กางเกงขาสั้น **garng·geng kâr·sâhn** shorts
กางเกงว่ายน้ำ **garng·geng wîe·nárm** swimming trunks
ก๊าซบิวเทน **gárt bihw·ten** butane gas
การขนส่ง **garn kôn·sòng** n transport
การเคลมประกัน **garn klem bprah·gahn** insurance claim
การจราจร **garn jah·rar·jorn** traffic
การจอง **garn jorng** reservation
การจ่ายเงิน **garn joe·ngern** payment
การเชื่อมต่อ **garn chûeam·dtòr** connection
การใช้ยา **garn chí yar** medication
การดูแล **garn doo·lae** supervision
การเดินทาง **garn dern·tarng** journey; trip
การติดเชื้อ **garn dtìht·chúea** infection
การติดต่อ **garn dtìht·dtòr** n contact
การทำร้าย **garn tahm·ríe** n attack
การประชุม **garn bprah·chuhm** meeting
การประชุมเป็นทางการ **garn bprah·chuhm bpehn tarng·garn** convention
การประชุมสัมมนา **garn bprah·chuhm sâhm·mah·nar** conference

การปล้น **karn bplôn** robbery
การรักษา **garn ráhk·sâr** treatment
การวัด **garn wáht** measurement
การส่ง **garn sòng** delivery
การสอบ **garn sòrp** examination
การแสดง **garn sah·daeng** performance; n show
กำกับ **gahm·gàhp** v direct
กำแพง **gahm·paeng** wall
กิน **gihn** eat
กินอาหาร **gihn ar·hârn** dine
กิโลกรัม **gih·loe·grahm** kilogram
กิโลเมตร **gih·loe·mét** kilometer
กีตาร์ **gee·dtâr** guitar
กีฬา **gee·lar** sport
กุญแจ **guhn·jae** key; padlock
เก็บ **gèhp** keep
เก็บรักษา **gèhp ráhk·sâr** save
เกม **gem** game
เกษียณ **gah·sêan** retired
เกสต์เฮาส์ **gét·hóu** guesthouse
เก่า **gòu** old
เก้าอี้เด็ก **gôu·êe dèhk** highchair
เก้าอี้ผ้าใบ **gôu·êe pâr·bi** deck chair
เกิด **gèrt** born
เกินไป **gern bpi** too (much)
เกียร์ **gear** gear
เกือบจะ **gùeap·jah** almost
แก้ไข **gâe·kî** alter (a garment)
แก่ง **gàng** rapids
แก้ว **gâew** glass
โกนหนวด **goen·nòart** shave (beard)
ใกล้ **glî** near
ใกล้ๆ **glî·glî** nearby

ไกด์(ทัวร์) **gí (toar)** n (tour) guide

ไกล **gli** far

## ข

ขนส่ง **kôn‑sòng** v transport

ขนาด **kah‑nàrt** size; portion

ขนาดรับประทาน **kah‑nàrt ráhp‑bprah‑tarn** dosage (medicine)

ขนาดสำหรับเด็ก **kah‑nàrt sâhm‑ràhp dèhk** children's portion

ข่มขืน **kòm‑kûeen** rape

ขโมย **kah‑moey** v steal; n theft, thief

ขยะ **kah‑yàh** trash

ขยับ **kah‑yàhp** move

ขยาย **kah‑yîe** enlarge

ขวด **kòart** bottle; jar

ขวดนมเด็ก **kòart‑nom dèhk** baby bottle

ขวา **kwâr** right (direction)

ขอโทษ **kôr‑tôet** apologize; sorry

ขอแสดงความยินดี **kôr sah‑daeng kwarm‑yihn‑dee** congratulations

ข้อกำหนดในการแต่งกาย **kôr gahm‑nòt ni garn dtaeng‑gie** dress code

ข้อความ **kôr‑kwarm** message

ข้อผิดพลาด **kôr pìht‑plârt** error

ข้อมูล **kôr‑moon** information

ของเก่า **kôrng‑gòu** antique

ของขวัญ **kôrng‑kwaˉhn** n present

ของที่ระลึก **kôrng‑têe‑rah‑lúek** souvenir

ของแท้ **kôrng táe** authenticity

ของฝาก **kôrng fàrk** gift

ของเล่น **kôrng‑lên** toy

ของเลียนแบบ **kôrng**

lean‑bàep imitation

ขอบคุณ **kòrp‑kuhn** thank

ขับ **kàhp** drive

ขา **kâr** leg

ขากรรไกร **kâr‑gahn‑gri** jaw

ขาเข้า **kâr‑kôu** arrivals

ขาออก **kâr‑òrk** departures

ข้างนอก **kârng‑nôrk** outside

ข้างใน **kârng‑ni** inside

ข้ามคืน **kârm kueen** overnight

ขาย **kîe** sell

ขายหมด **kîe mòt** sold out

ข่าว **kòw** news

ขี่ม้า **kèe már** horseback riding

ขึ้นเงิน **kûen‑ngern** v cash

เขต **kèt** region

เขตคนเดินถนน **kèt kon dern tah‑nôn** pedestrian zone [precinct BE]

เขตอนุรักษ์ **kèt àh‑núh‑ráhk** conservation area

เขตอยู่อาศัย **kèt yòo‑ar‑sî** residential zone

เข็มขัด **kêhm‑kàht** belt

เข็มขัดนิรภัย **kêhm‑kàht níh‑ráh‑pi** seat belt

เขา **kôu** horn (animal)

เข่า **kòu** knee

เข้า **kôu** v enter

เข้าใจ **kôu‑ji** understand

เข้าถึง **kôu‑tûeng** v access

เข้าระบบ **kôu rah‑bòp** log on

เขียน **kêan** write

แข็ง **kâng** hard (solid)

แข็งแรง **kâng‑raeng** strong (physical)

แข่งม้า **kàng már** horse racing
แขน **kâen** arm
แขนเสื้อ **kâen sûea** sleeve
ไขควง **kì·koarng** screwdriver
ไข่มุก **kì·múhk** pearl
ไข้ **kî** fever
ไข้หวัด **kî·wàht** n cold
ไข้หวัดใหญ่ **kî·wàht·yì** n flu

ค

คงที่ **kong·têe** constant
คน **kon** person
คนขับ **kon kàhp** driver
คนไข้ **kon kì** patient
คนเดินถนน **kon dern tah·nôn**
  pedestrian
คนตรวจตั๋ว **kon dtròart dtôar** ticket
  inspector
คนเป็นโรคเบาหวาน **kon bpehn
  rôek·bou·wârn** n diabetic
คนพิการ **kon píh·garn** disabled (person)
คนยกกระเป๋า **kon yók grah·bpôu**
  porter
คนอังกฤษ **kon ahng·grìht** British
  (person)
คม **kom** sharp
ครอบครัว **krôrp·kroar** family
ครับ? **kráhp?** yes
คริสตัล **kríhs·dtähn** crystal
ครีมกันแดด **kreem gahn·dàet** sunblock;
  sunscreen
ครีมแก้อักเสบ **kreem gâe àhk·sèp**
  antiseptic cream
ครีมโกนหนวด **kreem goen·nòart**

shaving cream
ครีมนวดผม **kreem nôart·pôm**
  conditioner (hair)
ครึ่ง **krûeng** half
คลอง **klorng** canal
คลับ **klàhp** club
คลับเต้นรำ **klàhp dtêhn·rahm** dance
  club
คลาสสิก **klárt·sìhk** classical
คลีนิก **klee·nìhk** clinic
คลื่น **klûeen** wave
คลื่นไส้ **klûeen·sî** nausea
ควบคุม **kôarp·kuhm** control
ควบคุมอาหาร **kôarp·kuhm ar·hârn** diet
ความช่วยเหลือ **kwarm chôary·lûea**
  assistance; help
ความดันเลือด **kwarm·dahn lûeat** blood
  pressure
ความปลอดภัย **kwarm bplòrt·pi** safety
ความยาว **kwarm yarw** length
ความร้อน **kwarm rórn** heat
ความรับผิดชอบ **kwarm
  ráhp·pìht·chôrp** responsibility
ความเร็ว **kwarm·rehw** n speed
ความสนใจ **kwarm sôn·ji** interest
  (hobby)
ความสัมพันธ์ **kwarm sâhm·pahn**
  relationship
ความสูง **kwarm·sôong** height
คอ **kor** neck
คอกเด็กเล่น **kôrk dèhk·lêhn** playpen
คอนแท็คเลนส์ **kohn·tàk·lehn** contact
  lens
คอนเสิร์ต **kohn·sèrt** concert

คอมพิวเตอร์ **kohm‧pihw‧dtêr** computer

คอร์สภาษา **kórt par‧sâr** language course

ค่ะ/ **kâh/** yes

คัน **kahn** itch

คับ **káhp** tight

ค่าเข้า **kâr kôu** admission charge

ค่าใช้จ่าย **kâr chí‧jie** allowance; n cost

ค่าบริการ **kâr bor‧rih‧garn** service charge; commission

ค่าบริการต่อหัว **kâr bor‧rih‧garn dtòr‧hûa** cover charge

ค่าผ่านทาง **kâr pàrn‧tarng** toll

ค่าผ่านประตู **kâr pàrn bprah‧dtoo** entrance fee

ค่าแสตมป์ **kâr sah‧dtaem** postage

คาสิโน **kar‧sih‧noe** casino

คำเตือน **kahm‧dtuean** warning

คำแปล **kahm‧bplae** translation

คำสั่ง **kahm‧sàhng** instructions

คิดเงิน **kíht‧ngern** v charge

คิดเงินเกิน **kíht‧ngern gern** overcharge

คิดว่า **kíht wâr** think

คิว **kihw** n line [queue BE]

คิ้ว **kíhw** eyebrow

คีม **keem** clamp

คีย์การ์ด **kee‧gárt** key card

คืน **kueen** return; give back

คืนเงิน **kueen ngern** v refund

คืนนี้ **kueen‧née** tonight

คือ **kuee** be

คุก **kúhk** prison

คุณ **kuhn** you

คุณภาพ **kuhn‧nah‧pârp** quality

คุมกำเนิด **kuhm‧gahm‧nèrt** contraceptive

คู่ **kôo** double; pair

คู่มือของที่ระลึก **kôo‧muee kôrng‧têe‧rah‧lúek** souvenir guide

คู่มือแหล่งบันเทิง **kôo‧muea làng bahn‧terng** entertainment guide

คู่สมรส **kôo sôm‧rót** spouse

คู่หมั้น **kôo‧mâhn** fiancé

เครือข่าย **kruea‧kìe** network

เครื่องโกนหนวดไฟฟ้า **krûeang goen‧nòart fi‧fár** electric shaver

เครื่องคิดเงิน **krûeang kít‧ngern** cash register

เครื่องช่วยฟัง **krûeang chôary‧fahng** hearing aid

เครื่องซักผ้า **krûeang sáhk‧pâr** washing machine

เครื่องดับเพลิง **krûeang dàhp‧plerng** fire extinguisher

เครื่องดื่ม **krûeang‧dùeem** n drink

เครื่องดูดฝุ่น **krûeang dòot‧fûhn** vacuum cleaner

เครื่องนอน **krûeang‧norn** bedding

เครื่องบิน **krûeang bihn** plane

เครื่องประดับ **krûeang bprah‧dàhp** jewelry

เครื่องปั้นดินเผา **krûeang‧ bpâhn‧dihn‧pôu** pottery

เครื่องแฟกซ์ **krûeang fàk** fax machine

เครื่องมือ **krûeang‧muee** equipment

เครื่องยนต์ **krûeang‧yon** motor

เครื่องล้างจาน **krûeang lárng‧jarn** dishwasher

เครื่องลายคราม **krûeang lie‧kram**

porcelain
เครื่องเล่นซีดี **krûeang lêhn see•dee** CD player
เครื่องสำอาง **krûeang sâhm•arng** cosmetic
เคาน์เตอร์ **kóu•dtêr** counter
เคาะ **kóh** knock
แคชเชียร์ **káet•chea** cashier
แคลอรี่ **kae•lor•rêe** calorie
โคเชอร์ **koe•chêr** kosher
โคมไฟ **koem•fi** lamp
ใคร **kri** anyone; who

## ฆ

ฆ้อน **kórn** hammer

## ง

งดงามมาก **ngót•ngarm mârk** magnificent
ง่วง **ngôarng** drowsy
งาน **ngarn** job
งานแต่งงาน **ngarn dtàng•ngarn** wedding
งานทำถนน **ngarn tahm tah•nôn** roadwork
งานปาร์ตี้ **ngarn bpar•dtêe** party
งานฝีมือ **ngarn fêe•muee** crafts
ง่าย **ngîe** easy
เงา **ngou** shadow
เงิน **ngern** currency; money; silver (metal)
เงินคืน **ngern•kueen** n refund
เงินบริจาค **ngern bor•rih•jàrk** donation
เงินปอนด์ **ngern•bporn** pound sterling
เงินมัดจำ **ngern máht•jahm** n deposit
เงินสด **ngern•sòt** n cash
เงินสเตอร์ลิง **ngern sah•dter•lihng** sterling silver
เงียบ **ngêap** quiet

## จ

จดหมาย **jòt•mîe** n mail [post BE]; letter
จบ **jòp** v end
จมน้ำ **jom•nárm** drown
จมูก **jah•mòok** nose
จริง **jihng** true
จริงจัง **jihng•jahng** serious
จอง **jorng** reserve
จอด **jòrt** v stop
จอดรถ **jòrt•rót** v park
จักรยาน **jàhk•grah•yarn** bicycle
จักรยานยนต์ **jàhk•grah•yarn yon** motorcycle
จัดระบบ **jàht rah•bòp** organize
จับ **jàhp** catch
จาก **jàrk** depart; from
จาน **jarn** dish; plate
จ่าย **jìe** pay
จำกัดความเร็ว **jahm•gàht kwarm•rehw** speed limit
จำได้ **jahm•dîe** remember
จำนวน **jahm•noarn** amount
จำเป็น **jahm•bpehn** essential; necessary
จี้ **jêe** mugging
จุกนม **jùhk•nom** pacifier [dummy BE]
จุด **jùht** spot (place; site)
จุดชมวิว **jùht chom wihw** viewpoint
จุดไฟ **jùht•fi** v light
จูบ **jòop** kiss

เจ **je** vegan
เจ็ทแล็ก **jéht•làk** jet lag
เจ็ทสกี **jéht sah•gee** jet-ski
เจ็บ **jèhp** pain; hurt
เจ็บคอ **jèhp•kor** sore throat
เจ้าของ **jôu•kôrng** owner
แจ้ง **jâeng** notify
แจ้งความ **jâeng•kwarm** report (to police)
แจ็ส **jáet** jazz
ใจดี **ji•dee** *adj* kind

ฉ

ฉีก **chèek** torn
ฉีดยา **chèet•yar** inject
ฉุกเฉิน **chùhk•chêrn** emergency

ช

ชกมวย **chók•moary** boxing
ชนิด **chah•níht** type
ช่วงออฟพีค **chôarng órp•péek** off-peak (ticket)
ช่วย **chôary** *v* help
ช่วยด้วย **chôary•dôary** help (command)
ช็อค **chóhk** shock
ช่องคลอด **chông•klôrt** vagina
ช่องทำน้ำแข็ง **chôhng tahm náhm•kâeng** freezer
ช้อน **chórn** spoon
ชอบ **chôrp** like
ช็อปปิ้ง **chóp•bpîhng** shopping
ชั่งน้ำหนัก **châhng náhm•nàhk** weigh
ชัน **chahn** steep
ชั้น **cháhn** floor (level)

ชั้นใต้ดิน **cháhn tîe•dihn** basement
ชั้นธุรกิจ **cháhn túh•ráh•gìht** business class
ชั้นบน **cháhn bon** upstairs
ชั้นประหยัด **cháhn bprah•yàht** economy class
ชั้นหนึ่ง **cháhn nùeng** first class
ชั่วโมง **chôar•moeng** hour
ช้า **chár** delay; slow
ช่าง **chârng** mechanic
ช่างตัดผม **chârng tàht•pôm** barber
ช่างทำผม **chârng tahm•pôm** hairdresser
ช่างทำแว่น **chârng tahm wân** optician
ชานชาลา **charn•char•lar** platform
ชาม **charm** bowl
ชายฝั่ง **chie•fàhng** coast
ชายหาด **chie•hàrt** beach
ชิ้น **chíhn** piece
ชิม **chihm** *v* taste
ชีวิต **chee•wíht** life
ชื้น **chúeen** damp
ชื่อ **chûee** name
ชื่อผู้ใช้ **chûee pôo•chí** username
ชุดกระโปรง **chúht grah•bproeng** dress
ชุดเป็นทางการ **chúht bpehn tarng•garn** formal dress
ชุดนอน **chúht•norn** pajamas
ชุดว่ายน้ำ **chút wîe•nárm** swimsuit
ชุดสูท **chúht sòot** suit
ชุน **chuhn** mend (clothes)
เช็ค **chéhk** *n* check [cheque BE]
เช็คเดินทาง **chéhk dern•tarng** traveller's check [traveller's cheque BE]
เช็คอิน **chéhk•ihn** check in

เช็คเอาท์ **chéhk·óu** check out

เช็ด **chéht** wipe

เช่า **chôu** hire; rent

เช้า **chów** morning

เชิญ **chern** invite

เชื่อถือได้ **chûea·tûee·dîe** reliable

เชือก **chûeak** rope

เชื่อมต่อ **chûeam·dtòr** connect

แชมพู **chaem·poo** shampoo

ใช้ **chí** use

ใช้จ่าย **chí·jìe** spend

ใช้ได้ **chí·dîe** valid

ใช้แล้วทิ้ง **chí láew tíhng** disposable

## ซ

ซองจดหมาย **sorng jòt·mîe** envelope

ซ่อม **sôhm** repair

ซ่อมรองเท้า **sôhm rorng·tów** shoe repair

ซักแห้ง **sáhk·hâeng** dry clean

ซ้าย **síe** left

ซ้ำอีกที **sáhm èek·tee** repeat

ซิการ์ **síh·gâr** cigar

ซิป **síhp** zipper

ซีดี **see·dee** CD

ซื้อ **súee** buy

ซุปเปอร์ **súhp·bpêr** premium (fuel)

ซุปเปอร์มาร์เก็ต **súhp·bpêr·mar·gêht**
  supermarket

เซ็กซ์ **séhk** sex (activity)

เซ็นชื่อ **sehn·chûee** v sign

เซรามิก **se·rar·mìhk** ceramics

## ค

ดนตรี **don·dtree** music

ด่วน **dòarn** urgent; express

ดอกไม้ **dòrk·míe** flower

ดอลลาร์ **dohn·lâr** dollar

ดัง **dahng** loud (noise); famous

ดั้งเดิม **dâhng·derm** original

ด่านเก็บค่าผ่านทาง **dàrn gèhp
  kâr·pàrn·tarng** toll booth

ด้านหน้า **dârn·nâr** front

ดำน้ำ **dahm·nárm** dive

ดิจิตอล **dih·jih·dtôhn** digital

ดี **dee** nice; good

ดีเซล **dee·sen** diesel

ดีมาก **dee mârk** great; very good

ดึง **dueng** pull

ดื่ม **dùeem** v drink

ดู **doo** look

เด็ก **dèhk** child

เด็กผู้ชาย **dèhk·pôo·chie** boy

เด็กผู้หญิง **dèhk·pôo·yǐhng** girl

เด็กอ่อน **dèhk·òrn** baby

เดิน **dern** walk

เดินป่า **dern bpàr** hike

เดินรถทางเดียว (วันเวย์) **dern·rót tarng
  deaw (wahn·we)** one-way (traffic)

เดือน **duean** month

แดด **dàet** sun (light)

แดดเผา **dàet pôu** sunburn

โดย **doey** by

โดยประมาณ **doey bprah·marn**
  approximately

ได้กลิ่น **dî·glìhn** v smell

ได้รับ **dî·ráhp** receive

ได้ยิน **dî·yihn** hear

ต
ตกแต่ง **dtòk‑dtàng** decorative
ตกปลา **dtòk‑bplar** fishing
ต้นขา **dtôn‑kâr** thigh
ต้นไม้ **dtôn‑mîe** tree
ตรง **dtrong** *adj* direct
ตรงข้าม **dtrong‑kârm** across; opposite
ตรงไป **dtrong‑bpi** straight (ahead)
ตรวจ **dtròart** *v* check
ตรวจสอบ **dtròart‑sòrp** examine
ตลก **dtah‑lòk** funny
ตลาด **dtah‑làrt** market
ตลาดนัด **dtah‑làrt náht** flea market
ต่อราคา **tòr rar‑kar** bargain
ต่อสู้ **dtòr‑sôo** fight
ต้อง **dtôhng** must
ต้องการ **dtôhng‑garn** need
ตอนเช้า **dtorn‑chów** morning
ตอนนี้ **dtorn‑née** now
ตอนบ่าย **dtorn‑bìe** afternoon
ตอนเย็น **dtorn‑yehn** evening
ตะกร้า **dtah‑grâr** basket
ตะกร้าช้อปปิ้ง **dtah‑grâr chóhp‑bpîhng** shopping basket
ตะคริว **dtah‑krihw** cramp (sports)
ตะไบขัดเล็บ **dtah‑bi kàht léhp** nail file
ตะหลิว **dtah‑lîhw** spatula
ตั้งแคมป์ **dtâhng‑káem** *v* camp
ตั้งท้อง **dtâhng‑tórng** pregnant
ตัด **dtàht** *v* cut
ตัดการเชื่อมต่อ **dtàht garn chûeam‑dtòr** disconnect
ตัวกรอง **dtoar grong** filter
ตัวต่อ **dtoar‑dtòr** wasp

ตั๋ว **dtôar** ticket
ตั๋วขากลับ **dtôar ka˘r‑glàhp** return ticket
ตั๋วขึ้นเครื่อง **dtôar kûen krûeang** boarding card
ตั๋วเที่ยวเดียว **dtôar têaw‑deaw** one‑way ticket
ตั๋วไปกลับ **dtôar bpi‑glàhp** round‑trip ticket
ตั๋วรถเมล์ **dtôar rót‑me** bus ticket
ตั๋วฤดู **dtôar rúe‑doo** season ticket
ตั๋วสำรอง **dtôar sâhm‑rorng** standby ticket
ตั๋วอิเล็กทรอนิกส์ **dtôar ee‑léhk‑tror‑nìhk** e‑ticket
ตา **dtar** eye
ตาชั่ง **dtar‑châhng** scale
ตารางเดินรถ **dtar‑rarng dern rót** schedule [timetable BE] (bus)
ต่างชาติ **dtàrng‑chârt** foreign
ต่างประเทศ **dtàrng‑bprah‑têt** foreign; abroad
ต่างหู **dtàrng‑hôo** earrings
ตาม **dtarm** follow
ตาย **dtie** dead
ต่ำ **dtàhm** low
ตำรวจ **dtahm‑ròart** police
ติดกับ **dtìt‑gàhp** next to
ติดต่อ **dtìht‑dtòr** *v* contact
ติดต่อกันได้ **dtìht‑dtòr gahn dîe** contagious (disease)
ติดทะเล **dtiht tah‑le** seafront
ตื้น **dtûeen** shallow
ตุ๊กตา **dtúhk‑gah‑dtar** doll

ตู้จดหมาย **dtôo jòt∙mîe** mailbox [postbox BE]

ตู้เซฟ **dtôo∙séf** n safe

ตู้โทรศัพท์ **dtôo toe∙rah∙sàhp** telephone booth

ตู้นอน **dtôo∙norn** sleeping car

ตู้เย็น **dtôo∙yehn** refrigerator

เต้นรำ **dtêhn∙rahm** dance

เต็นท์ **dtéhn** tent

เต็ม **dtehm** full

เตา **dtou** stove

เตารีด **dtou∙rêet** n iron

เตาอบ **dtou∙òp** oven

เติม **dterm** fill

เติมให้เต็ม **dterm hî dtehm** fill up

เตียง **dteang** bed

แต่ **dtàe** but

แตก **dtàek** break

แต่งงาน **dtàng∙ngarn** marry

แต่งหน้า **dtàng∙nâr** v make-up

แตร **dtrae** horn (car)

โต๊ะ **dtó** table

โต๊ะเช็คอิน **dtó chéhk∙ihn** check-in desk

ใต้ **dtîe** under

ไต **dti** kidney

ถ
___

ถนน **tah∙nôn** road; street

ถ้วย **tôary** cup

ถอน **tôrn** withdrawal

ถอนเงิน **tôrn∙ngern** withdraw (bank)

ถัง **tâhng** bucket

ถังขยะ **tâhng kah∙yàh** trash can

ถังน้ำมัน **tahng náhm∙mahn** fuel tank

ถัดไป **tàht∙bpi** next

ถ่าน **tàrn** charcoal

ถาม **târm** ask

ถ่ายเอกสาร **tìe èk∙gah∙sârn** photocopy

ถ้ำ **tâhm** cave

ถึง **tûeng** to (place)

ถือ **tûee** hold

ถุงขยะ **tûhng kah∙yàh** garbage bag

ถุงเท้า **tûhng∙tów** socks

ถุงน่อง **tûhng∙nôhng** panty hose

ถุงนอน **tûhng∙norn** sleeping bag

ถุงมือ **tûhng∙muee** gloves

ถุงยางอนามัย **tûhng∙yarng ah∙nar∙mi** condom

ถูก **tòok** cheap; right (correct)

ถูกกฎหมาย **tòok gòt∙mîe** legal

ถูกขโมย **took kah∙moey** stolen

ถูกต้อง **tòok∙dtôhng** correct

แถว **tâew** n row

ท
___

ทนายความ **tah∙nie∙kwarm** lawyer

ทราย **sie** sand

ทอง **torng** gold

ทองแดง **torng∙daeng** copper

ท่องเที่ยว **tôhng∙têaw** travel

ท้อง **tórng** stomach

ท้องถิ่น **tórng∙tihn** local

ท้องร่วง **tórng∙rôarng** diarrhea

ทะเล **tah∙le** sea

ทะเลสาบ **tah∙le∙sàrp** lake

ทั้งหมด **táhng∙mòt** all

ทัวร์ชมเมือง **toar chom mueang** sightseeing tour

ทัวร์เดินนำเที่ยว **toar dern nahm têaw** guided walk

ทัวร์ทางเรือ **toar tarng ruea** boat trip

ทัวร์นำเที่ยว **toar nahm•têaw** guided tour

ทัวร์ระยะสั้น **toar rah•yáh sâhn** excursion

ทัวร์วันเดียว **toar wahn•deaw** day trip

ท่าเรือ **târ•ruea** harbor

ทาง **tarng** way

ทางขึ้นสำหรับรถเข็นคนพิการ **tarng kûen sâhm•ràhp rót kêhn kon píh•garn** wheelchair ramp

ทางจักรยาน **tarng jàhk•grah•yarn** bike path; cycle route

ทางเดินชมธรรมชาติ **tarng dern chom tahm•mah•chárt** nature trail

ทางตัน **tarng•tahn** dead end

ทางเท้า **tarng•tów** sidewalk [pavement BE]

ทางเบี่ยง **tarng•bèang** detour

ทางม้าลาย **tarng•már•lie** pedestrian crossing [zebra crossing BE]

ทางหนีไฟ **tarng née fi** fire escape; fire exit

ทางหลวง **tarng•lôarng** highway [motorway BE]

ทางออก **tarng•òrk** n exit

ทางออกฉุกเฉิน **tarng•òrk chùhk•chêrn** emergency exit

ทำ **tahm** do

ทำความสะอาด **tahm kwarm•sah•àrt** v clean

ทำงาน **tahm•ngarn** work

ทำไม **tahm•mi** why

ทำร้าย **tahm•ríe** v attack

ทำเล็บเท้า **tahm léhp•tów** pedicure

ทำเล็บมือ **tahm léhp•muee** manicure

ทำสำเนา **tahm sâhm•nou** copy

ทำอาหาร **tahm ar•hârn** v cook

ทำเอง **tahm•eng** homemade

ทิศ **tíht** direction

ทิศตะวันตก **tíht dtah•wahn•dtòk** west

ทิศตะวันออก **tíht dtah•wahn•òrk** east

ทิศใต้ **tíht•dtîe** south

ที่เขี่ยบุหรี่ **têe kèar•buh•rèe** ashtray

ที่จอดรถ **têe•jòrt•rót** parking lot [car park BE]

ที่จอดรถแท็กซี่ **têe jòrt rót ták•sêe** taxi stand [rank BE]

ที่ชอบ **têe chôrp** favorite

ที่ดิน **têe•dihn** land

ที่ดูดส้วม **têe dòot•sôarm** plunger

ที่ตั้งแคมป์ **têe dtâhng•káem** campsite

ที่ทำการ ไปรษณีย์ **têe•tahm•garn bpri•sah•nee** post office

ที่ทำงาน **têe•tahm•ngarn** office

ที่นอน **têe•norn** mattress

ที่นอนอัดลม **têe•norn àht•lom** air mattress

ที่นั่ง **têe•nâhng** seat (on train, etc.)

ที่นั่งเด็ก **têe•nâhng dèhk** child seat

ที่นั่งริมหน้าต่าง **têe•nâhng rihm nâr•dtarng** window seat

ที่นั่น **têe•nâhn** there

ที่นี่ **têe•nêe** here

ที่ปิคนิค **têe bpíhk•níhk** picnic area

ที่เปิดกระป๋อง **têe bpèrt grah•bpôhng**

can [tin BE] opener

ที่เปิดขวด **têe bpèrt kòart** bottle opener

ที่เปิดจุกก๊อก **têe bpèr jùhk•góhk**
corkscrew

ที่พัก **têe•páhk** accommodation

ที่พักเยาวชน **têe•páhk
you•wah•chon** youth hostel

ที่พักริมทาง **têe•páhk rihm tarng**
rest area

ที่รับกระเป๋า **têe ráhp grah•bpôu**
baggage claim

ที่รับฝากเสื้อโค้ท **têe ráhp•fàrk
sûea•kóet** coat check

ที่รับแลกเงิน **têe ráhp lâek•ngern**
currency exchange office

ที่แล้ว **têe•láew** last (previous)

ที่ว่าง **têe•wârng** space; room

ที่สูบบุหรี่ **têe sòop•buh•rèe** smoking
area

ที่สูบลม **têe•sòop•lôm** air pump

ที่ใส่ของ **têe sì kôrng** compartment

ที่หนึ่ง **têe•nùeng** first

ที่ไหน **têe•nî** where

ที่อยู่ **têe•yòo** address

ที่อุดฟัน **têe•ùht•fahn** filling (dental)

ทีม **teem** team

ทีวี **tee•wee** TV

ทุก **túhk** every

ทุ่ง **tûhng** field

เทนนิส **tehn•níht** tennis

เทปนำเที่ยว **tép nahm•têaw** audio guide

เทอร์มินอล **ter•mih•nôrn** terminal

เท่านั้น **tôu•náhn** only

เท่าไหร่ **tôu•rì** how much; how many

เท้า **tów** foot

เที่ยง **têang** noon [midday BE]

เที่ยงคืน **têang•kueen** midnight

เทียน **tean** candle

เที่ยว **têaw** tour

เที่ยวเดียว **têaw•deaw** one way

เที่ยวบิน **têaw•bihn** flight

เที่ยวบินตรง **têaw•bihn trong** non-stop
flight

เที่ยวบินที่ **têaw•bhin têe** flight number

แท้ **táe** authentic; real; pure

แท็กซี่ **ták•sêe** taxi

แทนที่ **taen•têe** instead; replace

แทรก **sâek** insert

โทร **toe** v telephone

โทรศัพท์ **toe•rah•sàhp** call (phone);
phone; phone call

โทรศัพท์มือถือ **toe•rah•sàhp
muee•tûee** cell [mobile BE] phone

โทรศัพท์สาธารณะ **toe•rah•sàhp
sâr•tar•rah•náh** pay phone

ไทย **ti** Thai

ธ

ธนาคาร **tah•nar•karn** bank

ธนาณัติ **tah•nar•náht** money order

ธรรมชาติ **tahm•mah•chârt** nature

ธรรมดา **tahm•mah•dar** normal; regular;
typical

ธุรกิจ **túh•ráh•gìht** business

น

นก **nók** bird

นมผง (เด็ก) **nom•pông (dèhk)** formula

(baby)

นวด **nôart** massage

นอน **norn** sleep

นอนไม่หลับ **norn mî làhp** insomnia

น้อย **nóry** little; few

น้อยกว่า **nóry•gwàr** less

นักท่องเที่ยว **náhk•tôhng•têaw** tourist

นักศึกษา **náhk•sùek•sâr** student

นั่ง **nâhng** sit

นัด **náht** appointment

นั่น **nân** that

นา **nar** rice field

น่าเกลียด **nâr•glèat** ugly

นาง **narng** Mrs.

นาที **nar•tee** minute

นามบัตร **narm•bàht** business card

นาย **nie** Mr.

นาฬิกา **nar•lih•gar** clock

นาฬิกาข้อมือ **nar•lih•gar kôr•muee**
   watch

นาฬิกาปลุก **nar•li•gar bplùhk** alarm
   clock

นำ **nahm** lead

นำมา **nahm mar** bring

น้ำ **nárm** water

น้ำตก **náhm•dtòk** waterfall

น้ำพุ **náhm•púh** fountain

น้ำมัน **náhm•mahn** fuel

น้ำยาคอนแท็คเลนส์ **náhm•yar
   kohn•tàk•len** contact lens solution

น้ำยาล้างจาน **náhm•yar
   lárng•jarn** dishwashing liquid

น้ำหนัก **náhm•nàhk** weight

นิตยสาร **níht•tah•yah•sârn** magazine

นิ้ว **níhw** finger

นิ้วเท้า **níhw•tów** toe

นิ้วหัวแม่มือ **níhw hôar•mâe•muee**
   thumb

นี่ **nêe** this

เนคไท **néhk•tie** tie

เนินเขา **nern•kôu** hill

เนื้องอก **núea•ngôrk** tumor

เนื้อผ้า **núea•pâr** fabric

แน่นอน **nâe•norn** exact; sure

แนะนำ **ná•nahm** introduce; recommend
   suggest

ใน **ni** in

ในประเทศ **ni bprah•têt** domestic

ในไม่ช้า **ni•mî•chár** soon

ไนท์คลับ **ní•klàp** night club

ในลอน **ni•lôhn** nylon

บ

บกพร่อง **bòk•prôhng** faulty

บทเรียน **bòt•rean** lesson

บน **bon** on

บริการ **bor•rih•garn** service (work)

บริการฉุกเฉิน **bor•rih•garn
   chùhk•chêrn** emergency service

บริการซักรีด **bor•rih•garn
   sáhk•rêet** laundry service

บริการตนเอง **bor•rih•garn
   dton•eng** self-service

บริการโทรปลุก **bor•rih•garn toe
   bplùhk** wake-up call

บริการรับจอดรถ **bor•rih•garn ráhp
   jòrt•rót** valet service

บริการลูกค้า **bor•rih•garn lôok•kár**

customer service บริการอินเตอร์เน็ต **bor·rih·garn ihn·dter·nèht** internet service

บริษัท **bor·ríh·sàht** company

บริษัททัวร์ **bor·rih·sàht toar** travel agency

บริสุทธิ์ **bor·rih·sùht** innocent; pure

บวม **boarm** swelling

บ่อน้ำ **bòr·nárm** pond

บอก **bòrk** tell

บ่อย **bòhy** frequent; often

บ๋อย **bôhy** waiter

บังคับ **bahng·káhp** mandatory

บัญชีกระแสรายวัน **bahn·chee grah·sâe rie·wahn** checking account

บัญชีออมทรัพย์ **bahn·chee orm·sáhp** savings account

บัตร **bàht** card

บัตรเครดิต **bàht kre·dìht** credit card

บัตรจอดรถ **bàht jòrt·rót** parking ticket

บัตรโทรศัพท์ **bàht toe·rah·sàhp** phone card

บัตรโทรศัพท์แบบเติมเงิน **bàht toe·rah·sàhp bàep dterm·ngern** prepaid phone card

บัตรนักศึกษาสากล **bàht náhk·sùek· sâr·sâr·gon** International Student Card

บัตรประจำตัว **bàht·bprah·jahm·dtoar** identification

บัตรประจำตัวผู้เอาประกัน **bàht·bprah·jahm·dtoar pôo·ou·bprah·gahn** insurance card

บันได **bahn·di** ladder; stairs

บันไดเลื่อน **bahn·di·lûean** escalator

บัลเลต์ **bahn·lê** ballet

บาง **barng** some; thin

บางคน **barng·kon** someone

บางครั้ง **barng·kráhng** sometimes

บางที **barng·tee** perhaps

บางที่ **barng·têe** somewhere

บางอย่าง **barng·yàrng** something

บาดเจ็บ **bàrt·jèhp** injure

บาดแผล **bàrt·plâe** n cut

บ้าน **bârn** house

บาร์ **bar** bar

บาสเก็ตบอล **bárt·sah·gêht bohn** basketball

บิกินี่ **bih gih nêe** bikini

บิด **bìht** twist

บิน **bihn** fly

บิล **bihn** bill

บุหรี่ **buh·rèe** cigarette

เบนซิน **ben·sihn** gas [petrol BE]

เบรก **brèk** n brake

เบรกฉุกเฉิน **brèk chùhk·chêrn** emergency brake

เบอร์ต่อ **ber dtòr** extension (phone)

เบอร์โทรศัพท์ **ber toe·rah·sàhp** phone number

เบอร์แฟกซ์ **ber fàk** fax number

เบา **bou** adj light (weight)

เบาหวาน **bou·wârn** n diabetic

แบบเดียวกัน **bàep deaw·gahn** same

แบบฟอร์ม **bàep·form** form

โบสถ์ **bòet** church

ใบขับขี่ **bi kàhp·kèe** driver's license

ใบแจ้งความ **bi jâeng·kwarm** police report

ใบมีดโกน **bi mêet·goen** razor blade
ใบรับรอง **bi ráhp·rorng** certificate
ใบสั่งยา **bi sàhng·yar** prescription
ใบเสร็จ(รับเงิน) **bi·sèht (ráhp·ngern)** receipt

## ป

ปฏิกิริยา **bpah·dtìh·gih·rih·yar** reaction
ปฏิทิน **bpah·dtih·tihn** calendar
ปรอท **bpah·ròrt** thermometer
ประกันภัย **bprah·gahn·pi** insurance
ประกันสุขภาพ **bprah·gahn sùhk·kah·pârp** health insurance
ประจำเดือน **bpràh·jahm·duean** period (menstrual)
ประชาสัมพันธ์ **bprah·char·sǎhm·pahn** information desk
ประตู **bprah·dtoo** gate; door
ประตูทางออกขึ้นเครื่อง **bprah·dtoo tarng·òrk kûen krûeang** departure gate
ประเทศ **bprah·têt** country
ประภาคาร **bprah·par·karn** lighthouse
ประเภท **bprah·pêt** kind (type)
ประมาณ **bprah·marn** about
ประหลาด **bprah·làrt** bizarre
ปรับปรุง **bpràhp·bpruhng** improve
ปรับปรุงใหม่ **bpràhp·bpruhng mì** renovation
ปรึกษา **bprùek·sǎr** consult
ปลอดภัย **bplòrt·pi** *adj* safe
ปล่อย **bplòhy** let
ปลั๊กแปลงไฟฟ้า **bpláhk bplaeng**

**fi·fár** adapter
ปลาย **bplie** *n* end
ปลายทาง **bplie·tarng** destination
ปลุก **bplùhk** wake
ปวด **bpòart** sore
ปวดท้อง **bpòart·tórng** stomachache
ปวดประจำเดือน **bpòart bprah·jahm·duean** menstrual cramps
ปวดฟัน **bpòart·fahn** toothache
ปวดหลัง **bpòart·lǎhng** backache
ปวดหัว **bpòart·hǔa** headache
ปวดหู **bpòart·hǒo** earache
ปอด **bpòrt** lung
ปอดบวม **bpòrt·boarm** pneumonia
ป้อน **bpôrn** feed
ปอนด์ **bporn** pound (weight)
ปัจจุบัน **bpàht·juh·bahn** present (time)
ปัญหา **bpahn·hâr** problem
ปั๊ม **bpáhm** pump
ปั๊มน้ำมัน **bpáhm náhm·mahn** gas [petrol BE] station
ป่า **bpàr** forest
ปาก **bpàrk** mouth
ปากกา **bpàrk·gar** pen
ป้าย **bpîe** label; *n* sign
ป้ายรถเมล์ **bpîe rót·me** bus stop
ปิคนิค **bpíhk·níhk** picnic
ปิด **bpìht** *v* close; turn off; shut
ปี **bpee** year
เป้สะพายหลัง **bpê sah·pie lǎhng** backpack
เป็น **bpehn** be
เป็นของ **bpehn·kǒhng** belong
เป็นเจ้าของ **bpehn jôu·kôrng** own

เป็นที่นิยม **bpehn têe· níh·yom** popular

เป็นผื่นคัน **bpehn pùeen·kahn** rash

เป็นลม **bpehn·lom** faint

เป็นโสด **bpehn·sòet** single (unmarried)

เป็นหนี้ **bpehn·nêe** owe

เปรี้ยว **bprêaw** sour

เปลเด็ก **bple·dèhk** crib

เปลี่ยน **bplèan** v change

เปิด **bpèrt** turn on; open

เปิดดู **bpèrt·doo** browse

แปรงแปรงผม **bpraeng bpraeng·pôm** hairbrush

แปรงสีฟัน **bpraeng sêe·fahn** toothbrush

แปล **bplae** translate

โปรแกรม **bproe·graem** program

โปรแกรมส่งข้อความ **bproe·graem sòng kôr·kwarm** instant messenger

โปสการ์ด **bpóet·sah·gárt** postcard

ไป **bpi** go

ไปรษณีย์ด่วน **bpri·sah·nee dòarn** express mail

ไปรษณีย์อากาศ **bpri·sah·nee ar·gàrt** airmail

ผ

ผงซักฟอก **pông sáhk·fôrk** detergent

ผม **pôm** hair

ผลข้างเคียง **pôn·kârng·keang** side effect

ผลัก **plàhk** push

ผ่าตัด **pàr·dtàht** operation

ผ้าก็อซ **pâr·górt** gauze

ผ้าซาติน **pâr sar·dtin** satin

ผ้าปูที่นอน **pâr bpoo têe·norn** sheet

(bed)

ผ้าฝ้าย **pâr·fie** cotton

ผ้าพันคอ **pâr·pahn·kor** scarf

ผ้าพันแผล **pâr·pahn·plâe** bandage [plaster BE]

ผ้าม่าน **pâr·mârn** curtain

ผ้าลูกไม้ **pâr lôok·mí** lace

ผ้าห่ม **pâr·hòm** blanket

ผ้าอนามัยแบบสอด **pâr ah·nar·mi bàep·sòrt** tampon

ผ้าอ้อม **pâr·ôrm** diaper [nappy BE]

ผ่าน **pàrn** through

ผิด **pìht** wrong

ผิดกฎหมาย **pìht gòt·mîe** illegal

ผิดพลาด **pìht·plârt** mistake

ผิวหนัง **pîhw·nâhng** skin

ผู้จัดการ **pôo·jàht·garn** manager

ผู้ชาย **pôo·chie** man

ผู้โดยสาร **pôo·doey·sârn** passenger

ผู้นำ **pôo·nahm** leader (group)

ผู้แปล **poo·bplae** translator

ผู้สอน **pôo·sôrn** instructor

ผู้สูงอายุ **pôo·sôong·ar·yúh** senior citizen

ผู้ใหญ่ **pôo·yì** adult

ผู้อำนวยการ **pôo·ahm·noary·garn** director (company)

ผ้าเช็ดตัว **pâr·chéht·dtoar** towel

ผ้ายีนส์ **pâr·yeen** denim

ผ้าวูล **pâr woon** wool

ผ้าไหม **pâr·mɪ̌** silk

ผ้าอนามัย **pâr ah·nar·mi** sanitary napkin [pad BE]

ผ่าน **pàrn** v pass (drive)

เผ็ด **pèht** hot (spicy)

แผงขายหนังสือพิมพ์ **pâeng kîe nâhng-sûee-pihm** newsstand

แผน **pâen** plan

แผนที่ **pâen-têe** map

แผนที่ถนน **pâen-têe tah-nôn** road map

แผนที่รถไฟใต้ดิน **pâen-têe rót-fi tî-dihn** subway [underground BE] map

แผ่นพับ **pàen-páhp** brochure

แผนกของหาย **pah-nàek kôrng hîe** lost and found [lost-property office BE]

แผนกจำหน่ายตั๋ว **pah-nàek jahm-nìe dtôar** ticket office

แผนกต้อนรับ **pah-nàek dtôrn-ráhp** reception (desk)

แผนกรับจอง **pah-nàek ráhp-jorng** reservation desk

แผลพุพอง **plâe púh-porng** blister

## ฝ

ฝน **fôn** n rain

ฝนตก **fôn-dtòk** v rain

ฝังเข็ม **fâhng-kêhm** acupuncture

ฝาครอบเลนส์ **fâr-krôrp-lehn** lens cap

ฝากกระเป๋า **fàrk grah-bpôu** v check (luggage)

ฝากเงิน **fàrk-ngern** v deposit (bank)

ฝากไว้ **fàrk-wí** leave (deposit)

ฝาน **fârn** v slice

ฝึก **fùek** practice

ฝูงคน **fôong-kon** crowd

## พ

พจนานุกรม **pót-jah-nar-núh-grom** dictionary

พนักงาน **pah-náhk-ngarn** staff

พนักงานขาย **pah-náhk-ngarn kîe** shop assistant

พนักงานดับเพลิง **pah-náhk-ngarn dàhp-plerng** fire department [brigade BE]

พนักงานต้อนรับ **pah-náhk-ngarn dtôrn-ráhp** receptionist

พนักงานต้อนรับบนเครื่องบิน **pah-náhk-ngarn dtôrn-ráhp bon krûeang bihn** flight attendant

พนัน **pah-nahn** bet

พบ **póp** meet

พยากรณ์อากาศ **pah-yar-gorn ar-gàrt** weather forecast

พยาน **pah-yarn** witness

พยาบาล **pah-yar-barn** nurse

พรม **prom** carpet

พร้อม **prórm** ready

พระพุทธรูป **práh-púht-tah-rôop** Buddha image

พลั่ว **plôar** shovel

พลาสติก **plárt-sah-dtìhk** plastic

พวงกุญแจ **poarng guhn-jae** key ring

พอ **por** enough

พอดี **por-dee** fit

พ่อแม่ **pôr-mâe** parents

พัก **páhk** v rest; stay

พัฒนา **páht-tah-nar** develop

พัดลม **páht-lom** fan

พัสดุ **páht-sah-dùh** package [parcel BE]

พาโนรามา **par-noe-rar-mâr** panorama

พาราเซตามอล **par-rar-séht-dtar-môhn** acetaminophen [paracetamol BE]

พาย **pie** v row

พาสปอร์ต **párs·sàh·bpòrt** passport

พิการ **píh·garn** adj handicapped

พิการทางสายตา **píh·garn tarng sǎ·ry·dtar** visually impaired

พิการทางหู **píh·garn tarng hǒo** hearing impaired

พิพิธภัณฑ์ **píh·píht·tah·pahn** museum

พิมพ์ **pihm** print

พิเศษ **píh·sèt** special

พิวเตอร์ **pihw·dtêr** pewter

พี่เลี้ยงเด็ก **pêe·léang dèhk** babysitter

พื้นเมือง **púeen·mueang** native

พูด **pôot** talk; say; speak

เพชร **péht** diamond

เพนิซิลลิน **pe·níh·sih·lihn** penicillin

เพราะว่า **próh·wâr** because

เพศชาย **pêt·chie** male

เพศหญิง **pêt·yǐhng** female

เพิ่ม **pêrm** extra

เพิ่มเติม **pêrm·dterm** additional

เพื่อ **pêua** for

เพื่อน **pûean** friend

เพื่อนร่วมงาน **pûean·rôarm·ngarn** colleague

แพง **paeng** expensive

แพลง **plaeng** sprain

แพลตตินั่ม **pláet·dtih·nâhm** platinum

โพลีเยสเตอร์ **poe·lee·yét·dtêr** polyester

## ฟ

ฟองน้ำ **forng·nárm** sponge

ฟัน **fahn** tooth

ฟันปลอม **fahn·bplorm** denture

ฟิล์มถนอมอาหาร **feem tah·nôrm ar·hǎ·rn** plastic wrap [cling film BE]

ฟุตบอล **fúht·bohn** soccer [football BE]

เฟอร์นิเจอร์ **fer·nih·jêr** furniture

แฟกซ์ **fàk** fax

แฟลต **flàt** apartment [flat BE]

ไฟ **fi** fire; n light

ไฟฉาย **fi·chǐe** flashlight

ไฟแช็ก **fi·chák** lighter

ไฟฟ้า **fi·fár** electronic

## ภ

ภรรยา **pahn·rah·yar** wife

ภาพวาด **pârp·wârt** painting (picture)

ภาษาไทย **par·sâr ti** Thai (language)

ภาษาอังกฤษ **par·sâr ahng·grìht** English (language)

ภาษีมูลค่าเพิ่ม **par·se̖·e moon·kâr pêrm** sales tax [VAT BE]

ภาษีศุลกากร **par·sêe sǔhn·lah·gar·gorn** duty (tax)

ภูเขา **poo·kôu** mountain

ภูมิแพ้ **poom·páe** allergy

## ม

มรกต **mor·rah·gòt** emerald

มรสุม **mor·rah·sǔhm** monsoon

มอเตอร์ไซค์ **mor·dter·si** moped; motorcycle

มะเร็ง **mah·rehng** cancer

มังสวิรัติ **mahng·sàh·wíh·ráht** vegetarian

มัสยิด **máht·sah·yíht** mosque

มา **mar** come

มาถึง **mar•teung** arrive

มาเยี่ยม **mar•yêam** *v* visit

ม้า **már** horse

มาก **mârk** much; very

มากกว่า **mârk•gwàr** over (more than); more

มาตรฐาน **mârt•dtah•târn** standard

มาสคารา **márs•kar•râr** mascara

มินิบาร์ **míh•níh bar** mini-bar

มิสซา **míht•sar** mass (church)

มี **mee** have; contain

มีความสุข **mee kwarm•sùhk** happy

มีค่า **mee•kâr** valuable

มีชื่อเสียง **mee chûee•sêang** famous

มีซับไตเติล **mee sáhp•dti•dtêrn** subtitled

มีเสน่ห์ **mee sah•nè** attractive

มีด **mêet** knife

มีดโกน **mêet•goen** razor

มืด **mûeet** dark

มือ **muee** hand

มือสอง **muee•sôrng** secondhand

มุม **muhm** corner

มูลค่า **moon•kâr** value

เมนู **me•noo** menu

เมนูเด็ก **me•noo dèhk** children's menu

เมมโมรี่การ์ด **mem•moe•rêe gárt** memory card

เมาเครื่องบิน **mou krûeang•bihn** airsickness

เมารถ **mou rót** motion sickness

เมาเรือ **mou ruea** seasickness

เมื่อวาน **mûea•warn** yesterday

เมื่อไหร่ **mûea•rì** when

เมือง **mueang** town

เมื่อย **mûeay** stiff (muscle)

แม่น้ำ **mâe•nárm** river

แมลง **mah•laeng** bug; insect

แมลงกัดต่อย **mah•laeng gàht•dtòry** insect bite

แมลงสาบ **mah•laeng•sàrp** cockroach

โมง **moeng** o'clock

ไม่ **mî** no; not

ไม่กี่ **mî•gèe** a few

ไม่เคย **mî•kery** never

ไม่แพง **mî paeng** inexpensive

ไม่มีอะไร **mî mee ah•ri** nothing

ไม่สบาย **mî sah•bie** sick [ill BE]

ไม่ใส่ **mî sì** without

ไม้ **míe** wood (material)

ไม้กวาด **míe•gwart** broom

ไม้กอล์ฟ **míe•górf** golf club

ไม้แขวนเสื้อ **míe•kwâen•sûea** hanger; coat hanger

ไม้ถูพื้น **míe tôo•púeen** mop

ไม้เทนนิส **míe tehn•níht** racket (tennis)

ไมเกรน **mi•gren** migraine

ไมโครเวฟ **mi•kroe•wép** microwave (oven)

ย

ยกเลิก **yók•lêrk** cancel

ยกเว้น **yók•wéhn** except

ยอมรับ **yorm•ráhp** accept; approve

ย่อยนมไม่ได้ **yôry nom mî•dîe** lactose intolerant

ยังไง **yahng•ngi** how

ยา **yar** medicine

ยากันแมลง **yar gahn mah·laeng** insect
repellent

ยาชา **yar·char** anesthetic

ยานอนหลับ **yar norn·làhp** sleeping pill

ยาปฏิชีวนะ **yar
bpah·dtih·chee·wah·náh** antibiotics

ยาพิษ **yar·píht** poison

ยาระงับกลิ่นตัว **yar rah·ngáhp
glìhn·dtoar** deodorant

ยาระงับประสาท **yar rah·ngáhp
bprah·sàrt** sedative

ยาระบาย **yar rah·bie** laxative

ยาลดกรด **yar lót·gròt** antacid

ยาสีฟัน **yar sêe·fahn** toothpaste

ยาเส้น **yar·sên** tobacco

ยาเหน็บ **yar·nèhp** suppository

ยาก **yârk** difficult

ยาง **yarng** tire

ย่านใจกลางเมือง **yârn ji·glarng
mueang** downtown

ย่านช็อปปิ้ง **yârn
chóhp·bpîhng** shopping area

ย่านธุรกิจ **yârn túh·ráh·gìht** business
district

ยามไลฟ์การ์ด **yarm lí·gàrt** lifeguard

ยาว **yow** long

ยินดีต้อนรับ **yihn·dee dtôrn·ráhp**
welcome

ยีนส์ **yeen** jeans

ยืน **yueen** stand

ยืนกราน **yueen·grarn** insist

ยืนยัน **yueen·yahn** confirm

ยืม **yueem** borrow

ยุงกัด **yuhng·gàt** mosquito bite

ยุ่ง **yûhng** busy

ยูโรเช็ค **yoo·roe·chéhk** Eurocheque

เย็น **yehn** cool

เย็บ **yéhp** sew

เยี่ยมมาก **yêam·mârk** superb

แยก **yâek** separate

แยกกันอยู่ **yâek gahn yòo** separated
(marital status)

แยกตามรายการ **yâek dtarm rie·garn**
itemized

---

ร

รถ **rót** vehicle

รถเข็น **rót·kêhn** cart [trolley BE]

รถเข็นกระเป๋า **rót·kêhn grah·bpôu**
luggage cart [trolley BE]

รถเข็นคนพิการ **rót·kêhn kon píh·garn**
wheelchair

รถเข็นเด็ก **rót·kêhn dèhk** stroller [push-
chair BE]

รถเช่า **rót·chôu** car rental [hire BE]

รถบรรทุก **rót bahn·túhk** truck [lorry BE]

รถบัสทางไกล **rót báht tarng gli** long-
distance bus

รถพยาบาล **rót pah·yar·barn** ambulance

รถพ่วง **rót·pôarng** trailer

รถไฟ **rót·fi** train

รถไฟใต้ดิน **rót·fi tîe·dihn** subway
[underground BE]

รถเมล์ **rót·me** bus

รถยนต์ **rót·yon** car

รถราง **rót·rarng** tram

รถลาก **rót·lârk** tow truck

รถเสบียง **rót sah·beang** dining car

รบกวน **róp•goarn** bother; disturb

ร่ม **rôm** umbrella

รวม **roarm** merge; include

รวมค่าบริการ **roarm kâr•bor•rih•garn** service included

รสชาติ **rót•chârt** flavor; taste

รหัส **rah•hàht** code; password

รหัสประเทศ **rah•hàht bprah•têt** country code

รหัสพื้นที่ **rah•hàht púeen•têe** area code

รอ **ror** wait

รองเท้า **rorng•tów** shoe

รองเท้าแตะ **rorng•tów dtà** slippers; sandals

รองเท้าบู๊ท **rorng•tów bóot** boots

รองเทาผาใบ **rorng•tów pâr•bi** sneakers

ร้อน **rórn** *adj* hot

รอบ **rôrp** *n* round (golf)

รอบๆ **rôrp•rôrp** around

รอบกลางวัน **rôrp glarng•wahn** matinée

รอยฟกช้ำ **rory fók•cháhm** bruise

ระเบียง **rah•beang** balcony

ระมัดระวัง **rah•máht•rah•wahng** caution

ระยะทาง **rah•yáh•tarng** distance

ระวัง **rah•wahng** beware; careful

ระหว่าง **rah•wàrng** between; during

ระหว่างประเทศ **rah•wàrng bprah•têt** international

รัก **ráhk** love

รับ **ráhp** pick up

รับประกัน **ráhp•bprah•gahn** guarantee

ราคา **rar•kar** price; *v* cost

ร้านกาแฟ **rárn gar•fae** cafe

ร้านกิฟต์ช็อป **rárn gíp•chòhp** gift store

ร้านขายขนม **rárn kǐe kah•nôm** candy store

ร้านขายของชำ **rárn kǐe kôrng•chahm** grocery store

ร้านขายของที่ระลึก **rárn kǐe kôrng têe•rah•lúehk** souvenir store

ร้านขายของเล่น **rárn kǐe kôrng•lên** toy store

ร้านขายเครื่องกีฬา **rárn kǐe krûeang•gee•lar** sporting goods store

ร้านขายเครื่องมืออุปกรณ์ **rárn kǐe krûeang•muee ùhp•bpah•gorn** hardware store

ร้านงานฝีมือ **rárn kǐe ngarn•fěe•muee** craft shop

ร้านขายดอกไม้ **rárn kǐe dòrk•míe** florist

ร้านขายผักผลไม้ **rárn kǐe pàhk pôn•lah•míe** produce store

ร้านขายยา **rárn kǐe yar** pharmacy [chemist BE]

ร้านขายยาเปิด 24 ชั่วโมง **rárn kǐe yar bpèrt yêe•sihp•sèe chôar•moeng** all-night pharmacy [chemist BE]

ร้านขายรองเทา **rárn kǐe rorng•tów** shoe store

ร้านขายเสื้อผ้า **rárn kǐe sûea•pâr** clothing store [clothes shop BE]

ร้านขายเหล้า **rárn kǐe lôu** liquor store

ร้านขายอาหารสุขภาพ **rárn kǐe ar•hǎrn sùhk•kah•pârp** health food store

ร้านค้า **rárn•kár** store

ร้านค้าปลอดภาษี **rárn·kár bplòrt par·sêe** duty-free

ร้านเครื่องประดับ **rárn krûeang· bprah·dàhp** jeweler

ร้านซักรีด **rárn sáhk·rêet** laundromat [launderette BE]

ร้านซักแห้ง **rárn sáhk·hâeng** dry cleaner

ร้านทำเล็บ **rárn tahm·léhp** nail salon

ร้านเบเกอรี่ **rárn be·ger·rêe** bakery

ร้านหนังสือ **rárn nâhng·sŭee** bookstore

ร้านอาหาร **rárn ar·hârn** restaurant

รายการ **rie·garn** n list

รายการร้านค้า **rie·garn rárn·kár** store guide [directory BE]

รายละเอียด **rie·lah·èat** detail

รายวัน **rie·wahn** daily

ร้าว **róarw** fracture

ริมฝีปาก **rihm·fêe·bpàrk** lip

รีด **rêet** v iron

รีบ **rêep** hurry

รู **roo** hole

รู้จัก **róo·jàhk** know

รู้สึก **róo·sùek** feel

รู้สึกตัว **róo·sùek·dtoar** conscious

รู้สึกสนุก **róo·sùek sah·nùhk** enjoy

รูป **rôop** photograph

รูปแบบ **rôop·bàep** feature

รูปปั้น **rôop·bpâhn** statue

รูปร่าง **rôop·rârng** shape

รูมเซอร์วิส **room ser·wíht** room service

เร่ง **rêhng** rush

เร่งความเร็ว **rêhng kwarm·rehw** v speed

เร็ว **rehw** quick; fast

เริ่ม **rêrm** start; begin

เรียก **rêak** call (summon)

เรียนรู้ **rean·róo** learn

เรือข้ามฟาก **ruea kârm·fârk** ferry

เรือแคนู **ruea kae·noo** canoe

เรือชูชีพ **ruea choo·chéep** life boat

เรือเดินทะเล **ruea dern tah·le** ship

เรือพาย **ruea·pie** rowboat

เรือยนต์ **ruea·yon** motorboat

เรือยอชท์ **ruea·yórt** yacht

เรื่องตลก **rûeang dtah·lòk** joke

โรคไขข้อเสื่อม **rôek kĭ·kôr sùeam** arthritis

โรคเบาหวาน **rôek bou·wârn** diabetes

โรคแพ้อากาศ **rôek páe ar·gàrt** hay fever

โรคโลหิตจาง **rôek loe·hìht jarng** anemia

โรคหอบหืด **rôek hòrp·hùeet** asthma

โรคหัวใจ **rôek hôar·ji** heart condition

โรงพยาบาล **roeng pah·yar·barn** hospital

โรงยิม **roeng yihm** gym

โรงรถ **roeng·rót** garage

โรงแรม **roeng·raem** hotel

โรงละคร **roeng lah·korn** theater (play)

โรงหนัง **roeng·nǎ̌hng** movie theater [cinema BE]

โรแมนติก **roe·maen·dtìhk** romantic

ไร่องุ่น **rî àh·ngùhn** vineyard

ไร้สาย **rí·sǐe** wireless

---

ล

ลง **long** get off (bus, etc.)

ลด **lót** reduce

ลดราคา **lót rar·kar** clearance; sale

ลบ **lóp** delete
ลม **lom** air (tire); wind
ลมแดด **lom-dàet** sunstroke
ลมแรง **lom raeng** windy
ล้มลง **lóm-long** collapse
ล็อค **lóhk** lock
ล่องเรือ **lôhng-ruea** cruise
ล็อตเตอรี่ **lóht-dter-rêe** lottery
ล็อบบี้ **lóhp-bêe** lobby (theater, hotel)
ละคร **lah-korn** *n* play
ละลาย **lah-lie** dissolve
ล่า **lâr** hunt
ล่าม **lârm** interpreter
ลำคอ **lahm-kor** throat
ลำธาร **lahm-tarn** stream
ลำไส้ **lahm-sî** bowel
ลิตร **líht** liter
ลิ้น **líhn** tongue
ลินิน **lih-nihn** linen
ลิปสติก **líhp-sah-dtìhk** lipstick
ลิฟต์ **líhp** elevator [lift BE]
ลึก **lúek** deep
ลืม **lueem** forget
ลู่ม้าวิ่ง **lôo már wîhng** horsetrack
ลู่วิ่ง **lôo wîhng** racetrack
ลูกเต๋า **lôok-dtôu** *n* dice
ลูกบอล **lôok-bohn** ball
เล็ก **léhk** small
เลน **len** lane
เล่น **lêhn** *v* play
เล่นวินด์เซิร์ฟ **lêhn wihn-sérp** windsurfing
เลนส์ **lehn** lens
เล็บ **léhp** nail

เล็ม **lehm** trim
เลว **lew** bad
เลี้ยว **léaw** turn
เลือก **lûeak** choose
เลือด **lûeat** blood
เลือดออก **lûeat-òrk** bleed
แลกเงิน **lâek-ngern** *v/n* change (money)
แลกเปลี่ยน **lâek-bplèan** exchange
แล้ว **láew** already
แล้วก็ **láew-gôr** then (afterwards)
และ **lá** and
โลชั่นหลังโกนหนวด **loe-châhn lähng goen-nòart** aftershave
โลชั่นอาบแดด **loe-châhn àrp-dàet** suntan lotion
โลหะ **loe-hàh** metal

ว

วง (ดนตรี) **wong (don dtree)** band (music)
วลี **wah-lee** phrase
วอร์ดคนไข้ **wòrt kon-kî** ward (hospital)
วอลเล่ย์บอล **wohn-lê-bohn** volleyball
วัง **wahng** palace
วัดขนาด **wáht kah-nàrt** *v* measure
วัตถุประสงค์ **wáht-tùh bprah-sông** purpose
วัน **wahn** day
วันเกิด **wahn-gèrt** birthday
วันธรรมดา **wahn tahm-mah-dar** weekday
วันนี้ **wahn-née** today
วันพรุ่งนี้ **wahn prûhng-née** tomorrow
วันสุดสัปดาห์ **wahn sùht-sàhp-dar**

weekend
วันหยุด **wahn·yùht** vacation [holiday BE]
ว่าง **wârng** available; empty, free, vacant
วาดภาพ **wârt·pârp** v paint (picture)
ว่ายน้ำ **wîe·nárm** swim
วาล์ว **wow** valve
วิชา **wíh·char** course
วิดีโอเกม **wih·dee·oe·gem** video game
วิว **wihw** view
วีซ่า **wee·sâr** visa
วีซ่าเข้าประเทศ **wee·sâr kôu**
  **bprah·têt** entry visa
เว็ทสูท **wéht·sòot** wetsuit
เวลา **we·lar** time
เวลาทำการ **we·lar tahm·garn** opening
  hours
เวลาเยี่ยม **we·lar yêam** visiting hours
เวียนศีรษะ **wean sêe·sàh** dizzy
แว่นกันแดด **wân gahn·dàet** sunglasses
แว่นตา **wân·dtar** glasses (optical)

## ศ

ศาสนา **sàrt·sa·nâr** religion
ศึกษา **sùek·sâr** study
ศุลกากร **sǔhn·lah·gar·gorn** customs
ศูนย์การค้า **sôon·garn·kár** shopping mall
  [centre BE]
ศูนย์บริการทางธุรกิจ **sôon bor·rih·garn**
  **tarng túh·ráh·giht** business center

## ส

สกปรก **sòk·grah·bpròk** dirty
สกีน้ำ **sah·gee nárm** water skis
ส่ง **sòng** deliver; drop off; send

ส่งข้อความ **sòng kôr·kwarm** v text (SMS)
ส่งจดหมาย **sòng jòt·mǐe** v mail [post BE]
สด **sòt** fresh
สเตนเลส **sah·dten·lèt** stainless steel
สไตล์ **sah·dtie** style
สถานที่ **sah·tǎrn·têe** site; place
สถานที่ท่องเที่ยว **sah·târn·têe**
  **tôhng·têaw** sight (attraction)
สถานที่นัดพบ **sah·ta˘rn·têe**
  **náht·póp** meeting place
สถานทูต **sah·târn·tôot** embassy
สถานีขนส่ง **sah·târ·nee kôn·sòng** bus
  station
สถานีตำรวจ **sah·târ·nee**
  **dtahm·ròart** police station
สถานีรถไฟ **sah·târ·nee rót·fi** train
  [railway BE] station
สถานีรถไฟใต้ดิน **sah·târ·nee rót·fi tîe**
  **dihn** subway [underground BE] station
ส้น **sôn** heels
สนอร์กเกิล **sah·nórk·gêrn** snorkel
สนามกอล์ฟ **sah·nârm górp** golf course
สนามกีฬา **sah·nârm gee·lar** stadium
สนามเด็กเล่น **sah·nârm dèhk lên**
  playground
สนามเทนนิส **sah·nârm tehn·níht**
  tennis court
สนามบิน **sah·nârm·bihn** airport
สนุก **sah·nùhk** fun
สแน็คบาร์ **sah·nák bar** snack bar
สบายดี **sah·bie dee** fine (health)
สบู่ **sah·bòo** soap
สปอร์ตคลับ **sah·bpòrt kláhp** sports club
สปา **sah·bpar** spa

สมรภูมิ **sah·môr·rah·poom** battleground

สมาชิก **sah·mar·chíhk** member

สมุดโทรศัพท์ **sah·mùht toe·rah·sàhp** phone directory

สร้อยข้อมือ **sôry kôr·muee** bracelet

สร้อยคอ **sôry kor** necklace

สระกลางแจ้ง **sàh glarng·jâeng** outdoor pool

สระเด็ก **sàh dèhk** kiddie [paddling BE] pool

สระว่ายน้ำ **sàh wîe·nárm** swimming pool

สระว่ายน้ำในร่ม **sàh wîe·nárm ni rôm** indoor pool

สร้าง **sârng** build

สลัก **sah·làhk** engrave

สวดมนต์ **sòart·mon** prayer

สวน **sòarn** garden

สวนพฤกษศาสตร์ **sòarn prúek·sah·sàrt** botanical garden

สวนสนุก **sôarn sah·nùhk** amusement park; theme park

สวนสัตว์ **sôarn sàht** zoo

สวนสาธารณะ **sùan sâr·tar·rah·náh** *n* park

ส่วนตัว **sòarn·dtoar** private

ส่วนลด **sòarn·lót** discount; (price) reduction

สวม **sôarm** wear

ส้วมเคมี **sôarm ke·mee** chemical toilet

สวย **sôary** beautiful

สหรัฐอเมริกา **sah·hàh·ráht ah·me·rih·gar** United States

สหราชอาณาจักร **sah·hàh rârt·chah·ar·nar·jàhk** United Kingdom

ส้อม **sôrm** fork

สะกด **sah·gòt** spell

สะพาน **sah·parn** bridge

สะอาด **sah·àrt** *adj* clean

สั่ง **sàhng** order

สังเคราะห์ **sâhng·króh** synthetic

สัญชาติ **sân·chârt** nationality

สัญญาณไฟไหม้ **sâhn·yarn fi·mî** fire alarm

สัญลักษณ์ **sâhn·yah·láhk** symbol

สัตว์ **sàht** animal

สัตว์ป่า **sàht·bpàr** wildlife

สั้น **sâhn** short

สัปดาห์ **sàhp·dar** week

สัมมนา **sâhm·mah·nar** seminar

สาธารณะ **sâr·tar·rah·náh** public

สามี **sâr·mee** husband

สาย **sîe** late

สายการบิน **sîe·garn·bihn** airline

สายตายาว **sîe·dtar yow** far-sighted [long-sighted BE]

สายตาสั้น **sîe·dtar sâhn** near-sighted [short-sighted BE]

สำคัญ **sâhm·kahn** important; main

สำนักงานท่องเที่ยว **sâhm·náhk·ngarn tôhng·têaw** tourist office

สำรอง **sâhm·rorng** spare

สำหรับขาย **sâhm·ràhp kîe** for sale

สิ่งของ **sìhng·kôrng** thing

สี **sêe** color; paint

สี่แยก **sèe·yâek** intersection

สุขภาพ **sùhk·kah·pârp** health

สุดท้าย **sùht•tíe** last
สุนัข **suh•náhk** dog
สุนัขนำทาง **suh•náhk nahm•tarng** guide dog
สุสาน **sùh•sa̅rn** cemetery
สุเหร่า **suh•ròu** mosque
สุเหร่ายิว **suh•ròu yihw** synagogue
สูง **sôong** tall; high
สูตินรีแพทย์ **sôo•dtìh•nah•ree•pâet** gynecologist
สูบบุหรี่ **sòop buh•rèe** smoke
เส้น **sêhn** line
เส้นทาง **sêhn•tarng** route
เส้นทางเดินป่า **sêhn•tarng dern•bpàr** trail
เสาเต็นท์ **sôu dtéhn** tent pole
เสิร์ฟ **sèrp** serve
เสีย **sêa** break down; broken
เสียหาย **sêa•hĭe** damage
เสียงดัง **sêarng dahng** noisy
เสื้อกันฝน **sûea gahn fôn** raincoat
เสื้อกันลม **sûea gahn lom** windbreaker
เสื้อกันหนาว **sûea gahn nôw** sweater
เสื้อโค้ท **sûea•kóet** coat
เสื้อแจ็กเก็ต **sûea ják•gèht** jacket
เสื้อชูชีพ **sûea choo•chêep** lifejacket
เสื้อผู้หญิง **sûea pôo•yĭhng** blouse
เสื้อยกทรง **sûea yók•song** bra
เสื้อยืด **sûea yûeet** T-shirt
แสดง **sah•daeng** v show
แสดงรายการสิ่งของ **sah•daeng rie•garn sìhng•kôrng** declare
แสตมป์ **sah•dtaem** stamp
ใส่ **sì** put

หญ้า **yâr** grass
หน่วย **nòary** units
หนัก **nàhk** heavy
หนัง **nâhng** movie [film BE]; leather, skin
หนังสือ **nâhng•sŭee** book
หนังสือนำเที่ยว **nâhng•sŭee nahm•têaw** guide book
หนังสือพิมพ์ **nâhng•sŭee•pihm** newspaper
หนา **nâr** thick
หน้า **nâr** face
หน้ากาก **nâr•gàrk** mask
หน้าต่าง **nâr•dtàrng** window
หน้าผา **nâr•pâr** cliff
หน้าอก **nâr•òk** breast; chest
หนาว **nôw** adj cold
หมดแรง **mòt•raeng** exhausted
หมดสติ **mòt sah•dtìh** unconscious
หมวก **mòark** hat
หมวกแก๊ป **mòark gáp** cap
หมวกนิรภัย **mòark níh•ráh•pi** helmet
หมอ **môr** doctor
หมอเฉพาะทาง **môr chah•póh•tarng** specialist (doctor)
หมอเด็ก **môr dèhk** pediatrician
หมอฟัน **môr•fahn** dentist
หมอก **mòrk** fog
หมอน **môrn** pillow
หมั้น **mâhn** engaged
หมุด **mùht** peg
หมุดปักเต็นท์ **mùht bpàhk dtéhn** tent peg
หมู่บ้าน **mòo•bârn** village

หยด **yòt** drip

หย่า **yàr** divorce

หยาบคาย **yàrp•kie** rude

หยุด **yùht** v brake; stop

หรือ **rûee** or

หลงทาง **lông•tarng** lost

หลวม **lôarm** loose

หลอดไฟ **lòrt•fi** lightbulb

หลัง **lâhng** back; behind

หลังคา **lârng•kar** roof

หลังจาก **lâhng•jàrt** after

หลาย **lïe** many

หวัด **wàht** n cold

หวาน **wârn** adj sweet

หวี **wêe** comb

หอคอย **hôr•kory** tower

หอศิลป์ **hôr•sîhn** gallery

ห่อ **hòr** pack; wrap

ห่อไป **hòr bpi** to go [take away BE] (food)

ห้อง **hôhng** room

ห้องครัว **hôhng•kroar** kitchen

ห้องคอนเวนชั่น **hôhng kohn•wehn•châhn** convention hall

ห้องคู่ **hôhng•kôo** double room

ห้องเดี่ยว **hôhng•dèaw** single room

ห้องนอน **hôhng•norn** bedroom

ห้องน้ำ **hôhng•nárm** bathroom; restroom [toilet BE]

ห้องประชุม **hôhng bprah•chuhm** meeting room

ห้องพักผู้โดยสาร **hôhng páhk pôo•doey•sârn** waiting room

ห้องพักผู้โดยสารขาออก **hôhng páhk pôo•doey•sârn kâr•òrk** departure lounge

ห้องลองเสื้อผ้า **hôhng lorng** sûea•pâr fitting room

ห้องสมุด **hôhng sah•mùht** library

ห้องอาบน้ำ **hôhng àrp•nárm** n shower

ห้องอาหาร **hôhng ar•hârn** dining room

หัตถกรรม **hàht•tah•gahm** handicraft

หั่น **hàhn** v dice

หัว **hûa** head

หัวใจ **hûa•ji** heart

หัวใจวาย **hûa•ji wie** heart attack

หา **hâr** find

ห่าง **hàrng** away

ห้างสรรพสินค้า **hârng sàhp•pah•sîhn•kár** department store

ห้าม **hârm** prohibited

ห้ามสูบบุหรี่ **hârm sòop buh•rèe** no smoking

หาย **hïe** missing; lose (item)

หายใจ **hâi•ji** breathe

หิมะ **hìh•máh** snow

หิว **hïhw** hungry

หิวน้ำ **hïhw•nárm** thirsty

หุ้นส่วน **hûhn•sòarn** partner

หู **hôo** ear

หูหนวก **hôo•nòark** deaf

เหตุการณ์ **hèt•garn** event

เห็น **hêhn** see

เห็นด้วย **hêhn•dôary** agree

เหนียว **nêaw** tough (texture)

เหนือ **nêua** north

เหนื่อย **nùeay** tired

เหมาะสม **mòh•sôm** suitable

เหมือนกัน **mu̇ean•gahn** also; too

เหมือนกับ **mu ˘ean·gàhp** *v* like (same)

เหรียญ **rêan** coin

เหล็ก **lèhk** iron (metal)

เหล็กกล้า **lèhk·glâr** steel

แห้ง **hâeng** *adj* dry (clothes)

แหนบ **nàep** tweezers

แหวน **wâen** *n* ring (jewelry)

โหล **lôe** dozen

ให้ **hî** give

ให้นม **hî·nom** breastfeed

ให้ยืม **hî yueem** lend

ใหญ่ **yì** big; large

ใหม่ **mì** new

ไหมขัดฟัน **mî kàht·fahn** dental floss

ไหม้ **mî** burn

ไหล่ **lì** shoulder

---

## อ

องศา **ong·sâr** degree (weather)

อธิบาย **ah·tíh·bie** describe

อนุญาต **ah·núh·yârt** allow

อนุสาวรีย์ **ah·núh·sa ˘r·wah·ree** memorial

อนุสาวรีย์สงคราม **ah·núh·sa ˘r·wah·ree sông·krarm** war memorial

อบซาวน่า **òp sow·nâr** *v* sauna

อพาร์ตเมนต์ **ah·párt·méhn** apartment

อเมริกัน **ah·me·rih·gahn** American

อยากได้ **yàrk·dîe** want

อย่างไม่เป็นทางการ **yàrng mî·bpehn tarng·garn** informal

อยู่ **yòo** stay; live

อร่อย **ah·ròhy** delicious

อโรมาเทราปี **ah·roe·mâr**

เterารปี **te·rar·pêe** aromatherapy

อวยพร **oary·porn** *v* wish (bless)

ออก **òrk** out

ออกจาก **òrk·jàrk** *v* leave

ออกจากระบบ **òrk·jark rah·bòp** log off

ออกเสียง **òrk·sêang** pronounce

อ็อกซิเจน **óhk·sih·jên** oxygen

ออเคสตร้า **or·két·trâr** orchestra

อ่อน **òrn** light (color)

อะไร **ah·ri** what

อะไหล่ **ah·lì** replacement part

อัตโนมัติ **àht·tah·noe·máht** automatic

อัตราแลกเปลี่ยน **àht·dtrar lâek·bplèarn** exchange rate

อันตราย **ahn·dtah·rie** dangerous

อาการ **ar·garn** symptom

อาการท้องผูก **ar·garn tórng·pòok** constipation

อาการอักเสบ **ar·garn àhk·sèp** inflammation

อากาศ **ar·gàrt** weather

อาคาร **ar·karn** building

อาคารจอดรถ **ar·karn jòrt·rót** parking garage

อ่าง **àrng** sink

อ่างเก็บน้ำ **àrng·gèhp·nárm** reservoir

อาจจะ **àrt·jah** maybe

อาเจียน **ar·jean** vomit

อาชีพ **ar·chêep** profession

อ่าน **àrn** read

อาบแดด **àrp·dàet** sunbathe

อาบน้ำ **àrp·nárm** *v* bath

อาบน้ำฝักบัว **àrp·nárm fàhk·boar** *v* shower

อาหาร **ar·hârn** food; meal
อาหารกลางวัน **ar·hârn glarng·wahn** lunch
อาหารจานด่วน **ar·hârn jarn·dòarn** fast food
อาหารชุด **ar·hârn chúht** set menu
อาหารเช้า **ar·hârn chóu** breakfast
อาหารเด็ก **ar·hârn dèhk** baby food
อาหารเป็นพิษ **ar·hârn bpehn·píht** food poisoning
อาหารไม่ย่อย **ar·hârn mî yôry** indigestion
อาหารเย็น **ar·hârn yehn** dinner
อาหารว่าง **ar·hârn wârng** snack
อินซูลิน **ihn·soo·lihn** insulin
อินเตอร์เน็ต **ihn·dter·nèht** internet
อินเตอร์เน็ตคาเฟ่ **ihn·dter·nèht kar·fê** internet cafe
อีบูโปรเฟน **ee·boo·bproe·fen** ibu-profen
อีเมล์ **ee·mew** e-mail
อีเมล์แอดเดรส **ee·mew át·drét** e-mail address
อุณหภูมิ **uhn·hah·poom** temperature
อุดฟัน **ùht·fahn** filling (dental)
อุ่น **ùhn** warm
อุบัติเหตุ **uh·bàht·tih·hèt** accident
อุปกรณ์ดำน้ำ **ùhp·bpah·gorn dahm·nárm** diving equipment
อุปกรณ์เดินป่า **ùhp·bpah·gorn dern·bpàr** hiking gear
อุปรากร **ùhp·bpah·rar·gorn** opera
อุโมงค์ **uh·moeng** tunnel

อู่เรือ **òo ruea** dock
เอ็กซเรย์ **éhk·sah·re** x-ray
เอกอัครราชทูต **èk·àhk·kah·rârt·chah·tôot** ambassador
เอทีเอ็ม **e·tee·ehm** ATM
แอร์ **ae** air conditioning
แอสไพริน **áes·pi·rihn** aspirin
เอา **ou** take
เอาออก **ou òrk** remove
เอื้อม **ûeam** reach
โอเค **oe·ke** OK
โอนเงิน **oen·ngern** transfer (finance)
ไอ **i** cough
ไอโอดีน **i·oe·deen** iodine

## ฮ

ฮันนีมูน **hahn·nee·moon** honeymoon
ฮัลโหล **hahn·lôe** hello (phone)
ฮาลาล **har·larn** halal